Financing SMEs and Entrepreneurs 2020

AN OECD SCOREBOARD

OECD
BETTER POLICIES FOR BETTER LIVES

This document, as well as any data and map included herein, are without prejudice to the status of or sovereignty over any territory, to the delimitation of international frontiers and boundaries and to the name of any territory, city or area.

The statistical data for Israel are supplied by and under the responsibility of the relevant Israeli authorities. The use of such data by the OECD is without prejudice to the status of the Golan Heights, East Jerusalem and Israeli settlements in the West Bank under the terms of international law.

Please cite this publication as:
OECD (2020), *Financing SMEs and Entrepreneurs 2020: An OECD Scoreboard*, OECD Publishing, Paris, *https://doi.org/10.1787/061fe03d-en*.

ISBN 978-92-64-94815-0 (print)
ISBN 978-92-64-59853-9 (pdf)

Financing SMEs and Entrepreneurs
ISSN 2306-5257 (print)
ISSN 2306-5265 (online)

Photo credits: Cover © Shutterstock/Roman Gorielov

Corrigenda to publications may be found on line at: *www.oecd.org/about/publishing/corrigenda.htm*.

Preface

In today's global economy, SMEs and entrepreneurs are at the heart of the search for inclusive growth. Ensuring small firms have access to finance in the appropriate forms and volumes is a prerequisite for their development and growth. It also becomes critical for their survival in times of crisis, such as the one the world is currently facing in the context of the COVID-19 pandemic, which is having immediate and profound effects on SMEs.

Small businesses and the self-employed are extremely vulnerable to the disruptions caused by the public health crisis and related containment measures, including through disruptions to local markets, business networks, and global and local supply chains. In the short term, loss of revenues and liquidity shortages risk putting vast numbers of SMEs out of business. SMEs are also likely to be impacted strongly by a longer-term economic and financial downturn after the immediate public health crisis has passed. These factors will affect a number of key SME finance indicators going forward.

Financing SMEs and Entrepreneurs: An OECD Scoreboard was developed as a response to the 2008 financial crisis, which brought to the fore the need for timely data to underpin policymaking. In the years since the last global crisis, SME access to finance has improved: Interest rates have reached historically low levels, bank lending has picked up again, and credit conditions for SMEs have eased considerably.

The 2020 edition of the Scoreboard shows that SMEs are opting for alternative finance instruments like never before, while growth in straight debt volumes has been sluggish. This step towards financial diversification is in line with the G20/OECD High Level Principles on SME Financing. Online alternative finance activities have shown remarkable growth rates in virtually all participating Scoreboard countries. If these trends continue, SMEs can become more resilient and less vulnerable to changes in credit market conditions. However, these developments do not come without risks and challenges for policymakers and regulators around the globe, who need to ensure adequate levels of investor protection and promote a level playing field between different financing instruments.

The Scoreboard also documents policy developments since the financial crisis. These experiences may hold important lessons for policy makers today, as they put in place urgent measures to mitigate the severe liquidity shortages brought on by the COVID-19 pandemic and begin to address the medium-term impacts of a global recession.

This is no time for complacency. The emerging economic effects of the COVID-19 global pandemic are changing the outlook for global growth, affecting the operations of SMEs worldwide, as well as their ability to access finance for cash flow needs and longer-term investments. In addition, weak trade and investment flows and the reorganisation of supply chains could negatively impact the availability of credit and other forms of finance for SMEs in the years to come.

In this complex environment, the OECD will continue to monitor closely the trends in SME and entrepreneurship finance. This report will continue to evolve and expand, with coverage of additional countries in our analysis and the collection of more granular data on specific segments of the SME population. In this way, we can continue to support governments in ensuring that their policies keep up with fast-moving developments in SME finance.

Angel Gurría
OECD Secretary-General

Foreword

Financing SMEs and Entrepreneurs 2020: An OECD Scoreboard provides a comprehensive framework for policy makers and other stakeholders to monitor access to finance by SMEs and entrepreneurs. This report also constitutes a valuable tool to support the design and evaluation of policy measures, and to monitor the implications of financial reforms on access to finance and financing conditions for SMEs more generally. The 2020 report provides information about SMEs' and entrepreneurs' access to finance over the 2007-18 period. Based on data collected for the country profiles and information from demand-side surveys, it includes indicators on debt, equity and asset-based finance, as well as on financing framework conditions, complemented by information on recent public and private initiatives to support SME access to finance.

The 2020 report is the eight edition of this annual report. It presents data for 48 countries: Australia, Austria, Belarus, Belgium, Brazil, Canada, Chile, the People's Republic of China, Colombia, the Czech Republic, Denmark, Estonia, Finland, France, Georgia, Greece, Hungary, Indonesia, Ireland, Israel, Italy, Japan, Kazakhstan, Korea, Latvia, Lithuania, Luxembourg, Malaysia, Mexico, the Netherlands, New Zealand, Norway, Peru, Poland, Portugal, the Russian Federation, Serbia, the Slovak Republic, Slovenia, South Africa, Spain, Sweden, Switzerland, Thailand, Turkey, Ukraine, the United Kingdom and the United States.

Chapter 1 of this publication captures recent trends in SME and entrepreneurship finance, drawing on data received from experts from participating countries, as well as from external sources. It also provides an overview of major policy developments across Scoreboard countries. Chapter 2 puts the spotlight on a thematic issue of particular interest. This edition focuses on the evolution of SME financing policies since the financial crisis in 2008 and documents the shift from immediate crisis response measures to addressing more structural issues and putting in place the appropriate regulatory environment for Fintech. Chapter 3 contains profiles of SME and entrepreneurship developments, as well as relevant policies, for all 48 participating countries. The print edition of this publication includes a snapshot view with key facts and figures, while the more detailed, complete profiles, can be accessed online.

This publication was prepared by the SME and Entrepreneurship Division of the Centre for Entrepreneurship, SMEs, Regions and Cities (CFE/SMEE) under the guidance of the OECD Working Party on SMEs and Entrepreneurs (WPSMEE) and the WPSMEE Informal Steering Group on SME and Entrepreneurship Financing. The initial findings were discussed at the meeting of the WPSMEE Informal Steering Group on SME Finance on 10 and 11 September 2019, and a more advanced version of the report was presented at the 56th meeting of the WPSMEE on 16 and 17 October 2019. The final report was approved by written procedure on 17 January 2020 [CFE/SME(2019)11/CHAP1/FINAL, CFE/SME(2019)11/CHAP2/FINAL and CFE/SME(2019)11/CHAP3/ADD/FINAL].

Acknowledgements

This report was produced by the OECD Centre for Entrepreneurship, SMEs, Regions and Cities (CFE), led by Lamia Kamal-Chaoui, Director, as part of the programme of work of the Working Party on SMEs and Entrepreneurship. The development of *Financing SMEs and Entrepreneurs 2020: An OECD Scoreboard* is possible thanks to the country experts from participating OECD member and non-member countries who provided information for the country profiles (see below).

The development of the Scoreboard also benefited from the inputs of Delegates of the OECD Working Party on SMEs and Entrepreneurship (WPSMEE), chaired by Martin Godel (State Secretariat for Economic Affairs, Switzerland), and members of its Informal Steering Group on SME and Entrepreneurship Financing, chaired by Professor Salvatore Zecchini (Italy).

Data and input provided by Wiebke Bartz-Zuccala (CFE/SMEE), Jurgita Bucyte (LeasEurope), Felix Haas (European Association of Guarantee Institutions), Helmut Kraemer-Eis (European Investment Fund), Kenix Lee (World Federation of Exchanges), Gianluca Riccio (OECD Business and Industry Advisory Committee) and Tania Ziegler (Cambridge Centre for Alternative Finance) are gratefully acknowledged. Stefanie Fröhling and Tanja Wulf (German Federal Ministry for Economic Affairs and Energy) provided information on SME and entrepreneurship policies in Germany.

This report was prepared by Kris Boschmans, Policy Analyst (CFE/SMEE) under the supervision of Miriam Koreen (Senior Counsellor, CFE/SMEE) and Lucia Cusmano (Acting Head of Division, CFE/SMEE). Jules Beley, Erika Soki and Maria Zamyatina (Trainees, CFE/SMEE) contributed to the publication. Heather Mortimer-Charoy provided technical support and Francois Iglesias communications support.

Country expert team

Australia	Evan Holley	Department of Employment, Skills, Small and Family Business
	Elizabeth Yoo	Department of Employment, Skills, Small and Family Business
Austria	Florian Eichberger	Federal Ministry for Digital and Economic Affairs
Belgium	Johan Westra	Federal Ministry of Economy, SMEs, Self-employed and Energy
	Christophe Herinckx	Federal Ministry of Economy, SMEs, Self-employed and Energy
Belarus	Irina Babachenok	Ministry of the Economy
Brazil	Alfredo Gonçalves Nascimento	Special Secretary for Micro and Small Enterprises (SEMPE)
Canada	Richard Archambault	Innovation Science and Economic Development Canada
Chile	Manuel López Bugueño	Ministry for the Economy, Development, and Tourism
	David Alejandro Calderón Mora	Ministry for the Economy, Development, and Tourism
China	Wu Bao	China Institute for Small and Medium-sized Enterprises
	Renyong Chi	China Institute for Small and Medium-sized Enterprises
	Chenfei Jin	China Institute for Small and Medium-sized Enterprises
Colombia	Jose David Quintero Nieto	Ministry of Commerce, Industry and Tourism
Czech Republic	Veronika Reek	Ministry of Industry and Trade
	Lukeš Zdenek	Ministry of Industry and Trade
Denmark	Anna Guldborg Ølgaard	Ministry of Industry, Business and Financial Affairs
	Rasmus Borup Nielsen	Ministry of Industry, Business and Financial Affairs
Estonia	Karel Lember	Ministry of Economic Affairs and Communications
Finland	Eeva Alho	Ministry of Economic Affairs and Employment
France	Jean-Pierre Villetelle	Banque de France
	Simon Verna	General Directorate for Competitiveness, Industry and Services
Georgia	Tinatin Khulordava	Enterprise Georgia

Greece	Timotheos Rekkas	Hellenic Ministry for Economy and Development
	Athanasios Argyriou	Hellenic Ministry for Economy and Development
Hungary	Péter Pogácsás	Ministry of Innovation and Technology
Indonesia	Yonas Dian Hermanu	Ministry of Cooperative and SMEs
Ireland	Leona Cantillon	Department of Finance, Banking Policy Division
	Eric Gargan	Department of Finance, Banking Policy Division
Israel	Nir Ben-Aharon	Small and Medium Business Agency, Ministry of Economy
Italy	Sabrina Pastorelli	Bank of Italy
Japan	Daiji Hotihama	Small and Medium Enterprise Agency, Ministry of Economy, Trade and Industry
	Ryota Ochi	Small and Medium Enterprise Agency, Ministry of Economy, Trade and Industry
	Megumi Daiki	Small and Medium Enterprise Agency, Ministry of Economy, Trade and Industry
Kazakhstan	Anuar Ospanov	Damu Entrepreneurship Fund
	Adlet Kerimbekov	Damu Entrepreneurship Fund
Korea	Meeroo Kim	Korea Development Institute
	Suhan Kim	Korea Development Institute
	Juyeon Seo	Korea Development Institute
Latvia	Liene Bergholde	Ministry of Economics
Lithuania	Petras Dubinskas	Bank of Lithuania
Luxembourg	Cesare Riilio	National Institute for Statistics and Economic Studies
Malaysia	Farhana Sheikh Salim Alkhatib	SME Corporation Malaysia
Mexico	Octavio Gutiérrez	INADEM
	Luis Manuel Rodríguez Avila	INADEM
	Ivan Ornelas Diaz	INADEM
Netherlands	Liselotte Van Thiel	Ministry of Economic Affairs
	Pawel Bonilla	Ministry of Economic Affairs
New Zealand	Katie Sadetskaya	Ministry of Business, Innovation and Employment
	Saskia Berger	Ministry of Business, Innovation and Employment
Norway	Eirik Knutsen	Statistics Norway
	Øystein Jørgensen	Ministry of Trade, Industry and Fisheries
Peru	Daniel Jesus Vargas Canchan	Ministry of Production
Poland	Martyna Wieczorek	Ministry of Entrepreneurship and Technology
Portugal	António Almeida	Office of the Secretary of State of Economy and Regional Development
Russia	Evgeny Tcherbakov	Vnesheconombank
Serbia	Maja Gavrilovic	National Bank of Serbia
	Ana Ivkovic	National Bank of Serbia
Slovak Republic	Jakub Lukác	National Agency for SME Development
	Tatiana Smoronová	National Agency for SME Development
Slovenia	Tine Janžek	Bank of Slovenia
South Africa	Peter Makgetsi	National Treasury, Financial Sector Policy Unit
	Mulalo Mamburu	National Treasury, Financial Sector Policy Unit
Spain	Víctor García-Vaquero	Bank of Spain
Sweden	Andreas Kroksgård	Swedish Agency for Growth Policy Analysis
Switzerland	Samuel Turcati	State Secretariat for Economic Affairs
Thailand	Davina Kunvipusilkul	Bank of Thailand
Turkey	Ufuk Acar	KOSGEB
	Utku Macit	Ministry of Science, Industry and Technology
Ukraine	Olena Kravchenko	SME Development Office
	Andrii Remizov	Ministry for Development of Economy, Trade and Agriculture
United Kingdom	Matt Adey	British Business Bank
	Anthony Gray	British Business Bank
United States	Giuseppe Gramigna	Small Business Administration
	Henry Childs	Minority Business Development Agency
	Ryan Sun	Minority Business Development Agency

Table of contents

Tables

Figures

Boxes

Reader's Guide

Indicators

SME and entrepreneurship financing trends are monitored through core indicators, listed in Table 1, selected on the criteria of usefulness, availability, feasibility and timeliness (see Annex A for a detailed description). In detail, the core indicators describe and monitor the following key dimensions:

Table 1. Core indicators in Financing SMEs and entrepreneurs, 2020

Core indicators	Unit	What they show
The allocation and structure of bank credit to SMEs		
Outstanding business loans, SMEs	Volumes in national currency	SME demand for and access to bank credit. A stock indicator measuring the value of an asset at a given point in time, and thus reflecting both new lending, as well as bank loans that have accumulated over time along with loan repayments.
Outstanding business loans, total	Volumes in national currency	
Share of SME outstanding loans	% of total outstanding loans	
New business lending, total	Volumes in national currency	SME demand for and access to bank credit. It is a flow indicator, measured over one year, which tends to respond faster to short-term developments and is therefore more volatile than stocks.
New business lending, SMEs	Volumes in national currency	
Share of new SME lending	% of total new lending	
Short-term loans, SMEs	Volumes in national currency	The structure of SME debt, i.e. the share of outstanding credit with an initial maturity of less than one year and more than one year, respectively. This could be considered as a proxy to gauge the purpose of SME bank loans, i.e. for operational and investment needs.
Long-term loans, SMEs	Volumes in national currency	
Extent of public support for SME finance		
Government loan guarantees, SMEs	Volumes in national currency	These indicators illustrate the extent and uptake of government programmes and instruments supporting SMEs' access to finance.
Government guaranteed loans, SMEs	Volumes in national currency	
Direct government loans, SMEs	Volumes in national currency	
Credit costs and conditions		
Interest rate, SMEs	%	The cost of SME loans and how it compares to large firms.
Interest rate, large firms	%	
Interest rate spread	Percentage points	
Collateral, SMEs	% of SMEs needing collateral to obtain bank lending	Proxies the conditions SMEs face when applying for bank credit.
Percentage of SME loan applications	SME loan applications/ total number of SMEs, in %	The (unmet) demand for and utilisation of credit by SMEs, and willingness of banks to lend.

<table>
<tr><td>Rejection rate</td><td>1-(SME loans authorised/ requested), in %</td><td rowspan="2"></td></tr>
<tr><td>Utilisation rate</td><td>SME loans used/ authorised, in %</td></tr>
<tr><td colspan="3">Non-bank sources of finance</td></tr>
<tr><td>Venture and growth capital investments</td><td>Volumes in national currency and year-on-year growth rate in %</td><td rowspan="3">The take-up and ability to access non-bank finance instruments, including external equity for start-up, early development and expansion stages, as well as asset-based finance, such as leasing, hire purchases, factoring and invoice discounting.</td></tr>
<tr><td>Leasing and hire purchases</td><td>Volumes in national currency</td></tr>
<tr><td>Factoring and invoice discounting</td><td>Volumes in national currency</td></tr>
<tr><td colspan="3">Financial health</td></tr>
<tr><td>Non-performing loans, total</td><td>% of total business loans</td><td rowspan="2">The incidence of late or non-payments for SME loans, compared to the overall corporate sector. This proxies the (relative) riskiness of lending to SMEs.</td></tr>
<tr><td>Non-performing loans, SMEs</td><td>% of total SME loans</td></tr>
<tr><td>Payment delays, B2B</td><td>Number of days</td><td>The occurrence of payment delays in the B2B sector, i.e. the difficulty in paying and being paid, to capture the extent of cash flow problems.</td></tr>
<tr><td>Bankruptcies, SMEs</td><td>Number and year-on-year growth rate in %</td><td>A proxy for the overall business environment in which SMEs operate and the ability of small firms to survive economic downturns and credit crunches.</td></tr>
</table>

Data collection

The Scoreboard data are provided by experts designated by participating countries. Most of the indicators are derived from supply-side data provided by financial institutions, statistical offices and other government agencies. This is supplemented by national and regional demand-side surveys in order to provide a more comprehensive view of the evolution in financing trends and needs. Indicators cover access to finance for employer firms, that is, for SMEs which have at least one employee, and are operating a non-financial business. The data in the present edition cover the period 2007 to 2018, assessing trends over the medium term, both in the pre-crisis period (2007), the financial crisis (2008 and 2009) and the period afterwards. Specific attention is placed on developments occurring in 2017, 2018 and the first half of 2019. In addition, information on government policies to ease SMEs' access to finance is also collected on a systematic basis.

The published print version includes a chapter on emerging trends in SME and entrepreneurship finance, drawing on information provided by participating countries, a thematic chapter, focusing for this edition on the potential to collateralise SMEs' intangible assets, annexes, and a two-page snapshot for every participating country. This snapshot summarises the state of play regarding SME access to finance in each country, while the full country profiles will be available on the OECD website only.

Cross-country comparability

At the individual country level, the Scoreboard provides a coherent picture of SMEs' access to finance over time and monitors changing conditions for SME financing, as well as the impact of policies. There are limits to possible cross-country comparisons, however. Firstly, the statistical definition of an SME differs among participating countries; while the European Union definition is the most commonly used, participating countries outside of the Union usually define an SME differently, which complicates cross country comparisons (see Annex A for detailed definitions of SMEs across participating countries).

In addition, differences in definition and coverage for indicators hamper comparability, with a number of countries in which it is not possible to adhere to the "preferred definition" of the core indicators. A proxy has been adopted in these instances. For this reason, all country profiles include a table, which provides the definition adopted for each indicator and a reference to the data source. Despite these limitations, it is still possible to compare general trends across countries, though, as the differences in the exact composition of the single indicator are muted when evaluating rates of change.

Methodological advances and recommendations for data improvements

There are important methodological and structural improvements in recent editions of this report. More detailed information regarding the source and definition of core indicators have been provided for participating countries. Since June 2016, the Scoreboard data are available on the OECD.Stat website. Data on core indicators can be consulted, downloaded and put to further use, thereby addressing a longstanding demand to improve access to the data, and exposure of the publication to a wider audience. In addition, more information is provided on the uptake of financial instruments other than straight debt, and further endeavours will be undertaken in this area for future editions of the publication. Country profiles in the printed edition of this publication are abbreviated to two pages with key facts and the table with core indicators, while the full profiles remain available online. Finally, efforts are ongoing to increase the coverage of participating countries and to harmonise the data from already participating countries.

A summary of recommendations to further improve data collection and reporting of core indicators are outlined in Box 1 (see Annex A for a more detailed discussion), as well as in Chapter 1 of this publication. These are deemed necessary for countries to progress in the harmonisation of definitions and facilitate inter-temporal and cross-country analysis of trends in SME and entrepreneurship finance.

Box 1. Recommendations for improving the reporting of core indicators

1. Improve reporting of SME loan variables by:

- Systematically separating reporting of financial information for non-employer and employer-firms;
- Providing both stock and flow data for SME loans;
- Detailing the loans' composition, with indication of the different underlying products (e.g. overdrafts / lines of credit / leases / business mortgages or credit cards / securitised loans), and disclose such elements in the loan definition.

2. Fill gaps in available data and work towards more comprehensive information for other core indicators in the Scoreboard, including

- Offer more comprehensive information on government programmes that ease SMEs' access to finance.
- Provide data on non-performing loans for SMEs and for large firms, the latter to be used as a benchmark.
- Provide more comprehensive data on alternative sources of financing, including crowdfunding and business angel investments
- Collect information on SME loan fees, in addition to interest applied on the loans.
- Compile more complete information on the uptake and use of non-bank financing instruments, asset-based finance in particular.
- Detail the definition of collateral and improve reporting, using demand-side surveys to compensate for lack of supply-side data.

Acronyms and abbreviations

ADB	Asian Development Bank
AECM	European Association of Mutual Guarantee Societies
AUD	Australian dollar
B2B	Business-to-Business
B2C	Business-to-Customer
B2G	Business-to-Government
BIS	Bank for International Settlements
BLS	Bank Lending Survey
BRL	Brazilian rial
BYN	Belarusian ruble
CAD	Canadian dollar
CDS	Credit Default Swap
CGS	Credit Guarantee Scheme
CHF	Swiss franc
CLO	Collateralised debt obligation
CLP	Chilean peso
CNY	Chinese renminbi
COP	Colombian peso
CZK	Czech koruna
DKK	Danish krone
EBITDA	Earnings before interest, taxes, depreciation, and amortization
EBRD	European Bank for Reconstruction and Development
EC	European Commission
ECB	European Central Bank
EIB	European Investment Bank
EIF	European Investment Fund
ERP	European Rescue Programme
EU	European Union
EUR	Euro

EURIBOR	Euro Interbank Offered Rate
EVCA	European Venture Capital Association
FCI	Factors Chain International
G20	Group of 20
GBP	British bound
GDP	Gross domestic product
GEL	Georgian lari
GPFI	Global Partnership for Financial Inclusion
HUF	Hungarian forint
IDR	Indonesian rupiah
IFC	International Finance Corporation
IMF	International Monetary Fund
IPO	Initial public offering
IT	Information technology
JPY	Japanese yen
KRW	Korean won
KZT	Kazakhstani tenge
MFI	Micro-finance institution
MSME	Micro, small and medium-sized enterprise
MXN	Mexican peso
MYR	Malaysian ringgit
NFIB	National Federation of Independent Business
NIS	Israeli new shekel
NOK	Norwegian krone
NPL	Non-performing loan
NYSE	New York Stock Exchange
NZD	New Zealand dollar
OECD	Organisation for Economic Co-operation and Development
PCS	Prime collateralised securities
PE	Private equity
PEN	Peruvian nuevo sol
PLN	Polish zloty
R&D	Research and development
RSD	Serbian dinar
RSI	Risk Sharing Instrument
RUB	New Russian ruble
SAFE	Survey on the Access to Finance of Enterprises

SBA	Small Business Act
SEK	Swedish krona
SME	Small and medium-sized enterprise
THB	Thai baht
TRY	Turkish lira
UAH	Ukrainian hryvnia
UF	Unidad de Fomento
USAID	United States Agency for International Development
USD	United States dollar
VC	Venture capital
WB	World Bank
WPSMEE	Working Party on SMEs and Entrepreneurship
ZAR	South African rand

ISO Country Abbreviations			
AUS	Australia	**JPN**	Japan
AUT	Austria	**KAZ**	Kazakhstan
BEL	Belgium	**KOR**	Korea
BLR	Belarus	**LTU**	Lithuania
BRA	Brazil	**LUX**	Luxembourg
CAN	Canada	**LVA**	Latvia
CHE	Switzerland	**MYS**	Malaysia
CHN	People's Republic of China	**MEX**	Mexico
CHL	Chile	**NLD**	Netherlands
COL	Colombia	**NZL**	New Zealand
CZE	Czech Republic	**NOR**	Norway
DNK	Denmark	**PER**	Peru
ESP	Spain	**POL**	Poland
EST	Estonia	**PRT**	Portugal
FIN	Finland	**RUS**	Russian Federation
FRA	France	**SRB**	Serbia
GBR	United Kingdom	**SVK**	Slovak Republic
GEO	Georgia	**SVN**	Slovenia
GRC	Greece	**SWE**	Sweden
HUN	Hungary	**THA**	Thailand
IDN	Indonesia	**TUR**	Turkey
IRL	Ireland	**UKR**	Ukraine
ISR	Israel	**USA**	United States
ITA	Italy	**ZAF**	South Africa

Executive Summary

Financing SMEs and Entrepreneurs 2020: An OECD Scoreboard provides information on SME financing trends and policies for 48 countries around the world over the 2007-18 period. The Scoreboard includes indicators of debt, equity, asset-based finance and framework conditions for SME and entrepreneurship finance, complemented by demand-side information and recent developments in public and private initiatives to support SME finance. Taken together, these indicators form a comprehensive framework for policy makers and other stakeholders to evaluate the financing needs of SMEs. The Scoreboard also constitutes a valuable tool to support the design and evaluation of policy measures, and to monitor the implications of financial reforms on access to finance and financing conditions for SMEs.

The 2020 edition shows that macroeconomic trends as well as tightening credit conditions may have started to impact SME lending in some countries. Furthermore, at the time of publication, the global coronavirus (COVID-19) pandemic was producing immediate and profound effects, which will impact a number of SME finance indicators going forward.

The use of a diverse range of alternative financing instruments by SMEs, including asset-based instruments, online alternative finance and venture capital, continued to grow in 2018:

- Leasing and factoring volumes were up in a large majority of countries, in line with long-term trends. Growth in factoring accelerated in 2018;
- Online alternative finance activities were up by 54% in 2018 as a median value for participating countries, albeit often from a low base;
- Venture capital investments rose by 20.9% as a median value between 2017 and 2018, up from 0.4% in the previous year;
- Public listings on SME stock markets in 2018 were down compared to 2017, but activities remained high from a long-term perspective.

On the other hand, both new lending to SMEs and the outstanding stock of SME loans grew only modestly in 2018, with a significant drop in the median growth rate of these two indicators. SME loan shares declined modestly across both middle- and high-income countries in 2018. These developments raise questions related to possible substitution effects between alternative instruments and straight debt, as well as to SME demand.

The progressive shift from short-term to long-term SME lending continued in 2018, with long maturities outweighing short maturities in most countries. As a median value, more than half of all new SME loans were of a maturity of more than one year in 2018, as compared to less than one in five in 2008.

These developments in SME loans took place against the backdrop of generally favourable, though evolving, lending conditions. Collateral requirements and rejection rates declined in a majority of countries for which data is available. Payment delays remained roughly stable in 2018, and were below pre-crisis levels. Meanwhile, the number of SME bankruptcies decreased in 2018 for the sixth consecutive year, although, there is evidence that the decline is levelling off. At the same time, non-performing SME loans rose in a majority of participating countries in 2018, whereas non-performing loans for all businesses broadly stagnated, indicating a growing divergence between SMEs and large companies.

While interest rates declined in most middle-income countries, their median value rose very slightly in high-incomes economies, marking a break from previous years. This is in line with recent survey data indicating an uptick in the price of credit in some countries. Interest rate spreads between large enterprises and SMEs declined slightly in 2018.

The thematic chapter of this publication puts a spotlight on policy developments to facilitate SMEs' access to finance since the financial crisis. In the immediate aftermath of the financial crisis, policy makers around the world strengthened initiatives to ease access to debt instruments. Later, the focus shifted to support for specific sub-groups of the SME population facing distinct challenges to raise finance; improving delivery and eligibility criteria of existing policies; and supporting equity markets. Another important development relates to regulation, where the emphasis has shifted from guaranteeing financial stability to regulating the Fintech industry. Recent policy developments can be summarised as follows:

- Loan guarantees remain the most widespread instrument at the disposal of governments and private promotional institutions to tackle market failure in the area of SME finance, and loan guarantee volumes continued to rise in 2018.
- Support for equity instruments has developed through a variety of channels, and policymakers are seeking to increase SMEs' access to capital markets. In addition, an increasing number of jurisdictions have taken regulatory measures to foster and provide a framework for financial innovation.
- New developments include the implementation of open banking protocols in several jurisdictions. As part of these protocols, banks must allow their clients to share their financial information with other authorised providers, loosening these institutions' control on their clients' data.
- Financial support measures to enable SMEs to become active in foreign markets have been introduced or strengthened in recent years. In particular, there has been a focus on expanding knowledge and use of public export finance and export insurance instruments.
- Governments are also increasingly exploring the use of online tools, such as artificial intelligence, to inform entrepreneurs and small business owners about public support measures tailored for their business needs.

At the time of publication, policy makers across the world are taking action to dampen the impacts of the novel coronavirus (COVID-19) pandemic on SMEs. These measures take place in a financial context which was generally favourable for SMEs before the pandemic hit, but which was not sufficient to enable them to face the magnitude of the current shocks without government intervention. Many of the measures are aimed at enabling viable businesses to deal with temporary but severe liquidity shortages, stemming from the outbreak and the containment measures that were put in place in response. These include deferral of tax, social security, rent, utility and debt payments, faster payments for public procurement contracts, loan guarantees and direct lending to SMEs, grants and subsidies.

In light of the increasingly pessimistic macroeconomic outlook, governments need to remain extremely vigilant. The OECD will continue to monitor closely the short-term impacts of the coronavirus pandemic on the availability of finance, along with the effectiveness of policy responses. It will also assess longer-term implications to support governments in taking appropriate actions for their SMEs.

1. Recent Trends in SME and Entrepreneurship Finance

This document contains the draft of Chapter 1 of Financing SMEs and Entrepreneurs 2020: An OECD Scoreboard. It analyses trends in SME and entrepreneurship finance over 2007-18, based on data collected for the country Scoreboards and information from demand-side surveys. A short overview of the global business environment sets the framework for the analysis of SME financing trends and conditions, focusing in particular on the changes that occurred in 2018 and the first half of 2019. The chapter concludes with an overview of government policy responses put in place to improve SME access to finance in light of recent developments.

Business environment and macroeconomic context

In 2019, global economic dynamism weakened amidst trade tensions, policy uncertainty and declines in business and consumer confidence in both high-income countries and emerging countries. At the start of 2020, growth rates were well below the figures for the last three decades, although financial conditions had eased and inflation was set to remain moderate. Global GDP slowed to 3.5% in 2018, 2.9 in 2019 and was projected to slip further to a below-trend rate of 2.4% in 2020, before the coronavirus (COVID-19) global pandemic. Significant downward risks to the global economy included an escalation of trade tensions, rising geopolitical strains, disruptions to the supply of oil, a sharper than expected slowdown in China and the United Kingdom's exit from the European Union (OECD, 2019[1]).

At the time of publication, the spread of the coronavirus (COVID-19) is sounding a major alarm bell for growth prospects and significantly raises the probability of the cyclical downturn becoming more severe. Global GDP forecasts will be revised downwards, possibly turning negative, with businesses facing shocks in both supply and demand. Financial markets would likely be impacted severely in this scenario. Government bond yields in many countries have reached all-time lows, as markets have become more risk-averse (OECD, 2020).

Trade and business investment

The growth in global trade saw a steep drop from 5.5% in 2017 to 3.9% in 2018 and 1.2% in 2019 and may turn negative in 2020 (OECD, 2019[1]). Trade volumes fell, reflecting weak external and internal demand in Europe and import slowdown in China. Additionally, trade is being affected by a proliferation of tariffs and subsidies around the world and an increasing unpredictability of trade policies. Global supply chains have also come under considerable strain because of the COVID-19 pandemic (OECD, 2020).

The anticipated trade forecast is consistent with the dim investment outlook in many economies. High levels of uncertainty, especially related to the spread of the novel coronavirus, downward-revised GDP growth forecasts and a decline in business dynamism in some countries are all leading to reduced incentives to invest. Aggregate investments growth in G20 economies (excluding China) declined from an annualised rate of 5% at the beginning of 2018 to 1% in the first half of 2019. Both corporate investments and infrastructure investments are projected to remain well below the long-term average in 2019 and 2020. In 2018, the stock of foreign direct investments (FDI) fell for the first time since 2011, with a sharper contraction in 2019 (OECD, 2019[1]).

Financial conditions

Financial conditions remained accommodative in 2018 and 2019, buffering the effects of the slowdown. In the major advanced economies, central banks either paused monetary policy normalisation or added modest stimulus. Both short- and long-term interest rates have fallen in many areas of the world in recent years. Long-term interest rates are at especially low levels in a historical perspective, giving a boost to business activity in different sectors of economy (see Figure 1.1).

Financial market conditions improved, with signals of a more favourable monetary policy helping reverse the repricing of risk seen in late 2018. Equity markets have strengthened, with long-term yields on government bonds declining and corporate and emerging-market bond spreads narrowing (OECD, 2019[1]). However, trade tensions brought significant volatility to asset prices. Despite weaker global demand, oil prices increased in 2018 as a result of supply restrictions by OPEC and Russia and sanctions applied to Iran and Venezuela.

Moreover, financial vulnerabilities are also mounting. The debt of non-financial corporations is high by historical standards and its quality worsening. A market shock could trigger a wide sell-off of corporate bonds, especially for the high proportion that are currently rated just above non-investment grade. The record level of government and corporate debt trading at negative yields, as well as the low (and sometimes even negative) gap between long- and short-term assets are indicative of an unconventional monetary policy and a flight to safety by investors.

The spread of the COVID-19 virus also has financial implications. SMEs in need of finance, especially those with a relatively risky profile such as innovative businesses and start-ups, will likely find it increasingly hard to obtain external finance. In addition, liquidity shortages will probably become more common, as supply chains are interrupted and firms may face lower revenues and unexpected expenses. The IMF, for example, expects credit conditions to tighten and borrowing costs to rise (IMF, 2020).

Figure 1.1. Monetary policy is accommodative

Short-term versus long-term interest rates between 2009 and 2019

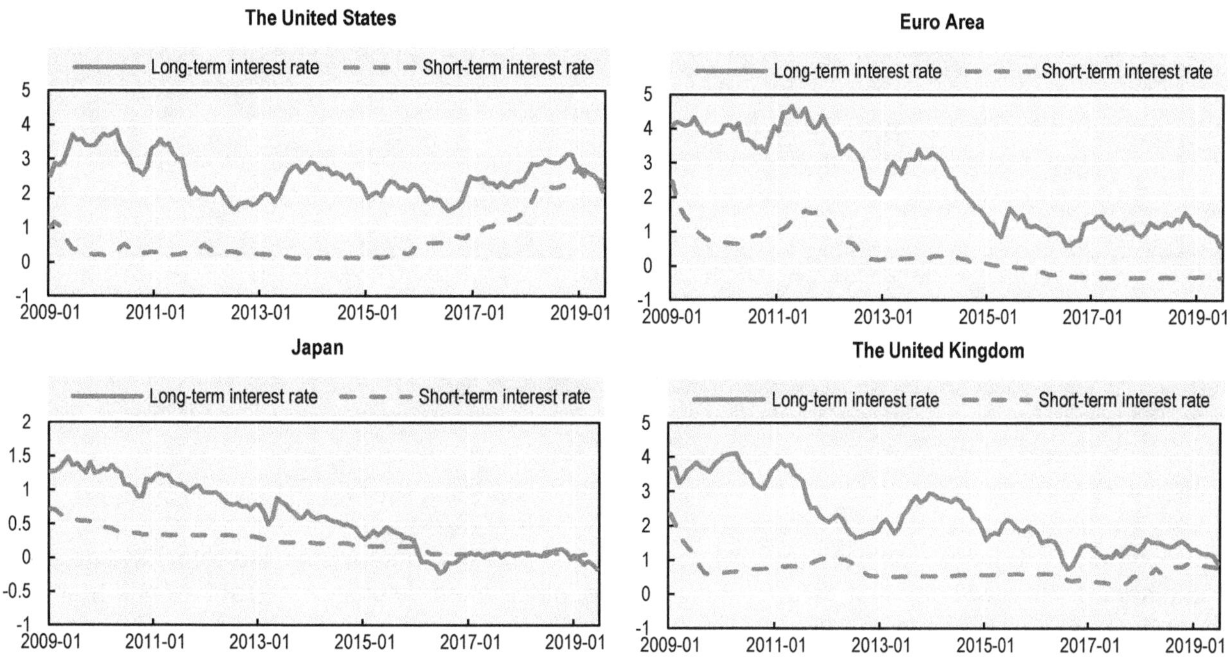

Source: OECD Main Economic Indicators (Finance).

StatLink https://doi.org/10.1787/888934115426

Lending to SMEs

Growth in new SME lending has been sluggish for most participating countries. After modest growth in 2017, the median growth rate fell in 2018. The growth in stocks of outstanding SME loans (measured by median values) has been declining since 2015 and stood at 0.77% in 2018. Overall, demand for finance remained broadly stable at low levels, holding back stronger growth in lending. This is also evidenced by recent survey data.

New SME loans

New SME loans showed a mixed picture in 2018. The median growth rate decreased to 0.69% in 2018 from 3.06% in 2017 (see Figure 1.2).

Figure 1.2. New SME loans, growth rates

Year-on-year growth rate, as a percentage

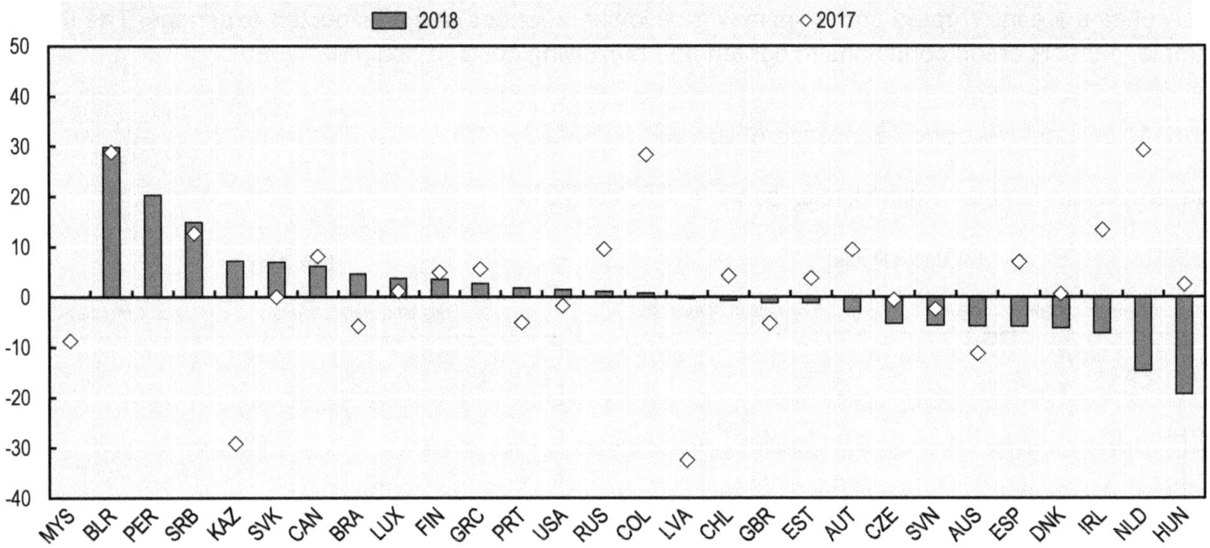

Note: The 2017 growth rate for Peru (132.92%) is not depicted. All data are adjusted for inflation using the OECD GDP deflator. Data for non-OECD countries were extracted from the World Development Indicators from the World Bank.
Source: Data compiled from the individual country profiles.

StatLink https://doi.org/10.1787/888934115445

Growth in new SME loans was positive in 14 countries that provided data for this indicator, and negative in 13 others. It is noteworthy that data for individual countries often display significant swings from one year to the next. For example, in Chile, Denmark, Estonia, Hungary, Ireland, the Netherlands and Spain, the growth rate turned negative in 2018, sometimes sharply. By contrast, Portugal showed a positive growth rate for the first time since 2012, from -5.14% to 1.74%. The United States also reversed a consecutive 2-year negative growth rate trend in 2018.

All seven middle-income countries with data available for this indicator showed positive growth rates in 2018. After four consecutive years of decline, new lending to SMEs in Brazil grew by 4.52% in 2018. For its part, Belarus showed a remarkable increase in new lending in 2018, at 29.81%. There is a marked difference between middle-income and high-income countries over the 2015-18 period, with growth rates considerably higher in the former. This marks a difference with the 2013-15 period where no clear trend could be observed (see Figure 1.3).

Figure 1.3. Growth in new SME lending, 2008-18

Median year-on-year growth rate, as a percentage

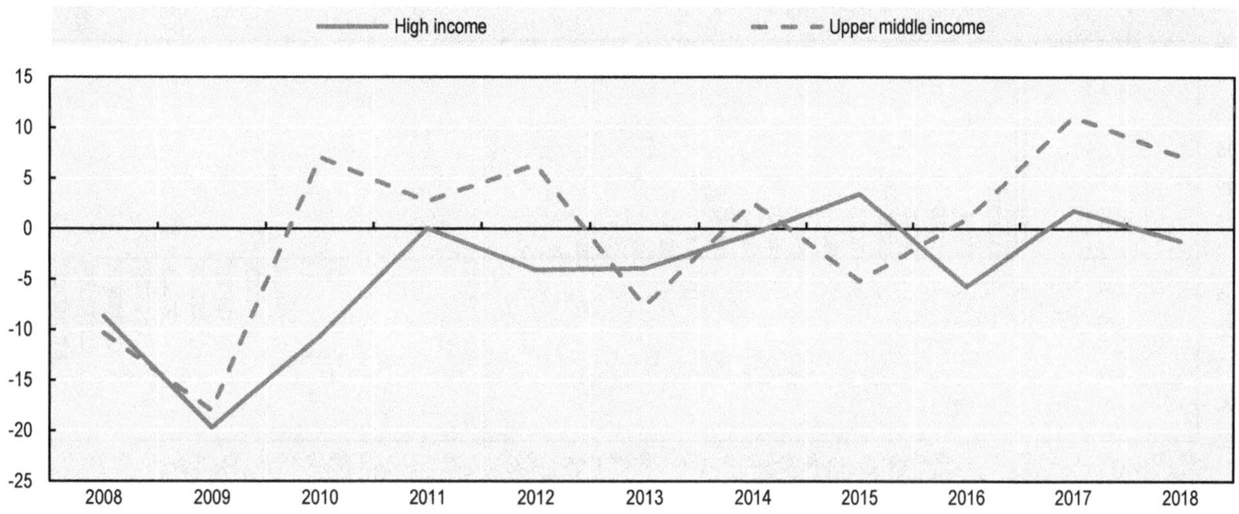

Notes: All data are adjusted for inflation using the OECD GDP deflator. Data for non-OECD countries were extracted from the World Development Indicators from the World Bank

Source: Data compiled from the individual country profiles

StatLink https://doi.org/10.1787/888934115464

Outstanding stock of SME loans

The stock of SME loans grew in 20 out of 36 countries that provided data for this indicator (see Figure 1.4), while the Scoreboard median value of the year-on-year growth in outstanding SME loans decreased from 2.02% in 2017 to 0.77% in 2018. Outstanding SME loan growth turned positive in 2018 in Hungary and Peru and turned negative in Australia, Estonia, the Netherlands and Spain. In Chile, the Czech Republic, New Zealand, Serbia, South Korea and Switzerland, growth in the outstanding SME loans gained further momentum in 2018.

While both new and outstanding SME loans are used to describe developments in the credit market, the latter is influenced by the pace of loan repayments, changes in loan maturity and fluctuations in non-performing loans, thus causing occasional divergence between the two indicators. For example, in the Czech Republic the outstanding stock of SME loans increased by 1.79% in 2017 and 2.95% in 2018, while new SME loans were down -0.65% in 2017 and -5.30% in 2018. On the other hand, the outstanding stock of SME loans in Greece went down by -8.19% in 2017 and -8.50% in 2018, while new SME loans increased by 5.48% in 2017 and 2.65% in 2018.

Additionally, in many countries there has been an upward trend in the share of long-term loans compared to short-term credit. This can partly explain the divergent trends in flow and stock data, since loans of greater maturity remain in the data for outstanding loans for a longer period.

Figure 1.4. Growth in outstanding SME business loans

Year-on-year growth rate, as a percentage

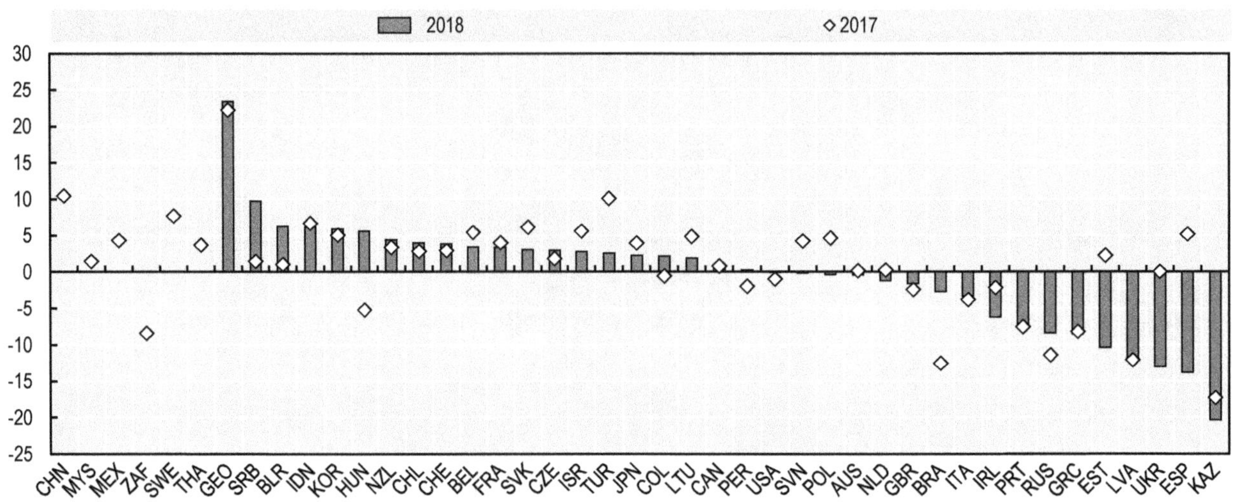

Note: Data is not available for Ukraine in 2017. All data are adjusted for inflation using the OECD GDP deflator. Data for non-OECD countries were extracted from the World Development Indicators from the World Bank.
Source: Data compiled from the individual country profiles.

StatLink https://doi.org/10.1787/888934115483

SME loan shares

SME loan shares vary significantly across countries, for both stock and flow data. Defined as the share of SME loans to total business loans, they help to situate indicators on SME lending in the context of general business lending trends. The share of outstanding SME business loans ranged from around 20% or less in Canada, Chile, France, Indonesia, Peru, Russia and the United States, to levels of more than 70% in Korea, Latvia, Portugal and Switzerland. SME loan shares are negatively correlated with the absolute size of countries and their economies, reflecting the generally stronger presence of large firms in larger economies. However, the correlation of SME loan shares with income is positive: high-income countries tend to exhibit higher SME loan shares.

The 2018 median value of the SME loan share for participating middle-income countries stood at 30.42%, compared to 52.52% for high-income countries.[1] This may reflect a stronger preference of the banking sector in middle-income economies to lend to large enterprises. In these economies, the financial system is often less developed and fewer options are available to SMEs and entrepreneurs. Finally, there are also demand-side dynamics, as SMEs in middle-income countries are known to be more likely to refrain from applying for credit even though they need it (Abraham and Schmukler, 2017[2]). China represents a notable exception, both in terms of its size and income level, with 64.96% of corporate loans flowing to SMEs in 2017.

The median value for SME loan shares provides some insight into overall trends. It declined from 41.6% in 2007 to a low of 37.9% in 2013, indicating more problematic access to bank credit for SMEs compared to large enterprises over this period. After 2013, the share of outstanding SME loans rose again, in line with recovery; nonetheless, it stood at 40.41% in 2018, below its pre-crisis level, and below 2017 figures. The decrease in 2018 was most strongly observed among high-income countries, but was also present in middle-income countries.

Figure 1.5. SME loan shares

As a percentage of total outstanding business loans

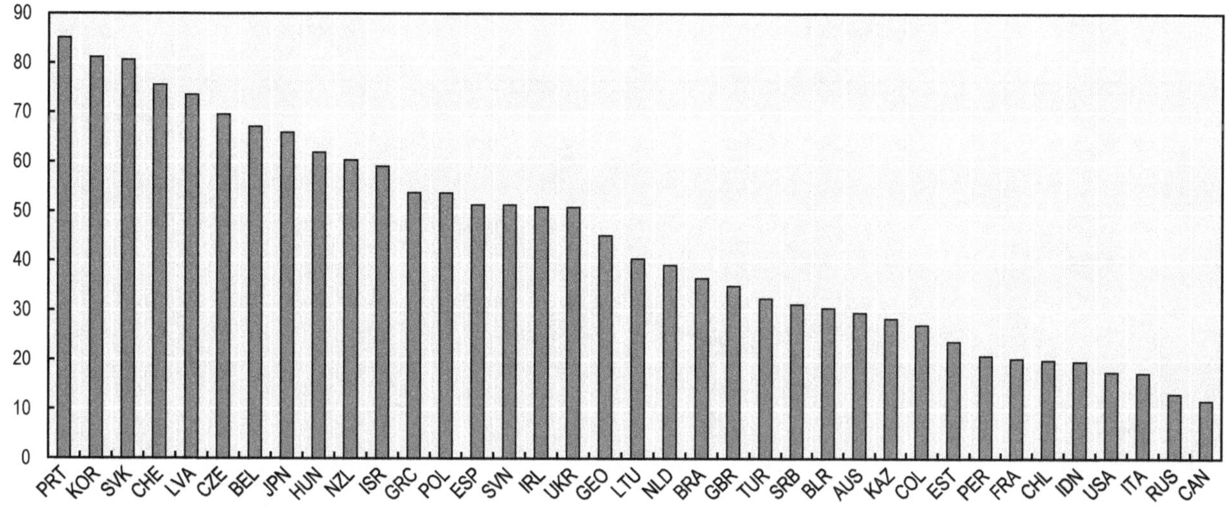

Source: Data compiled from the individual country profiles.

StatLink https://doi.org/10.1787/888934115502

This indicator should be interpreted carefully and in context. An increase in SME loan shares can sometimes reflect changes in large firms' financing opportunities and strategies, rather than increased access to finance for SMEs. This is especially the case during periods of lending contraction, when large enterprises can be expected to be resorting to other forms of finance. In addition, demand-side factors also play a large role in these developments, as does better access for SMEs to alternative financing instruments. Nonetheless, the sharp decline in this ratio between 2017 and 2018 may reflect the start of a shift in SMEs' access to finance.

Short-term versus long-term lending

Generally, data on loan maturities reveal a progressive shift in the SME loan portfolio from short-term to long-term over the past decade, and 2018 data confirm this trend. Short-term loans, defined as loans with an initial maturity of less than one year, such as overdrafts and lines of credit, are typically used to provide working capital.[2] Long-term loans can be more often related to investment initiatives, but can also indicate a strategy used by SMEs to lock in lower interest rates. This trend is most evident for new lending activities; all eight countries for which data are available show a shift to longer-term lending over the last decade. Between 2007 and 2009, only 1 out of 5 new loans were long-term, while between 2016 and 2018, half of the new loans were long-term, even though there is some cross-country variability.

Out of 30 Scoreboard countries that provide data on the maturity of SME loans, 22 relate to loan stock. Data from these countries also show an increase in loan maturities over the last decade. In these countries, more than 7 out of 10 SME loans in stock are long-term on average both for middle- and high-income countries (see Figure 1.6.).

Figure 1.6. Share of long-term SME loans

Median values, as a percentage of all SME loans

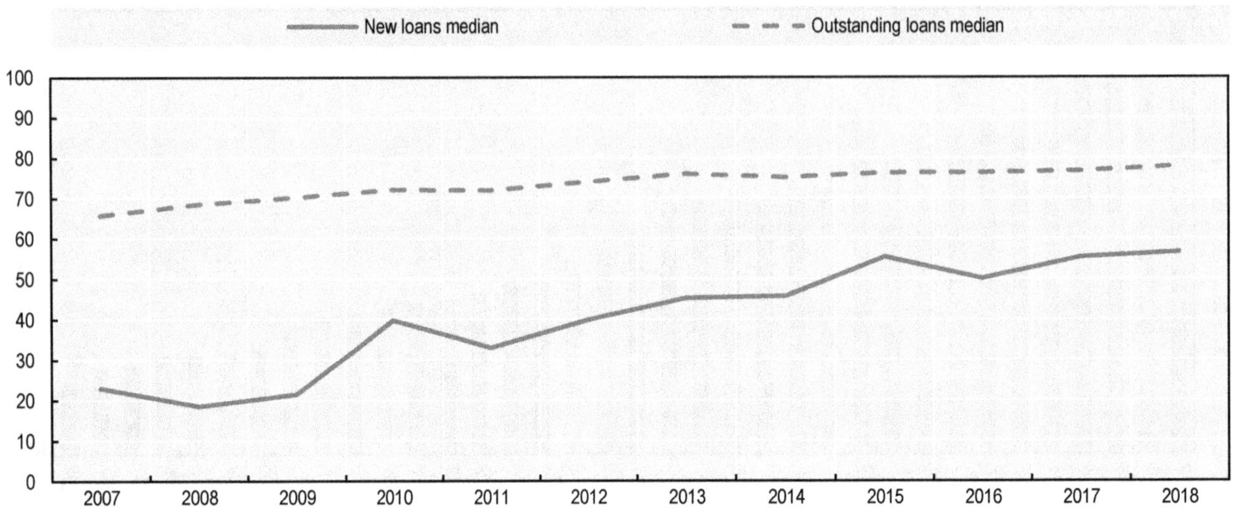

Note:Outstanding loans indicators were calculated based on data from Belarus, Belgium, Brazil, Canada, China, Colombia, Estonia, France, Greece, Indonesia, Italy, Kazakhstan, Latvia, Malaysia, the Netherlands, Poland, Portugal, Serbia, Slovak Republic, Slovenia Sweden and Ukraine. The variables for new loans were calculated based on data provided by Austria, Chile, Czech Republic, Denmark, Finland, Hungary, Ireland and Spain. Data for Korea were not included as it refers to all businesses, while data for Mexico were not included as it refers to loans provided by INADEM only. All data are adjusted for inflation using the OECD GDP deflator. Data for non-OECD countries were extracted from the World Development Indicators from the World Bank.

Source: Data compiled from the individual country profiles. Classification of countries by income group follows the World Bank criteria.

StatLink https://doi.org/10.1787/888934115521

Several factors may be driving this shift. Small businesses may find it easier now than in the past to use other sources of finance, such as factoring, online sources and especially retained earnings and cash flow for their short-term financing needs, while relying more heavily on straight debt for their investment needs. In addition, long-term lending may have become more attractive in the low-interest rate environment in recent years. Another possible explanation is related to the recovery of corporate investments from a low point in the direct aftermath of the financial crisis.

Credit conditions for SMEs

This section describes credit conditions for SMEs and entrepreneurs based on data on the cost of bank finance, collateral requirements and rejection rates. It also draws on findings from supply-side and demand-side surveys. Overall, available evidence suggests that demand for loans has remained broadly stable in recent years and collateral requirements and credit rejections remained at low levels. Data on credit conditions diverge across countries of different income levels. This is especially the case for interest rate figures.

Interest rates

The cost of bank credit varies considerably among Scoreboard countries. Figure 1.7 depicts interest rates, both in nominal and real terms (adjusted for inflation). In 2018, SME interest rates were highest in Peru, followed closely by a number of other middle-income economies, both for nominal as well as real rates. Five countries (Peru, Brazil, Colombia, Mexico and Ukraine) had nominal interest rates superior to 17%.

Chile and New Zealand were the only high-income economies with interest rates close to 10%, well above the median of 4.08%. As in previous years, SME interest rates were lowest in European countries like Belgium, France, Hungary and Sweden, where real interest rates were negative.

Figure 1.7. SME interest rates, 2018

As a percentage

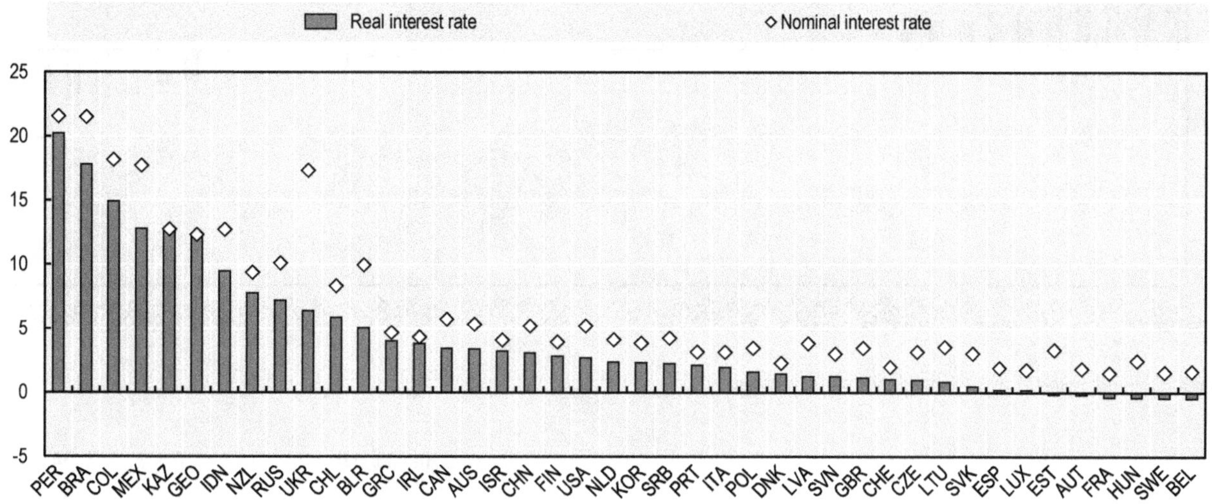

Note: Definitions differ across countries. Detailed information on sources and definitions is available in the full country profiles. Nominal interest rates were adjusted using World Bank data on inflation. Data from Ukraine for 2017 are missing
Source: Data compiled from the individual country profiles.

StatLink https://doi.org/10.1787/888934115540

For the first year in a decade, the median growth rate in nominal interest rates among Scoreboard countries was positive, if very low, at 0.02 percentage points. Significant increases occurred in economies such as Colombia (+2.80 percentage points), Finland (+1.17 percentage points) and Georgia (+1.94 percentage points), which in some cases constitutes a reversal of trends in previous years. Survey data for the euro area show that most SMEs report an increase in interest rates, for the first time since 2013-14 (see section on survey data below). Meanwhile, decreases were strongest in middle-income countries, such as Brazil (-3.60 percentage points), Kazakhstan (-0.95 percentage points) and Peru (-1.50 percentage points), where interest rates remain at comparatively high levels.

Figure 1.8. SME interest rates, growth rate

Nominal rates, percentage points

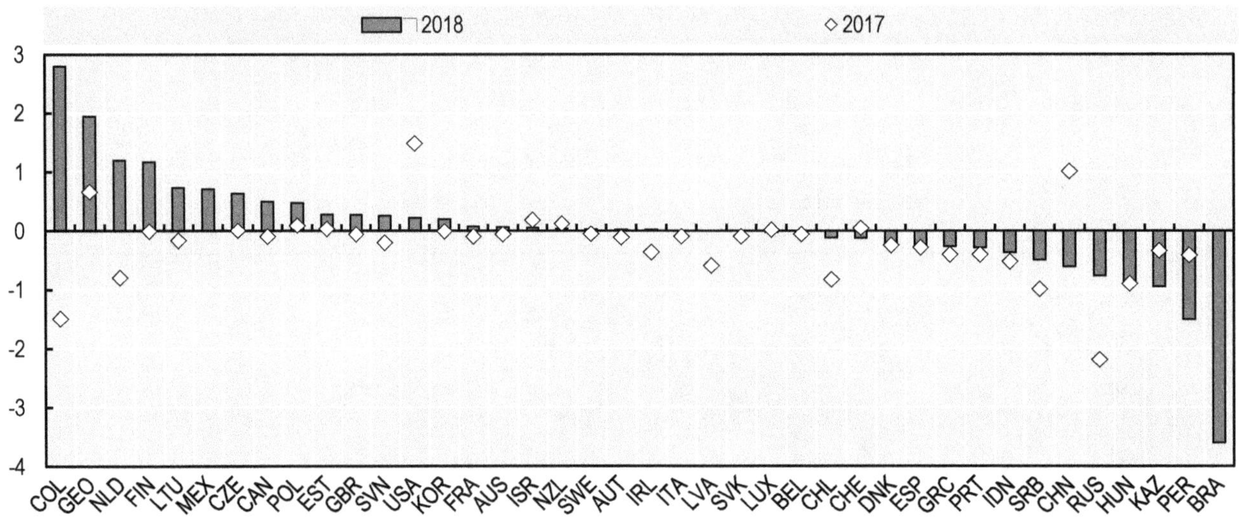

Source: Data compiled from the individual country profiles.

StatLink https://doi.org/10.1787/888934115559

Figure 1.9 shows a divergence between middle-income economies and high-income economies, with the former's interest rates continuing to decrease, while the latter's interest rates are stagnating or increasing slightly. This shows that there may only be limited room for further interest rate reductions in many high-income countries, given that central bank interest rates are already at unprecedented lows, and that monetary policies have started to tighten in some participating economies.

Further decreases in the interest rate from already low levels may not spur SMEs to borrow more. Indeed, analysis of the current data indicate no significant relationship between SME credit volumes and interest rates. This is in line with research that shows that monetary policy becomes less (or even not) effective in stimulating bank lending when interest rates are at a low enough level. Micro-level data even suggest that subdued lending may be the result of the impact that low interest rates have on banks' profitability (Borio and Gambacorta, 2017[3]).

Figure 1.9. Growth in SME interest rates

Median value, nominal rates, as a percentage

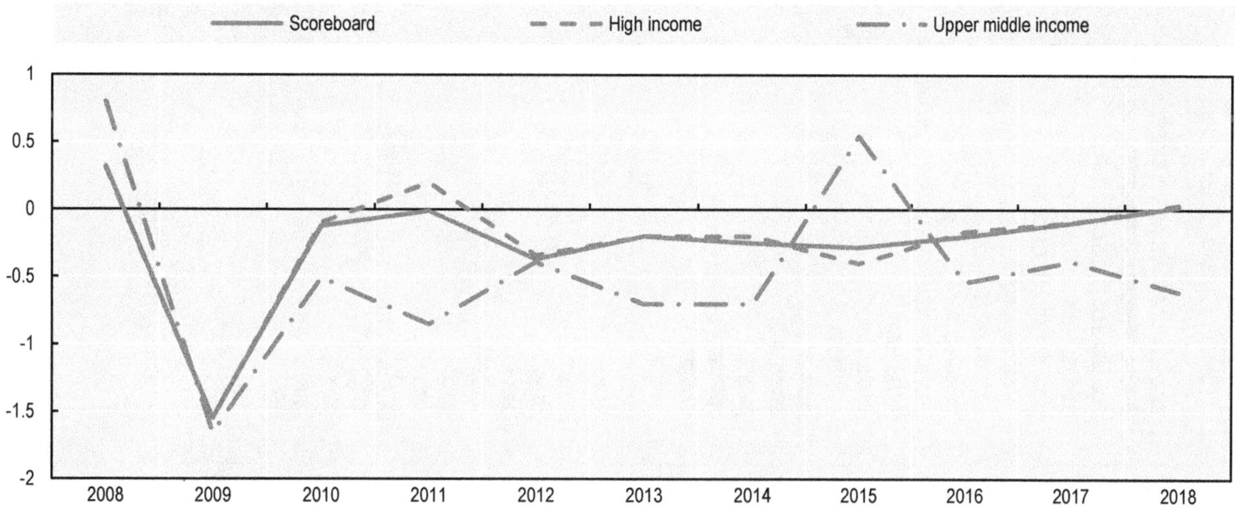

Source: Data compiled from the individual country profiles

StatLink https://doi.org/10.1787/888934115578

The interest rate spread between loans to SMEs and large enterprises offers additional insights regarding SME credit conditions. Typically, SMEs are charged higher interest rates than large enterprises, given their inherently riskier profiles. A narrowing interest rate spread generally indicates more favourable lending conditions for SMEs, while a widening spread indicates tighter lending conditions. Overall, interest rate spreads declined in 2018 in most countries, a reversal of the trend in 2017. The decline was strongest in Brazil and Mexico (countries with high interest rates), but was also significant in high-income countries like Lithuania (-1.08 percentage points).

The 2018 interest rate spread was higher in countries with higher interest rates, standing at more than 10 percentage points in Brazil and Peru. On the other hand, countries with low SME interest rates, such as Belgium and France, typically exhibit a low interest rate spread between small and large firms. Ukraine was the only country with a negative interest rate spread in 2018.

Figure 1.10. Interest rate spreads between loans to SMEs and to large firms

Nominal rates, percentage points

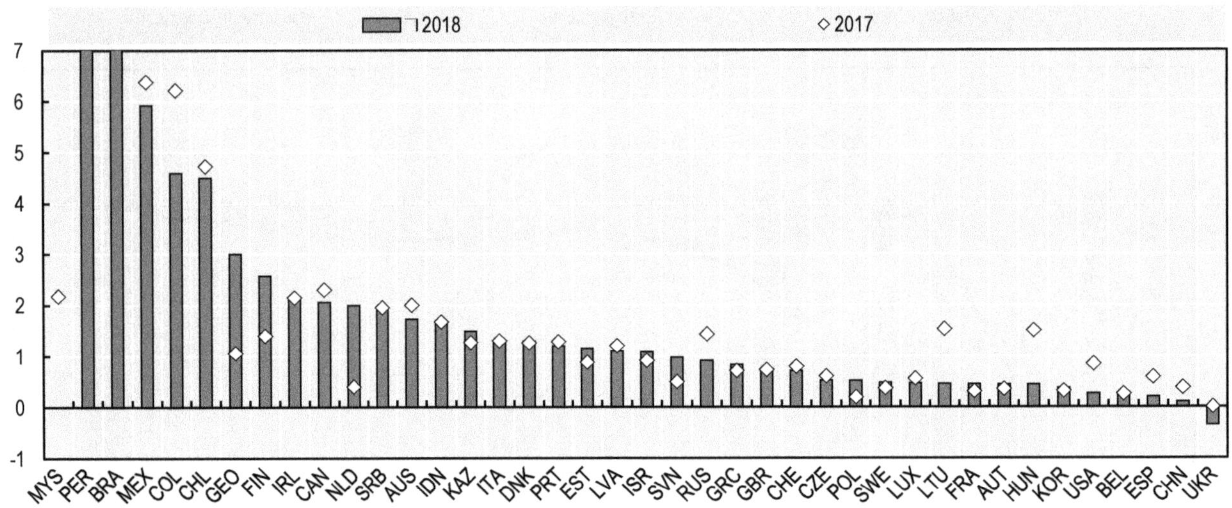

Note: Data for Brazil and Peru are not depicted, due to the scale. Peru: 2017 – 14.64 percentage points; 2018 – 13.72 percentage points. Brazil: 2017 – 16.10 percentage points; 2018 – 12.90 percentage points.
Source: Data compiled from the individual country profiles.

StatLink https://doi.org/10.1787/888934115597

Collateral requirements

Data on collateral requirements come from demand-side surveys, whose methodology, sample and questions asked differ from one country to the other. Cross-country comparisons should therefore be made with caution, and reporting improvements are needed to better assess the evolution in SME financing conditions in this respect.

While the database on collateral is relatively small, most countries experienced a decline in collateral requirements in 2018. Out of the fifteen countries that provided data for 2017 and 2018, ten experienced a decline in collateral requirements (expressed as a percentage of SMEs requiring collateral to access bank credit), while five experienced an increase or a stagnation (see Figure 1.11). This decrease was strongest in Finland and in Greece (respectively -3.00 and -5.05 percentage points). The decrease in collateral requirements coincided with an increase in the SME interest rate in Finland, illustrating the well-established negative relationship between collateral and interest rates (Degryse, Karapetyan and Karmakar, 2019[4]). Indeed, pledging collateral often allows SMEs to obtain lower interest rates on loans.

Figure 1.11. Collateral requirements

By country (left), median growth rate (right)

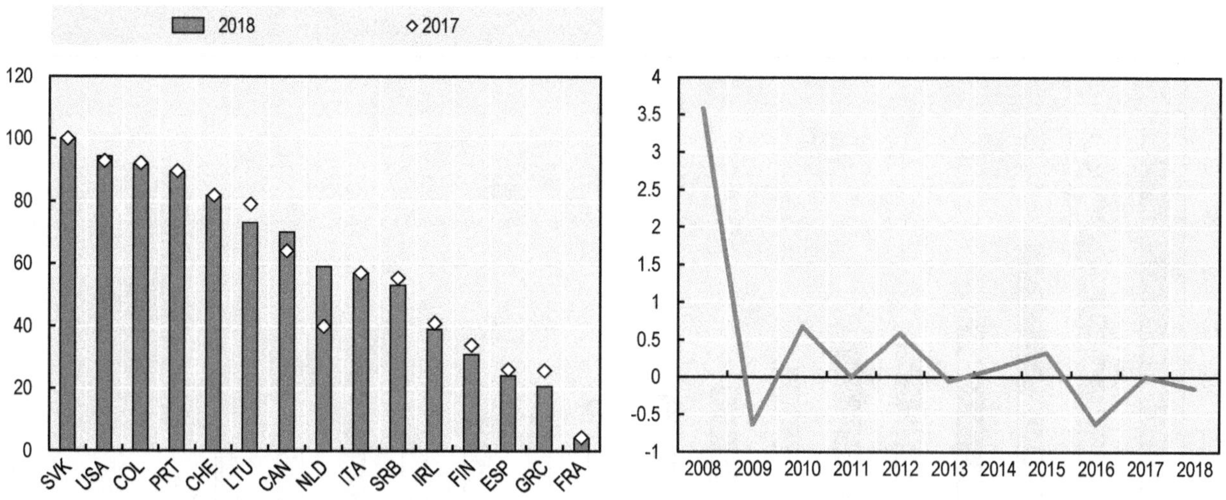

Source: Data compiled from the individual country profiles.

StatLink https://doi.org/10.1787/888934115616

SME loan applications

Data on loan applications come from demand-side surveys. Like with collateral requirements, cross-country comparisons should be made with caution, and reporting improvements are needed to better assess the evolution in SME financing conditions.

About one-fourth of SMEs applied for credit over the last six months, showing that the majority of SMEs do not seek external financing. This figure has remained stable over the past four to five years, suggesting that the demand for credit has been relatively constant over the reference period. There are however large cross-country differences, with Chinese SMEs far more likely to apply for credit (58.36%) than their counterparts in Indonesia, for example (3.35%). Also notable is the decrease in SME loan applications in the Netherlands, from 18% in 2017 to 12.80% in 2018 (-5.20 percentage points).

Figure 1.12. SME Loan applications

As a percentage

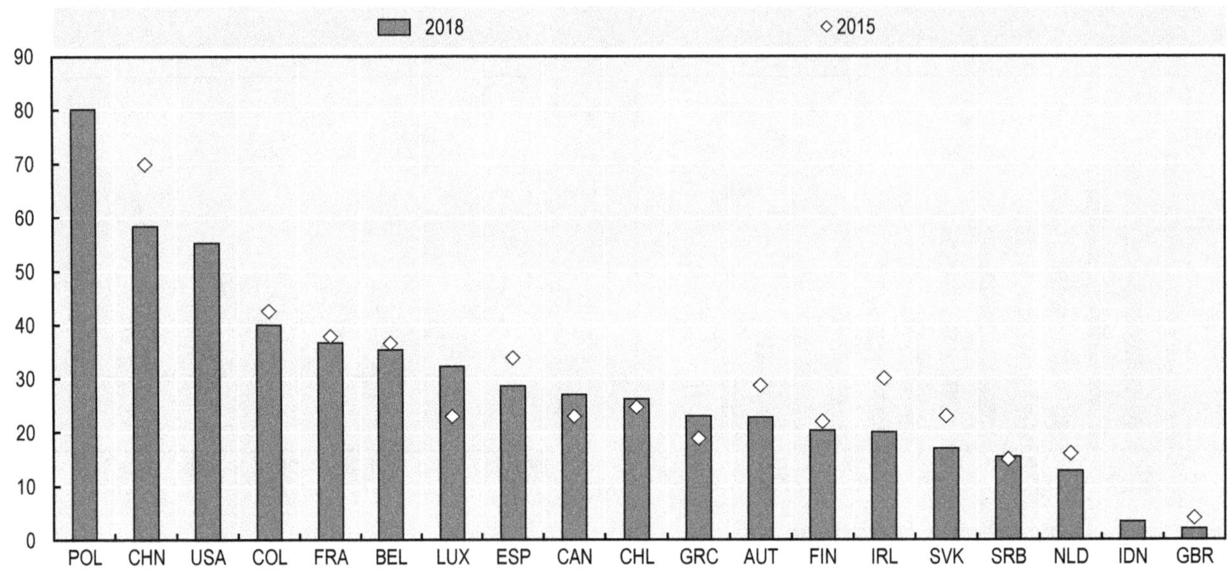

Note: Definitions differ across countries. Detailed information on sources and definitions is available in the full country profiles. Data for Chile, Poland, the United Kingdom and the United States are from 2017

Source: Data compiled from the individual country profiles

StatLink https://doi.org/10.1787/888934115635

Rejection rates

Rejection rates help to shed light on the supply of credit to SMEs and gauge the overall financing conditions they face. Higher rates of rejection are indicative of constraints in the credit supply and suggest that demand for loans is not being met, either because the terms and conditions of the loan offers are deemed unacceptable, the average creditworthiness of loan applications has deteriorated, or banks are rationing credit. Nevertheless, rejection rates should be analysed in the context of new lending trends, in order to have a more comprehensive perspective on SME access to finance. Data on rejection rates are usually gathered from demand-side surveys, with limited comparability across countries, however.

Overall, 2018 saw a decrease in the rejection rate in most Scoreboard countries, consistent with the increase in new lending. Twelve countries that provided data for the indicator reported a decrease in rejection rates, while six others reported an increase (Figure 1.12). The rejection rate decreased by 3.28 percentage points (looking at the median value for countries which provided data), broadly in line with the modest decrease in rejection rates since 2012, but a reversal of the 2017 trend. The rate remains high in countries such as the United States (32.70%), but it experienced a significant drop since 2017 (-12.10 percentage points). A similar trend can be observed in Serbia, with an 11.47 percentage point drop year-on-year. In other countries such as Lithuania, the rejection rate increased significantly (+11.40 percentage points, reaching 27%), suggesting a tightening of credit conditions and possible changes in risk assessment standards.

Figure 1.13. Rejection rates

As a percentage

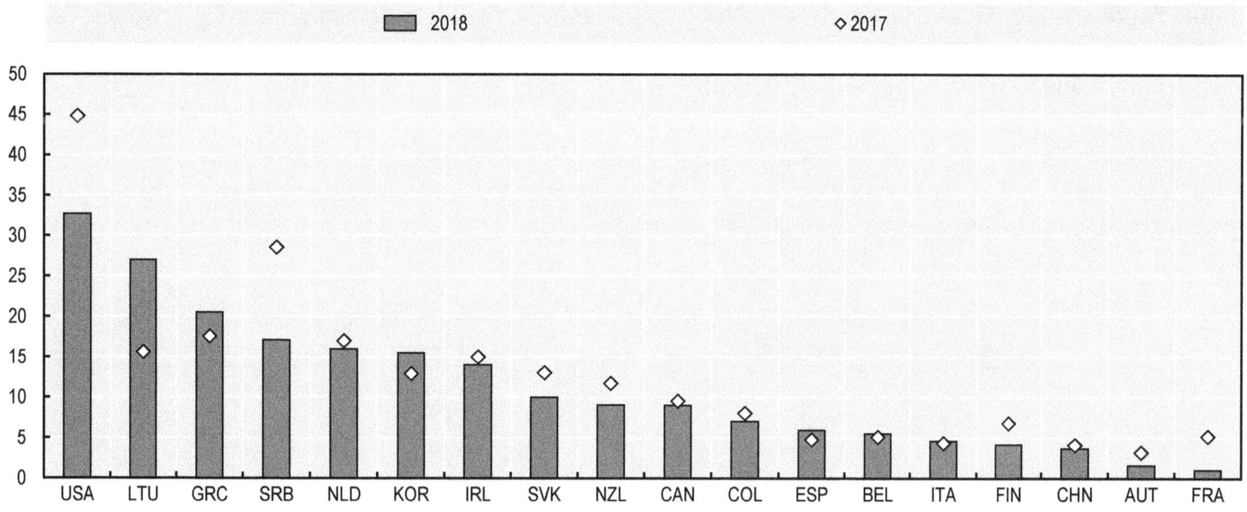

Source: Data compiled from the individual country profiles

StatLink https://doi.org/10.1787/888934115654

Additional evidence on credit conditions from survey data

Survey data indicate that credit conditions have remained relatively loose. In addition, there are indications that SMEs continue to consider that bank finance is relatively available, especially in comparison with the post-crisis period. While these surveys provide important insights, the comparability across different survey exercises is limited. The section on Recommendations for data improvements provides guidance for improvements in this area.

Euro area

The survey on the access to finance of enterprises (SAFE) provides data on financial situation of the firm, need for and availability of external financing. It is conducted twice a year: once by the ECB, covering the Euro area, and once in cooperation with the European Commission, covering all EU economies and some additional countries. Surveys from H2 2018 and H1 2019 show a small uptick in loan availability following a marked decline in 2018, while documenting a decrease in the share of companies reporting increased interest rates. Indeed, the net share of firms reporting an increase in interest rates dropped to -8.93% in H1 2019 compared to 2.89% in H1 2018 (Figure 1.14).

Applications for bank loans decreased in H1 2019 after having broadly remained constant over the 2011-18 period. In H1 2019, 25.96% of SMEs applied for a bank loan (versus 27.12% in H1 2018). The rate of fully successful loan applications reached 71.88% (versus 73.93% in H1 2018), while the rejection rate picked up to 6.45% (versus 4.88% in H1 2018). At the same time, 29% of SMEs signalled higher levels of other costs of financing, such as charges, fees and commissions, a figure that remained stable compared to 2018 (ECB, 2019[5]).

Large firms continue to benefit from better access to finance compared to SMEs. The share of large enterprises that applied and successfully obtained a loan continues to be higher (the success rate in H1 2019 was 87%), while the rejection rate is lower (1% in H1 2019) (ECB, 2019[5]). The difference in the average interest rate charged to large enterprises for credit lines compared to SMEs stood at 170 basis points, a difference which remained stable in 2019.

Generally, SMEs expect a moderate improvement in their access to external finance in the months to come. There are significant differences in SMEs' perspectives across different countries, however, with a few countries such as Spain expecting financing conditions to worsen, while in several others, SMEs expect conditions to remain the same (ECB, 2019[5]).

Figure 1.14. ECB Survey on SME access to finance

Selected indicators, as a percentage of total SMEs surveyed

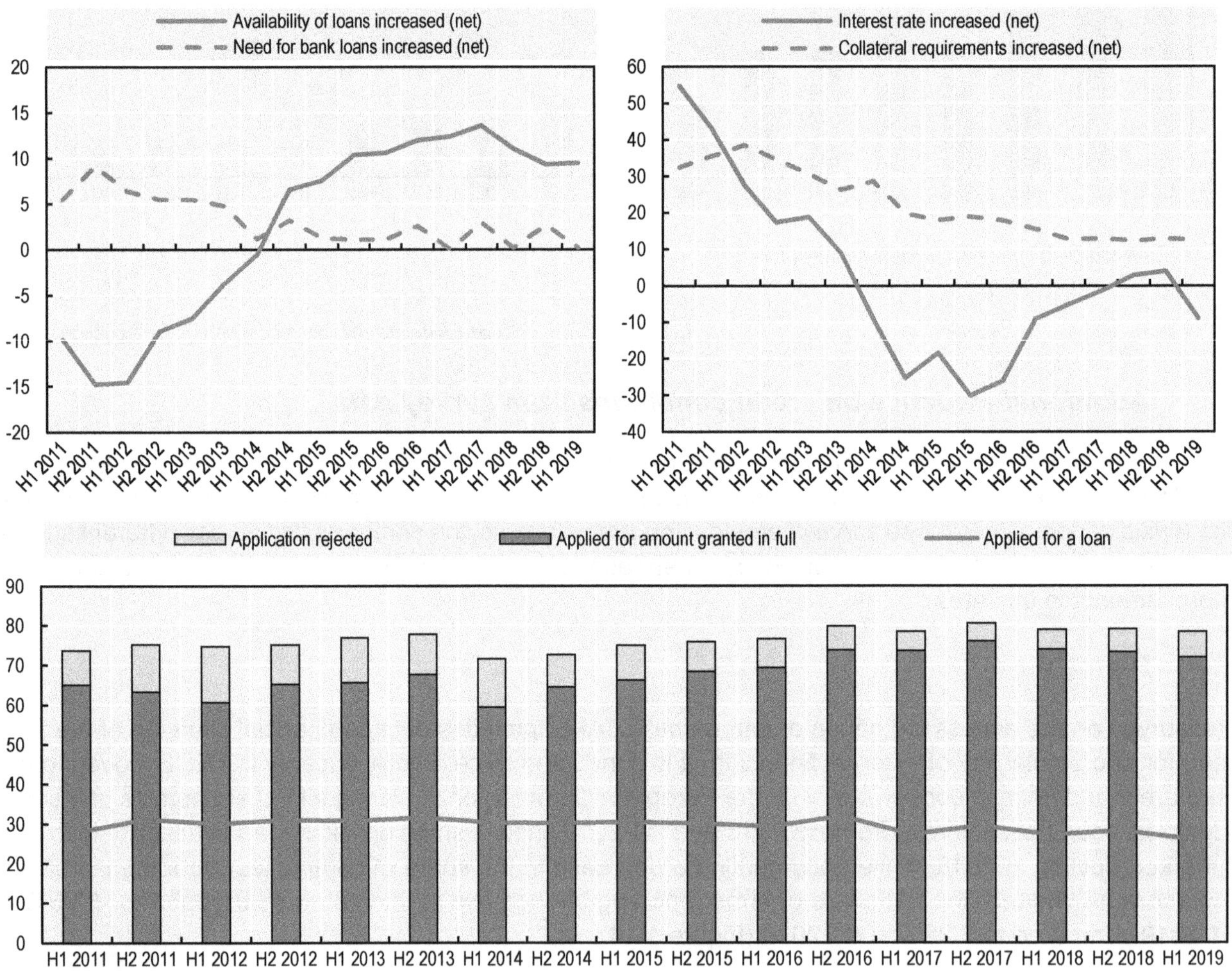

Note: The net percentage is the difference between the percentage of firms reporting that the given factor has improved and the percentage reporting that it has deteriorated or the difference between the percentage reporting that it had increased and the percentage reporting that it has decreased. H1 2019 refers to round 19 (April to September 2019), published in November 2019. H2 2018 refers to round 20 (October 2018 to March 2019), published in May 2019. The timeline is the same for previous rounds.
Source: (European Central Bank, 2019[6]).

StatLink https://doi.org/10.1787/888934115673

United States

In the United States, the National Federation of Independent Business (NFIB) Research Foundation collects Small Business Economic Trends data on a monthly basis since 1986. Evidence from this survey shows that the financial crisis had a marked impact on reported loan availability, which bottomed out in 2007, and steadily recovered afterwards to levels broadly comparable to the pre-crisis period. From the beginning of 2015 to October 2018, credit availability remained broadly constant.

The October 2018 survey illustrates that only 2% of surveyed small businesses in the United States stated that financing was their main concern (stable from October 2017), and only 4% reported that their financing needs were not being met (+1 percentage point from October 2017), indicating the relative ease and affordability of accessing credit. (Dunkelberg and Wade, 2018[7]).

The United States Federal Reserve Board surveys senior loan officers on their banks' lending practices on a quarterly basis, including a question on the evolution of credit standards for approving small business loans or credit lines[3]. According to the October 2018 survey, respondents indicated that they slightly eased their standards and terms on commercial and industrial (C&I) loans to large and mid-sized firms. However, they left their standards unchanged for small firms, citing increased competition from other lenders as the main reason for easing, as well as a less uncertain economic outlook and an increased tolerance for risk.

The survey also includes a question on SMEs' demand for loans[4]. For most of 2016 and the first half of 2017, demand for credit in the United States weakened. According to the October 2018 survey, a modest net percentage of domestic banks reported weaker demand for loans from all firms (United States Federal Reserve Board, 2018[8]).

Japan

In Japan, perceived lending attitudes deteriorated sharply between 2008 and 2009, according to the TANKAN survey, a quarterly poll on business confidence published by the Bank of Japan[5]. Between 2010 and 2015, financing conditions loosened, and from 2015 onwards, lending attitudes for small and medium-sized enterprises have largely remained constant and accommodative (see Figure 1.15). It is noteworthy that the perceived lending attitudes for large and medium-sized enterprises have become largely similar in recent years, in contrast with the pre-crisis period, when medium-sized firms faced tighter credit conditions. The gap between small and large firms has remained large, however (Bank of Japan, 2019[9]).

Figure 1.15. Lending attitudes in Japan

Diffusion index, in percentage points

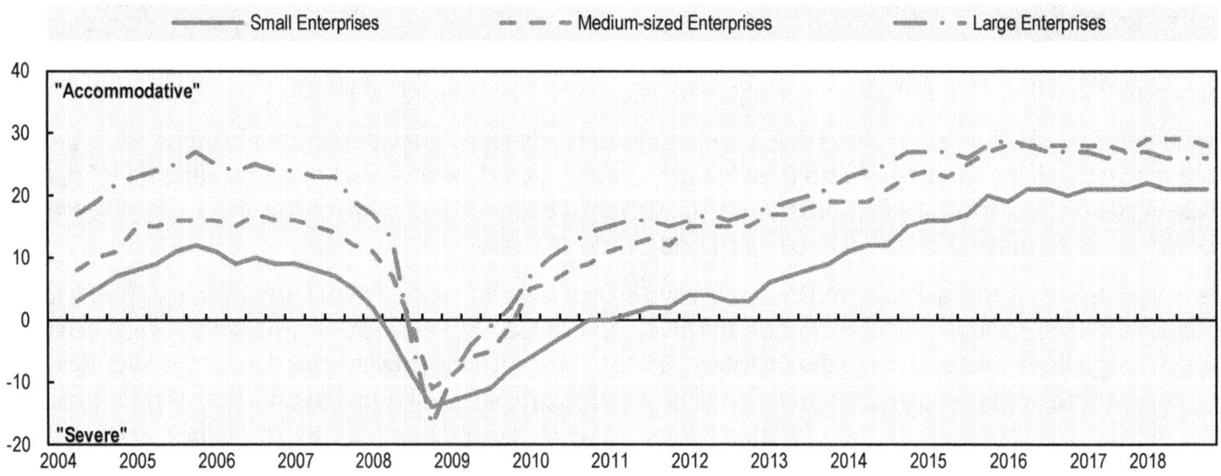

Note: Diffusion index of "Accommodative" minus "Severe", percentage points.
Source: Bank of Japan.

StatLink https://doi.org/10.1787/888934115692

United Kingdom

Responses to Bank of England Credit Conditions Survey suggest no change in availability of credit in first three quarters of 2019, following an improvement in 2018.[6] On the other hand, more recent data illustrate an uptick in interest rates since the second half of 2017.

Asset-based finance

Asset-based finance comprises all forms of finance that are based on the value of specific assets, rather than on the cash flow/creditworthiness or debt capacity of firms, and represents a well-established alternative for many SMEs. Within this category, leasing and hire purchases on the one hand, and factoring and invoice discounting on the other are the most well-known and widely used instruments in most countries under study. In the case of leasing and hire purchases, the owner of an asset provides the right to use of the asset (like motor vehicles, equipment or real estate) for a specified period of time in exchange for a series of payments. Factoring and invoice discounting are financial transactions, whereby a business sells its accounts receivable to another party at a discount.

Leasing and hire purchases

Data for 2018 show a considerable increase in leasing and hire purchase activities, in line with developments in previous years. In 24 out of 33 countries where data on leasing and hire purchase activities is available, inflation-adjusted volumes rose in 2018, continuing the trend documented since 2014. The year-on-year growth rate, as a median value, stood at 3.75% in 2018, compared to 5.79% in the previous year. Colombia, Kazakhstan, Lithuania, the Netherlands, Poland, Portugal, Russia and Slovenia exhibited year-on-year growth rates superior to 10%. At the country level, leasing figures are quite volatile from one year to the next.

Figure 1.16. Leasing and hire purchases, growth rate

As a percentage

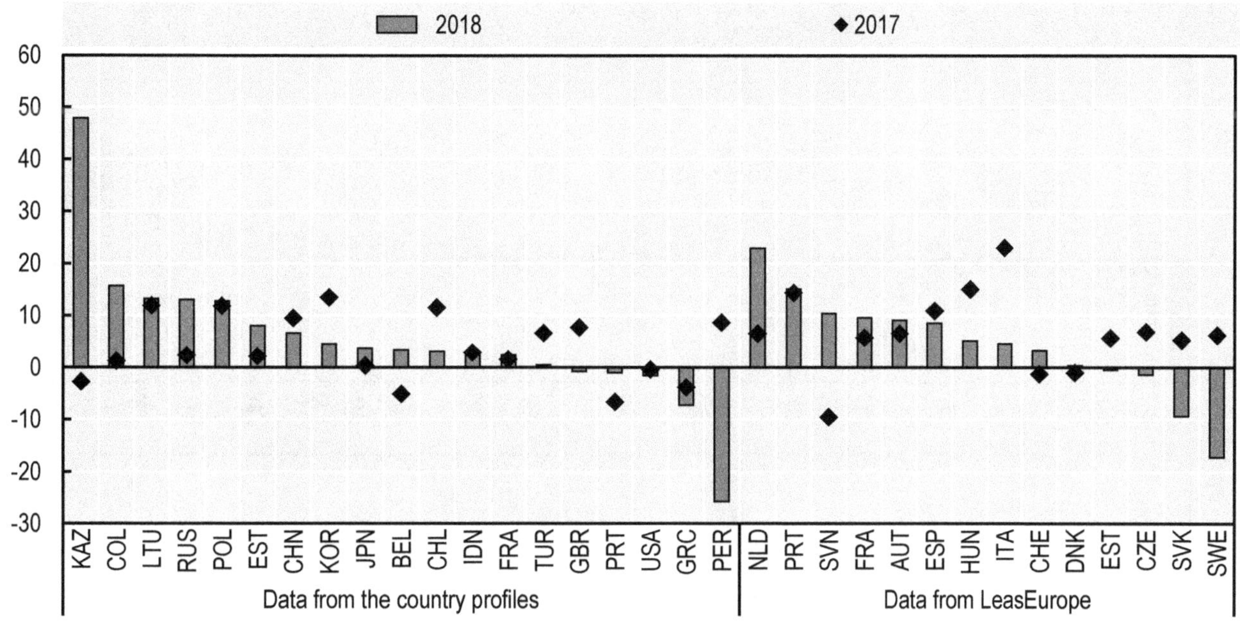

Note: When several associations existed for one country, figures were summed and growth rates were recalculated. Data are adjusted for inflation using the OECD GDP deflator. Data from non-OECD countries are adjusted for inflation using the deflator from the World Bank World Development Indicators.

Source: Data compiled from the individual country profiles, from the LeasEurope Annual Survey 2018 and from the LeasEurope Annual Survey 2017.

StatLink https://doi.org/10.1787/888934115711

Factoring[7]

Since 2010, factoring volumes have been rising in the majority of Scoreboard countries. The highest median growth rates were 15.34% and 13.77%, in 2010 and 2011 respectively, suggesting that factoring provided an alternative for finance-constrained SMEs following the crisis. From 2012 to 2017, the median growth rate remained positive, although growth slowed. Growth picked up in 2018, with a median growth of 8.42% and volumes up in 31 out of 45 countries. Significant cross-country variations can be observed, with Canada, Switzerland and Turkey showing a strong decline at -58.42%, -84.63% and -33.03% respectively. In Korea on the other hand, volumes nearly doubled in 2018 (see Figure 1.17).

Figure 1.17. Factoring growth rates by country and Scoreboard median

Year-on-year growth, as percentage

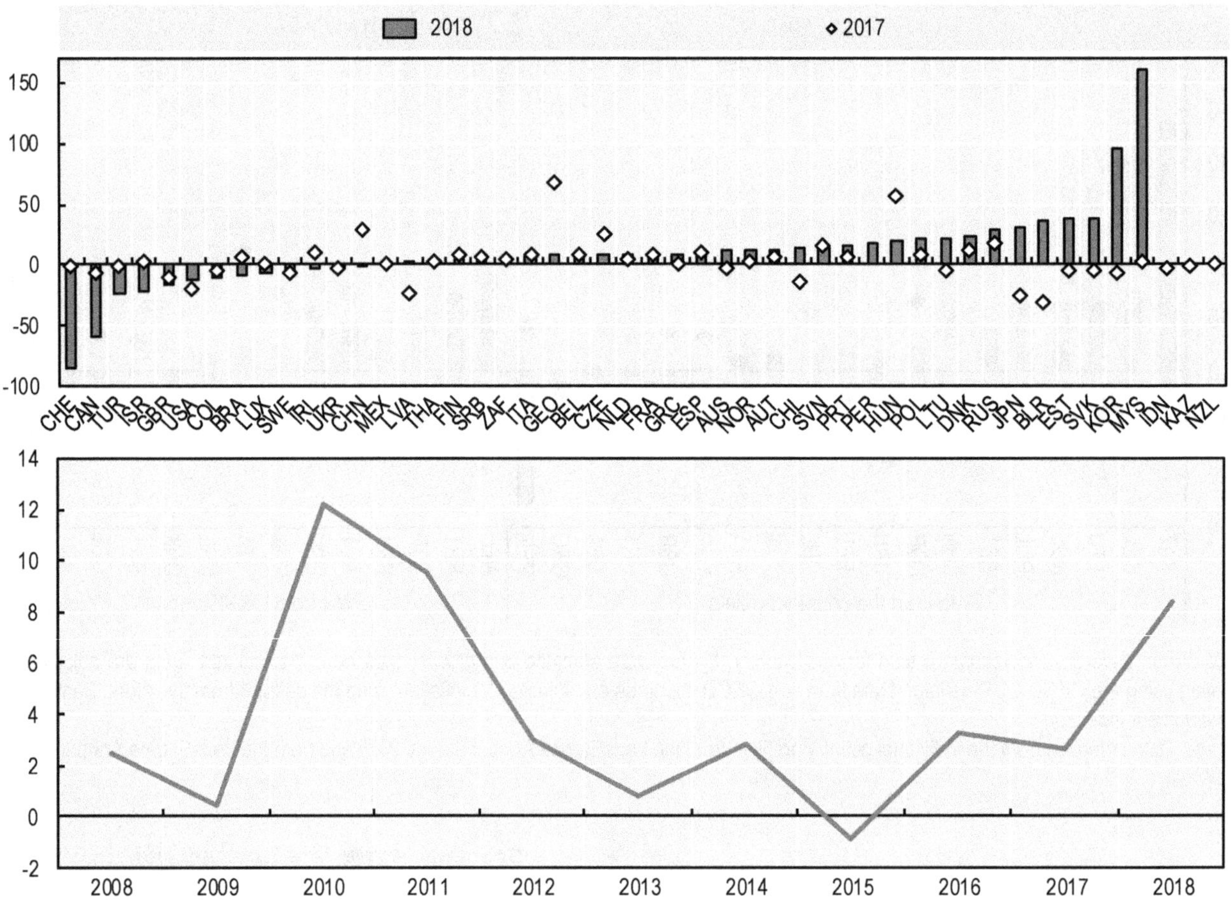

Note: All data are adjusted for inflation using the OECD GDP deflator. Data for non-OECD countries were extracted from the World Development Indicators from the World Bank. Due to the scale, the 2018 figure for Malaysia (+ 167.87%) is not represented.
Source: Factors Chain International (2019).

StatLink https://doi.org/10.1787/888934115730

Self-financing

Self-financing plays an important role in SME financing, although its significance varies across countries, firm size and age, as well as type of business activity. On average, start-ups are more likely to rely on internal funding compared to mature firms, given that they have lower levels of tangible assets, a less established reputation, longstanding relationship with a financial institution and track record (Paroma and Mann, 2010[10]). Empirical studies have shown that almost a third of all SMEs in the EU rely solely on internally generated sources of revenue for their day-to-day operations and investments (Moritz, Block and Heinz, 2017[11]).

According to the ECB's *Survey on the Access to Finance of Enterprises in the euro area,* internal funds were considered an important alternative source of finance by one-fourth of European SMEs surveyed between October 2018 and March 2019. Likewise, 18% of firms pointed funds from family, friends or related companies as relevant sources of financing for them. In recent years, internal funds seem to have become an increasingly important source of finance, with possible implications for the demand for credit. For instance, in the euro area the proportion of SMEs citing sufficient internal funds as a reason for not applying for loans has been rising steadily, from 35% in 2014 to 43% in 2019. At the same time, the proportion of SMEs not applying for bank loans because they were "discouraged" has declined from 8.4% in 2014 to 4.2% in 2019, suggesting that the use of internal funds only is not driven by mounting difficulties to access credit (European Central Bank, 2019[6]).

The BACH database, hosted by the Central Bank of France, provides comparable data on the aggregate financial ratios of SMEs in twelve countries from the euro area that are part of current Scoreboard exercise. Recent evidence from this database suggests that, on average, SMEs' profitability continued to increase over the 2013-17 period. The observed trend may indicate an increased availability of funds for self-financing purposes, as measured by EBITDA (earnings before interest, taxes, depreciation and amortisation) to net turnover ratio for the median SME operating in a country (see Figure 1.18.).

Figure 1.18. Profitability ratios for European SMEs, 2013-17

EBITDA to net turnover ratio, median value for each country

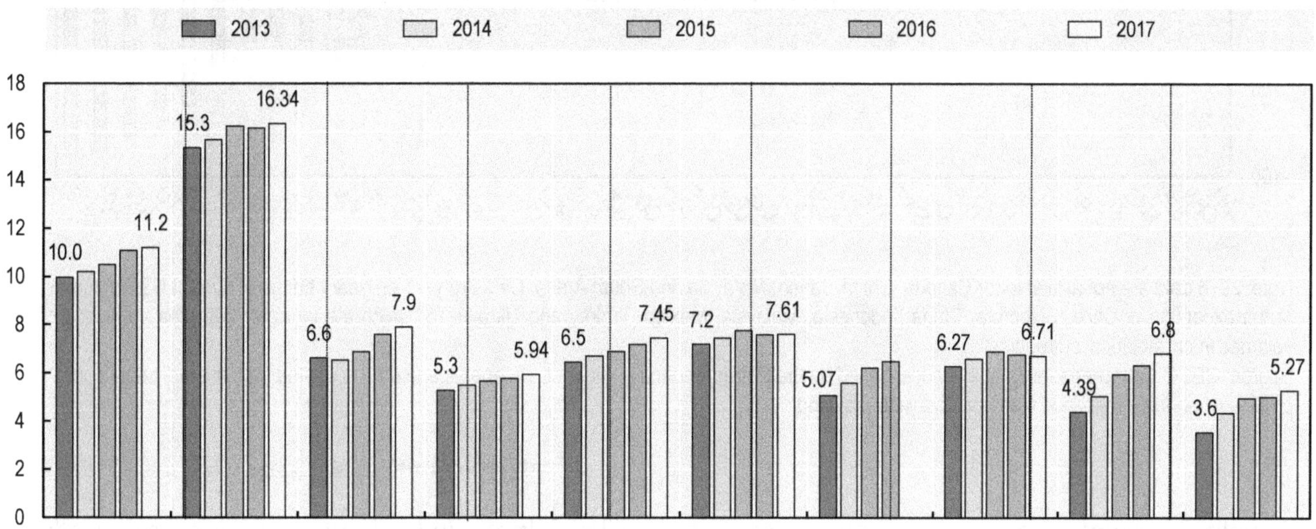

Note: This ratio assesses the profitability of a company by comparing its revenue with its earnings, giving the remaining earnings after all operating expenses in percentage
Source: Bank for the Account of Companies Harmonized (BACH) – Banque de France

StatLink https://doi.org/10.1787/888934115749

Equity instruments and private debt

Venture capital investments, listings on stock exchanges, private debt and business angel investments are discussed in this section.

Venture capital

The median growth rate of venture capital investments increased in 2018, at 20.86%. This contrasts with the 2011-15 period, when median volumes fell, but it is in line with 2017 developments. It is important to keep in mind that data on VC investments are highly volatile, especially for smaller countries, where a single deal may impact overall volumes considerably (as the data for Latvia and Luxembourg illustrate, for example). In the United States, the largest market by far, for instance, volumes rose by 11% in 2017 and by 57% in 2018, after dropping by 6.3% in 2016.

Figure 1.19. Venture capital investments

Year-on-year growth rates, as a percentage

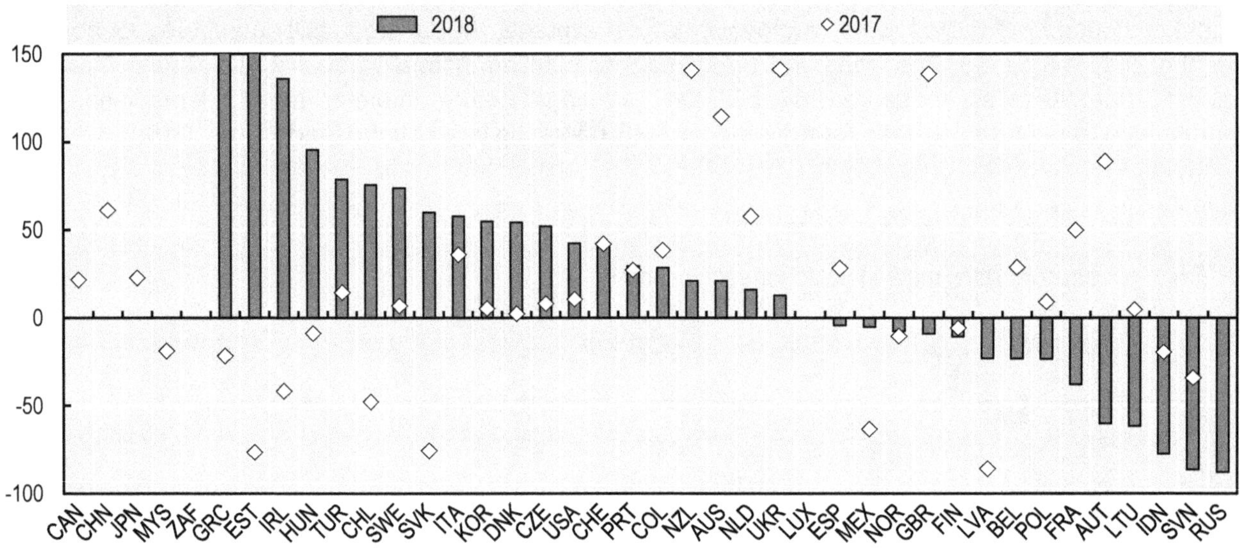

Note: 2018 data are not available for Canada, China, Japan, Malaysia and South Africa. Data are year-on-year change of current USD volumes, at the exception of Chile, Colombia, China, Indonesia, Malaysia, Mexico, Turkey and Ukraine for which the indicator captures variations of volumes in current local currencies.
Source: OECD Entrepreneurship at a Glance, based on the Entrepreneurship Finance Database, and data compiled from the individual country profiles when the information was not otherwise provided.

StatLink https://doi.org/10.1787/888934115768

Country-level data hide more granular trends at the local level. Indeed, VC activities are mostly concentrated in cities rather than in countries, which prompts the question of the most relevant unit of observation. While US cities still dominate global VC deals, the share of all VC deals conducted in these cities has been declining for approximately fifteen years, and other hubs, especially in upper middle-income economies, are showing strong growth rates, albeit from low base levels (Florida and Hathaway, 2018[12]).

Government interventions have played a decisive role in the recovery of VC investments in recent years. In Europe in particular, government agencies are the most important source of VC funds (BPIFrance et al., 2016[13]). This was the case in Denmark (Rogers, 2016[14]) and the United Kingdom (UK Finance, 2018[15]), among other countries.

Private debt

Private debt is a relatively recent instrument that has experienced a strong expansion since the global financial crisis, following tightened regulation on commercial banks and durably low interest rates. Specialised loan funds operate through an originator, typically unconnected to a banking institution, which originates a portfolio of SME loans. Many of the legal and institutional features of this instrument are similar to the private equity market, with the crucial difference that it engages in debt. While commercial banks tend to operate on the low-risk, low-yield end of the financing spectrum, alternate lenders cover its entire range. The private debt market is especially relevant for larger and more mature SMEs facing a major transition, such as a change in ownership, expansion into new markets and/or activities, or acquisitions.

Global fundraising activities declined between 2017 and 2018, but remain high in a historical context. In 2018 for the fourth consecutive year, fundraising activities surpassed USD 100 billion, the level observed in 2008. As in previous years, most fundraising in 2018 took place in the United States, which was responsible for 62% of volumes raised. Europe was the second region with the most fundraising, accounting for 33% of total volumes. The private debt market remains relatively underdeveloped in Asia and even more so in other regions of the world (see Figure 1.20) (McKinsey, 2019[16]).

Figure 1.20. Global private debt fundraising

As a percentage share of world total in 2018 (left) and in USD billion (right)

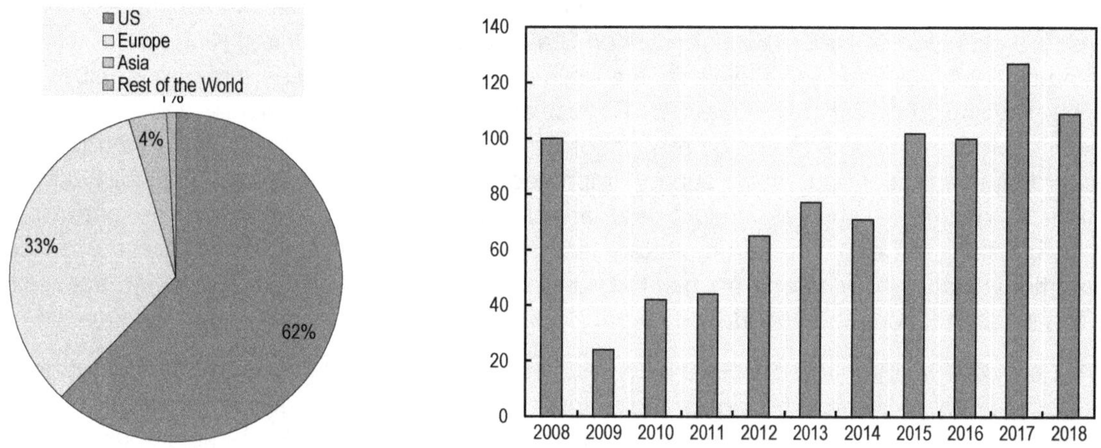

Source: Preqin and McKinsey.

StatLink https://doi.org/10.1787/888934115787

Capital that has been committed for the private debt market, but not yet deployed (so-called "dry powder") rose by 11.1% between 2017 and 2018, reaching a new post-crisis record. Although these numbers are not SME-specific, many of the investments are taken up by smaller enterprises. According to a recent survey, around half of the capital raised is allocated to SMEs and mid-market borrowers (Alternative Credit Council, 2018[17]).

Business angel investments

Business angel (BA) investing is an important source of financing for early-stage start-ups, especially those which do not have own resources and/or are unable to access bank credit, but are not yet ripe for venture capital funding. Angel investors tend to be wealthy individuals, or groups of them, who provide financing, typically their own funds, in exchange for convertible debt or ownership equity. Business angel investors typically play an active role in the management of businesses they invest in, and they thereby can offer business expertise, access to a network and other non-financial benefits to companies they invest in. This enables entrepreneurs to scale up to a stage where venture capitalists may step in. It represents a potential means of narrowing the financing gap for early-stage, innovative SMEs, but is not suitable for all firms' profiles (OECD, 2016[18]).

Data collection on business angel investments suffers from many shortcomings (OECD, 2016[18]). As a result, the so-called "visible market" only accounts for a minority of the whole market, and trends may be hard to analyse. Indeed, many business angel deals remain private. In Europe, there is a lack of accessible and reliable data on business angel activities.

In the United States, the Center for Venture Research has been assessing the state of business angel investments since 2002. In 2017, volumes decreased by 3.7% compared to 2017, reaching USD 23.1 billion (Center for Venture Research, 2019[19]). Activities were traditionally concentrated in Boston, New York and San Francisco, but the geography of business angels is increasingly diverse, with 63% of the business angels considered to be outside of these three hubs, according to a recent study (Huang et al., 2017[20]). The same report concludes that business angels are more diverse than venture capitalists in terms of gender and geography.

Listings on stock exchanges

Listings on public stock exchanges constitute another means of attracting external sources of finance, and are especially relevant for larger SMEs. Many junior stock markets (also known as second-tier stock markets) are modelled on NASDAQ in the United States and AIM in the United Kingdom. They act both as screening devices until firms are eligible for the main market, and as providers of opportunities for venture capitalists wishing to divest (exit) (Granier, Revest and Sapio, 2019[21]). While accessing finance from external investors represents the prime reason for SMEs to become listed, other factors often play a role, too, according to a recent large-scale survey. Improved creditworthiness and the possibility of opening up other sources of finance, such as straight debt, are stated by almost one half and one fourth of surveyed SMEs, respectively. In addition, non-monetary factors such as brand recognition and more visibility are also commonly stated (World Federation of Exchanges & Milken Institute, 2017[22]). SME access to capital markets also aims to reduce dependence on bank finance and increase the diversity of financing sources.

Table 1.1 provides an overview of specialised vehicles for SME markets of Scoreboard countries on stock exchanges that typically provide less onerous information and due diligence requirements. In several cases, there is more than one SME market in a country, and a few SME markets span more than one country. The market capitalisation of most of these markets represents only a very small fraction of the capitalisation of the national stock exchange, with the exception of Ireland, Japan and Korea. 2018 developments include a general decrease in market capitalisations year-on-year, with only Bursa Malaysia's LEAP Market showing a positive trend. Meanwhile, the number of listed firms has broadly stagnated since 2017, mechanically reducing the average market capitalisation on these markets.

Table 1.1. SME markets on stock exchanges, 2018

	Exchange	Name of the Market	Domestic market cap (USD millions)	% change 2017/2018	Number of listed companies	% change 2017/2018
BEL, FRA, NLD, PRT, GRB	Euronext	Euronext Growth	11696.23	-0.23	206	0.05
CAN	TMX Group	TSX Venture	33311.81	-0.19	1974	0.00
CHN	Hong Kong Exchanges and Clearing	Growth Enterprise Market	23774.25	-0.34	389	0.20
DEN, EST, FIN, LVA, SWE	Nasdaq Nordic Exchanges	First North	17826.49	0.05	348	0.34
GRC	Athens Stock Exchange	ATHEX Alternative Market (EN.A)	123.31	-0.02	12	0.00
IRL	Irish Stock Exchange	Enterprise Securities Market	5991.99	-0.10	24	0.09
JPN	Japan Exchange Group	JASDAQ	75693.13	-0.25	726	-0.03
JPN	Japan Exchange Group	Mothers	45448.89	-0.03	276	0.11

	Exchange	Name of the Market	Domestic market cap (USD millions)	% change 2017/2018	Number of listed companies	% change 2017/2018
KOR	Korea Exchange	Kosdaq	204700.52	-0.23	1279	0.05
LUX	Luxembourg Stock Exchange	Euro MTF	1735.49	-0.32	125	0.00
MYS	Bursa Malaysia	ACE Market	2825.46	-0.21	119	0.03
MYS	Bursa Malaysia	LEAP Market	222.57	3.24	13	5.50
NZL	NZX Limited	NZAX	188.28	-0.37	13	-0.19
NZL	NZX Limited	NXT	45.93	-0.42	2	-0.33
NOR	Oslo Stock Exchange	Oslo Axess	631.29	-0.66	17	-0.29
POL	Warsaw Stock Exchange	NEWCONNECT	1968.66	-0.29	387	-0.05
RUS	Moscow Exchange	Innovations and Investments Market	5196.87	-0.13	10	0.00
ZAF	Johannesburg Stock Exchange	Alternative Exchange	1427.45	-0.15	46	0.18
ESP	BME Spanish Exchanges	MAB Expansion	13403.11	0.16	105	0.19
THA	The Stock Exchange of Thailand	Market for Alternative Investment (mai)	7367.98	-0.27	159	0.06
TUR	Borsa Istanbul	BIST Emerging Companies	188.76	-0.83	17	0.00
TUR	Borsa Istanbul	Watchlist	152.82	-0.49	27	-0.13
GBR	LSE Group	AIM	124109.46	..	1036	-0.02

Note: This table excludes exchanges from countries which are not part of the Scoreboard exercise as well as exchanges that are not member of the World Federation of Exchanges.
Source: WFE Annual Statistics Guide 2018.

Online alternative finance

Online alternative finance is a mean of soliciting funds from the public for a firm or project through an online platform. It comprises different kinds of activities, broadly categorised in three categories (debt-based, equity-based and non-investment). The data in this section refer to business activities and thus excludes certain activities (such as online lending to households).

Debt-based online alternative finance encompasses business, property and consumer (when applicable for SMEs) loans which come from peer-to-peer activities, institutional funders, or directly from the platform. It also includes invoice trading and debt-based securities.

Equity activities include equity-based, revenue-sharing and real estate crowdfunding.

Non-investment online alternative finance includes reward-based crowdfunding, whereby backers provide funding to individuals, projects or companies in exchange for non-monetary rewards or products, and donation-based crowdfunding, whereby donors provide funding to individuals, projects or companies based on philanthropic or civic motivations with no expectation of monetary or material return.

Globally, debt-based activities account for 96.4% of online alternative finance volumes, equity activities for 3.0%, and non-investment activities for 0.6%.

The online alternative finance market for businesses (aggregating the various instruments) has expanded rapidly in recent years. In 2018, the median inflation-adjusted growth rate for participating countries for which data are available stood at 54% (see Figure 1.21). Growth rates are especially high in emerging economies and small economies, where activities remain relatively modest.

In some more mature and developed markets, the growth rate is beginning to stabilise. In Australia and the United Kingdom, for instance, 2018 growth rates amounted to 6% and 9% respectively. In 12 countries, online alternative finance contracted, often by more than half. The wide discrepancy in growth rates indicates a strong volatility in the market. China is a case in point; in 2018, its online alternative finance market for businesses, the largest in the world both in absolute and relative terms, experiencing a contraction of 57% following a regulatory crackdown by the authorities (see Figure 1.21). The market also plummeted by 77% in Korea, another relatively developed market, following mounting concerns about dubious or outright fraudulent behaviour by some platforms active in the country.

Figure 1.21. Growth in the online alternative finance market for businesses

As a percentage, year-on-year growth

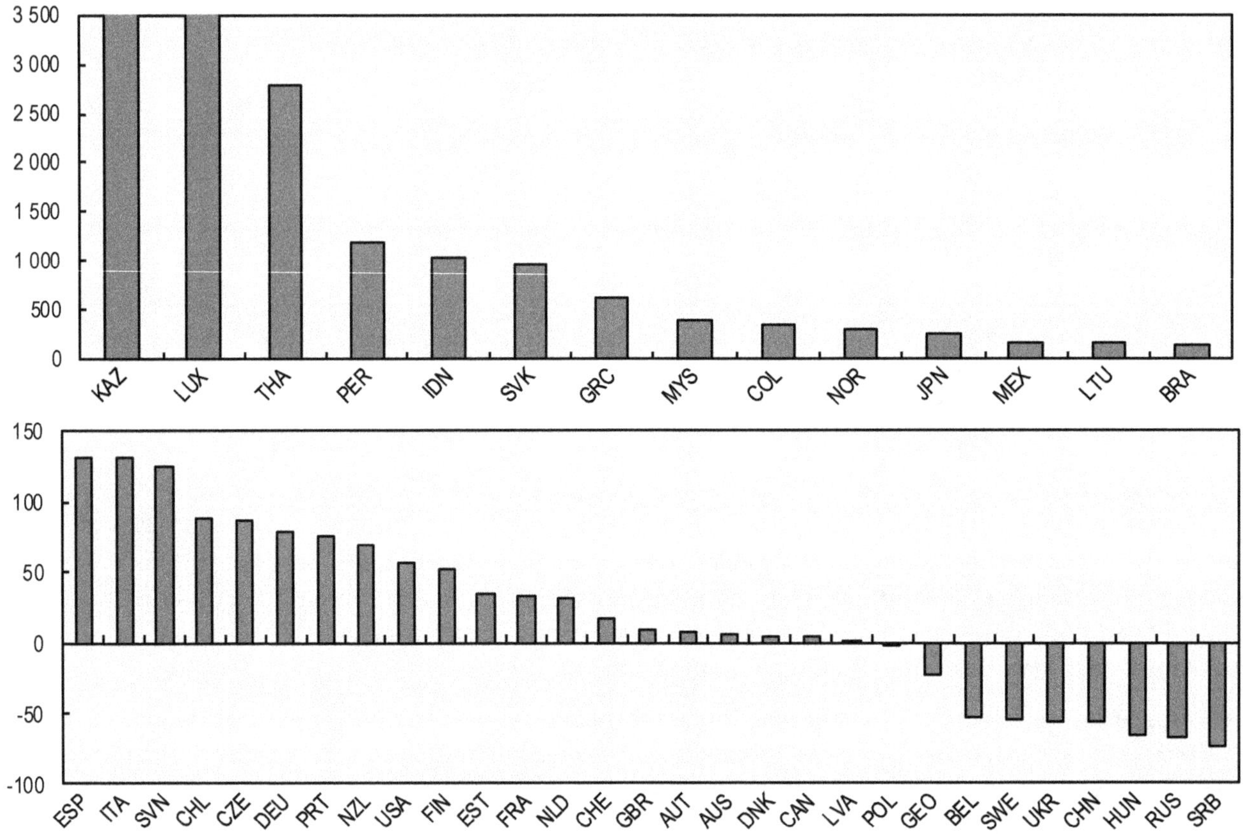

Note: All the data are expressed in USD. Volumes are adjusted for inflation using the OECD deflator. Due to the scale, growth rates for Kazakhstan (421761.6%) and Luxembourg (5182.2%) are not depicted. Growth rates for Israel could not be calculated due to missing 2017 data.

Source: Regional reports of the Cambridge Centre for Alternative Finance at the University of Cambridge.

StatLink https://doi.org/10.1787/888934115806

Box 1.1. Online alternative finance markets in China

China continues to dominate the global online alternative finance market, but saw a strong contraction of P2P lending volumes in 2018 following a regulatory crackdown by the authorities. Some platforms in the largely unregulated P2P market in China had insufficient guarantees in terms of capital requirements and loss provisions for investors, and others were considered to be fraudulent.

In the wake of extremely rapid growth, policy makers' concern about investor and consumer protection, and about financial stability, mounted. As early as 2016, a cap on borrowing from P2P platforms was put into place as part of the *Interim Rules on the Business Activities of Online Lending Information Intermediaries*, and various inspections of existing P2P platforms were carried out to increase supervision. Since then, additional rules have been put in place. As a result, many non-compliant platforms, whether fraudulent or incapable of producing guarantees in terms of investor and consumer protection, have closed.

This led to a sharp contraction in the market in 2018 and the first half of 2019. According to the China Banking and Insurance Regulatory Commission (CBIRC), only 427 P2P platforms were still operating as of October 2019, against 6 000 in 2015. A registration programme is being designed for the remaining platforms, with strict conditions for eligibility. This should strengthen the market and ensure that interests of investors and firms seeking finance are safeguarded.

China's crackdown illustrates the regulatory challenges inherent to online alternative finance, and the importance of an appropriate regulatory framework and oversight.

Source: (Business Insider, 2019[23]), (South China Morning Post, 2019[24]), (Reuters, 2019[25]).

Overall, online alternative finance activities for for-profit businesses continue to be strongly concentrated in a few countries. Despite a sharp decline in 2018, China has the largest market by far, representing 62.5% of global volumes of online alternative finance, followed by the United States and the United Kingdom with shares of 20.5% and 7.5% respectively (see Figure 1.22). These countries are followed by Japan (1.2%), Australia (1.1%) and Israel (0.9%).

The share of volumes in continental Europe remain relatively modest in comparison, with France the most active market (with a global share of 0.6%), followed by Italy (0.6%) and the Netherlands (0.5%). Latin America accounts for a small share of global online alternative finance volumes: Peru accounts for 0.4% of the global market, while Chile accounts for 0.2% of total volumes.

Figure 1.22. The online alternative finance market for businesses by region, 2018

As a percentage of total volumes

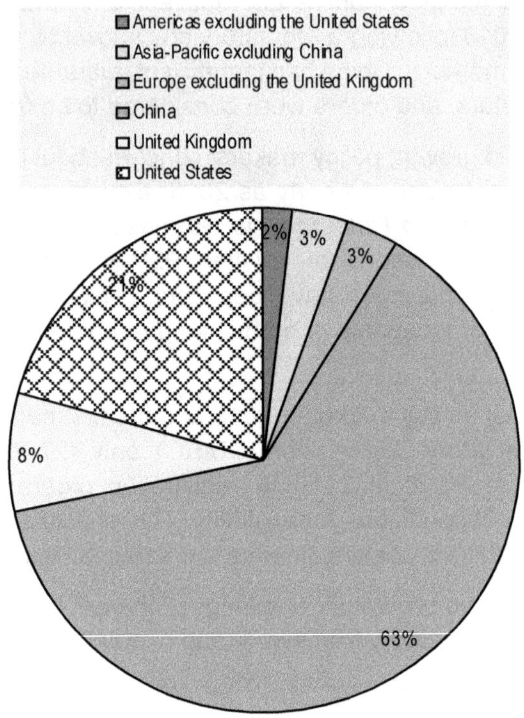

Note: All the data are expressed in USD.
Source: Regional reports of the Cambridge Centre for Alternative Finance at the University of Cambridge.

StatLink https://doi.org/10.1787/888934115825

Relative to GDP, China still has the largest online alternative finance market, followed by the United Kingdom, Estonia and Israel. In these countries, market volumes amount to more than 0.15% of GDP, compared to the median value for all countries of 0.0168% (see Figure 1.23).

Figure 1.23. Online alternative finance business volumes, 2018

As a percentage of GDP

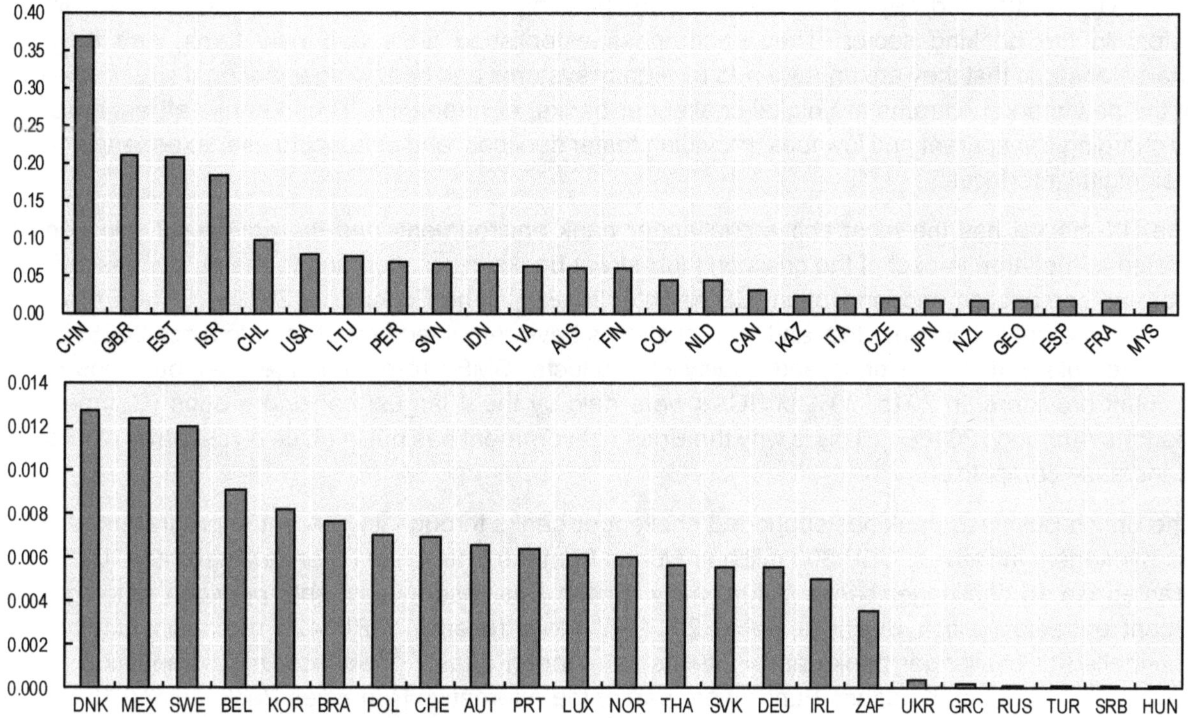

Note: All the data are originally expressed in USD. Volumes are adjusted for GDP using yearly GDP data from the International Monetary Fund (IMF).

Source: Regional reports of the Cambridge Centre for Alternative Finance at the University of Cambridge. (IMF, 2019[26]).

StatLink https://doi.org/10.1787/888934115844

It is important to note that, although online alternative finance represents one avenue for financial innovation to deliver financial services to SMEs', there are many other channels. Box 1.2 puts a spotlight on challenger banks.

Box 1.2. Challenger banks are gaining ground among SMEs

In the UK market and beyond, challengers are pushing for competition. Challenger banks are new actors in the banking sector. They encompass established firms and new firms, and their core characteristic is that they are unburdened by legacy systems and heavy organisational structures. Many of the new market entrants are digital challenger banks, or neobanks. These banks attract customers by charging transparent and low fees, providing faster services, and enhancing user experience through their digital interfaces.

The UK market has the most active challenger bank environment, and the drivers for this trend are related to the large impact of the crisis on high-street banks' reputation and to the authorities' efforts to promote competition and innovation (CBInsights, 2018[27]) (The Economist, 2019[28]). The British SME banking market is concentrated, and market shares have remained broadly stable since 2005. Despite considerable variation in price and quality of products, SMEs rarely change their business current account providers. In 2015, 80% of BCAs were held by the 4 largest banking groups (Competition & Markets Authority, 2016[29]). This is why the British government has put in place a vast array of initiatives to increase competition.

The British Business Bank has supported challenger banks through its guarantee programmes as well as investment initiatives. GBP 300 million of loans from the Enterprise Finance Guarantee (EFG) were granted via 16 challenger banks. Additionally, British Business Investments provided funding to two recent entrants (British Business Bank, 2017[30]). More recently, GBP 425 million in funding were channelled to challenger banks and Fintechs to broaden quality of service and competition in SME banking in the United Kingdom. Funds were part of the Alternative Remedies Package and 15 financial providers gained access to funding between GBP 5 and GBP 120 million.

Challenger banks are on the rise in other markets and numbered more than 100 globally in 2018 (Caplain, 2018[31]). The German bank N26, launched in 2013, currently has 3.5 million customers in 22 European countries and the United States. Bunq, a Dutch challenger, has expanded to 5 European markets since its launch in 2015. Both firms also offer business accounts with different targets: Bunq offers features for employers and N26 targets freelancers and the self-employed. The Finnish bank Holvi focuses only on freelancers and small business owners. It has partnered with the Estonian e-Residency Programme and offers accounts for these location-independent entrepreneurs. The bank, backed by BBVA since 2016, reported 150 000 customers.

In Asia, Korea's Kakao Bank has 10 million customers 2 years after its launch, and it is the second most-used banking app in the country (Min-kyung, 2019[32]). WeBank, China's first private and digital-only bank, was authorised in 2014. It markets SME and consumer loans and reported more than 100 million active users in 2018. VoltBank (Australia) was the first digital challenger bank to be granted a full banking license in the country in January 2019, removing the cap on deposits that limited its operations. It was the first license granted in the country since 2000, meaning almost 2 decades without new entrants. In Brazil, neobanks have recently started to target small business, going beyond their consumer accounts. Neon, Inter, Original all offer corporate accounts. NuBank, which has 8.5 million customers and holds 5 million current accounts after the product's launch in 2017, started its business account pilot in July 2019.

Source: (British Business Bank, 2017[30]), (Caplain, 2018[31]), (CBInsights, 2018[27]), (Competition & Markets Authority, 2016[29]), (Min-kyung, 2019[32]), (The Economist, 2019[28]).

Payment delays, bankruptcies and non-performing loans

Payment delays declined in 2018, following an established trend since 2013. Bankruptcies also remained on a downward path in 2018, with a negative median bankruptcy growth rate for the sixth consecutive year. Data on NPLs show an upward trend for SME loans and a downward trend for large business loans.

Payment delays

The 2018 data on payment delays shows a decline in twelve countries for which data are available and an increase in three countries, with another four countries remaining constant. The decline varies significantly across countries. Greece and Portugal experienced strong decreases in their payment delays, of fourteen and eight days respectively. The median value for all Scoreboard countries stood at 19.77 days, while the average stood at around 15 days, suggesting that the data are skewed by outliers, especially among upper middle-income countries. The OECD median (10.79 days) stood slightly lower than the EU median (11.39 days). Overall, the median payment delay has experienced a strong decrease since 2013, and it appears to be recovering pre-crisis levels.

Figure 1.24. Payment delays by country and evolution in number of days (median value)

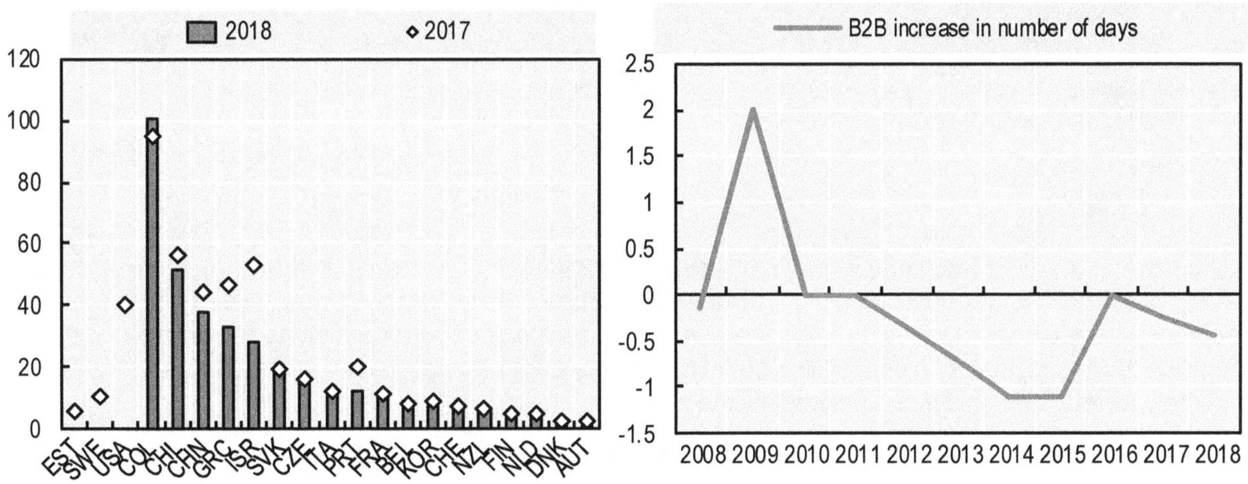

Note: Definitions differ across countries. Detailed information on sources and definitions is available in the full country profiles.
Source: Data compiled from the individual country profiles.

StatLink https://doi.org/10.1787/888934115863

Bankruptcies

In 2018, the number of bankruptcies decreased in 21 out of 33 countries for which data are available. The median year-on-year change in bankruptcies was negative for the sixth consecutive year, with a 1.93% decline in 2018. Overall, the decline in bankruptcies appears to be levelling out, from almost -7% in 2014 to -1.8% in 2018. There seems to be a convergence across countries, as evidenced by a decline in the standard deviation in growth rates since 2015. For the first time since 2014, the median growth rate was negative within all country groups in 2018 (OECD, EU, World Bank high income and World Bank upper-middle income). This decrease is particularly strong in middle-income countries.

Figure 1.25. SME Bankruptcies, growth rate

As a percentage

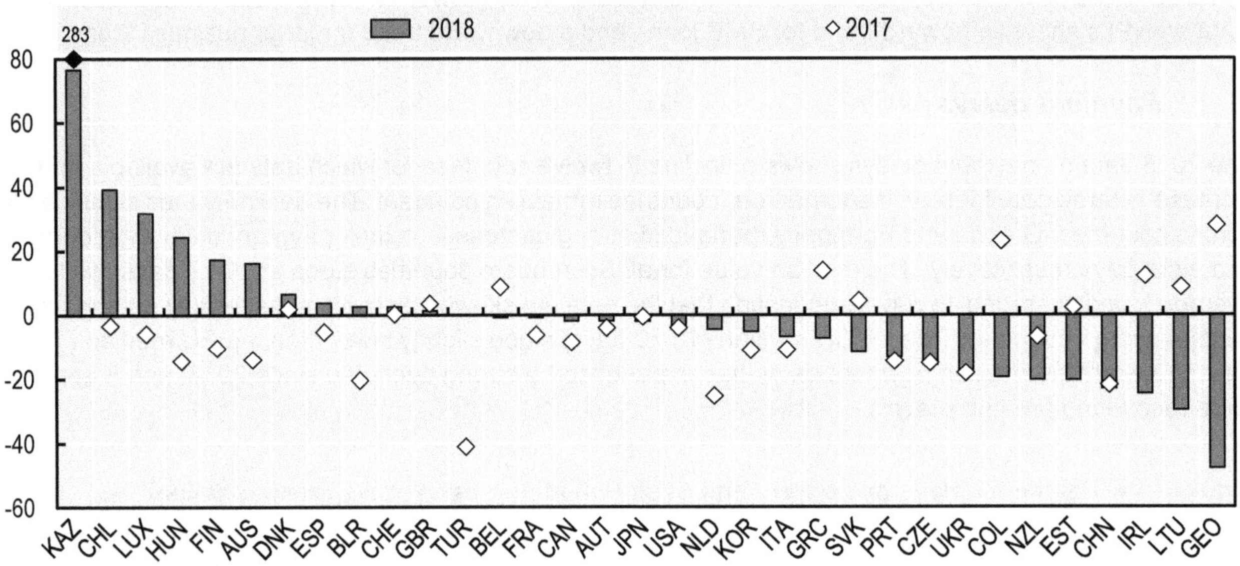

Note: Definitions of the indicator vary across jurisdictions. In addition to this, some countries provide bankruptcy data for all firms rather than for SMEs. Others still provide bankruptcy rates. 2017 data for Kazakhstan are not represented due to the scale (+283.33%).
Source: Data compiled from the individual country profiles.

StatLink https://doi.org/10.1787/888934115882

While bankruptcy time series by country are broadly indicative of firms' cash flow, there are important differences in the length and complexity of bankruptcy procedures between countries. This means that insolvent enterprises are not declared bankrupt at the same stage or under the same conditions in different countries. Bankruptcies upon court ruling constitute a very common approach to firm closure or liquidation in some countries, but this is not universally the case.

Moreover, legal and regulatory reforms that were introduced over the reference period can affect the figures. In addition, approaches to counting bankruptcies vary between countries (some of which do not distinguish between SMEs and other firms). This greatly hinders cross-country comparability and represents a weakness in the evidence base.

Non-performing loans (NPLs)

NPLs are overall more prevalent among SMEs than in the general business population (see Figure 1.26). Since the crisis, NPLs for all firms are on the decline, but there is no clear trend for SMEs. The difference in NPL rates between the two groups increased in 2018, and more generally since the crisis in most countries.

Figure 1.26. Median rate of NPLs by firm type, 2007-18

As a percentage

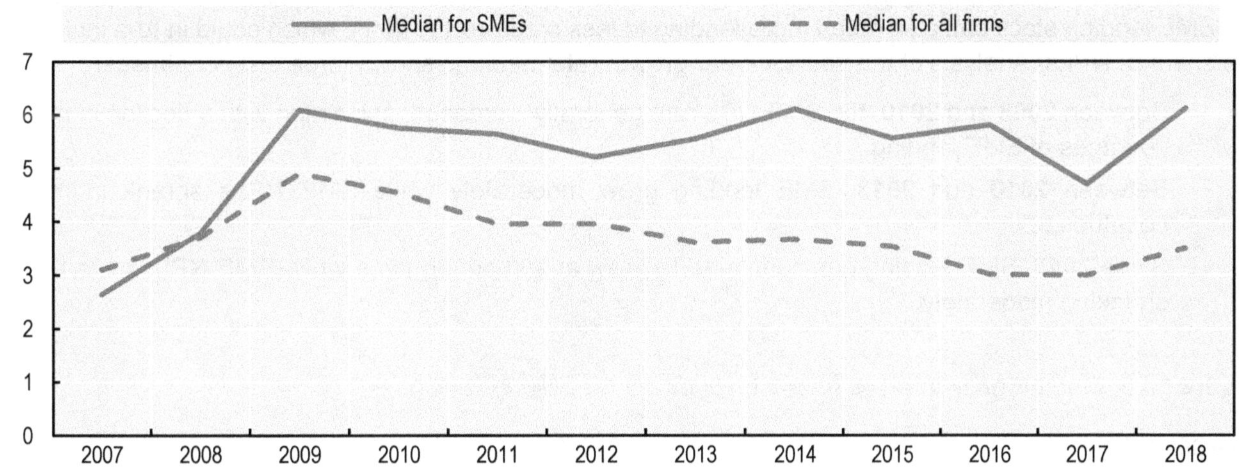

Note: Data for the Czech Republic, Malaysia and Russia were removed from the indicator for all firms due to differences in the definition of non-performing loans.
Source: Data compiled from the individual country profiles.

StatLink https://doi.org/10.1787/888934115901

Discrepancies in NPL ratios among high-income economies can be attributed to asymmetric effects of the financial crisis, which affected the financial industry harder in some countries than in others (European Commission, 2019[33]). This is evidenced for example by the high NPL rates in Greece and Portugal, two countries that were hit hard by the crisis. In addition, differences between national insolvency regimes and the exact definition of when a loan is non-performing can explain part of the variability observed.

Figure 1.27. NPL rates for SMEs, 2017-18

As a percentage

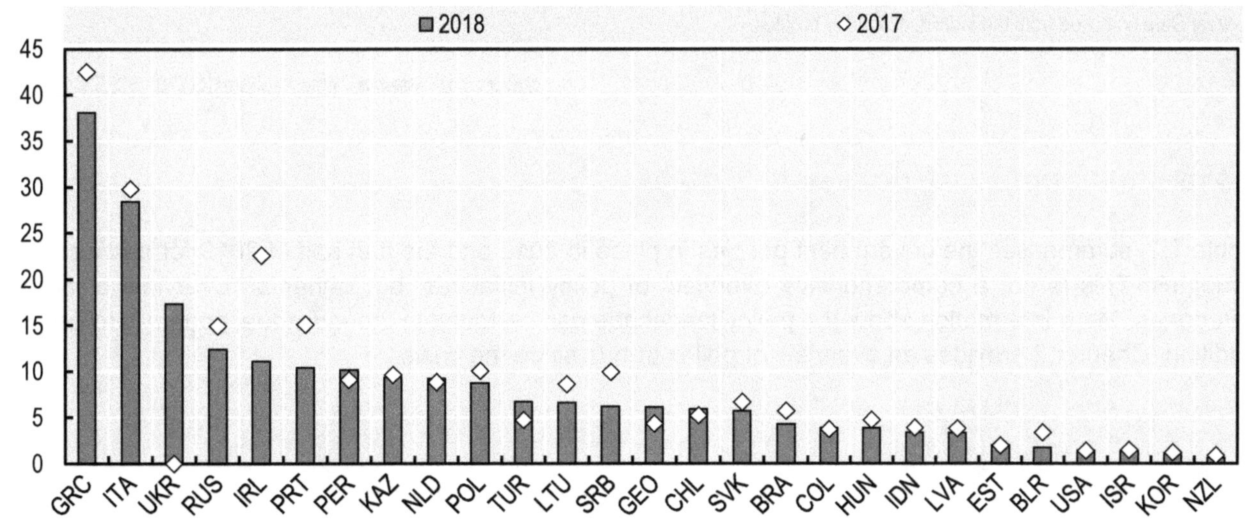

Note: Definitions of NPLs vary – see full country profiles for details.
Source: Data compiled from the individual country profiles.

StatLink https://doi.org/10.1787/888934115920

A higher share of NPLs hinders banks' capacity to provide credit, because it decreases banks' profitability. This automatically widens the financing gap for firms. The data for 2018 show that the relationship between the rate of NPLs and SME lending stock is not necessarily negative, especially when corrected for GDP. The relationship is also strongly affected by outliers and causal relationships are unclear: an increase in the SME lending stock can also mean more lending to less creditworthy firms, which could in turn increase the share of NPLs. Analysis of the year-on-year growth rate medians shows three distinct phases:

- Between **2008** and **2010**, the SME NPL rate generally increased, coinciding with a decline in many countries of SME lending;
- Between **2010** and **2013**, SME lending grew moderately while SME NPLs shrank in many countries;
- Since **2013**, SME lending has continued to grow at a subdued pace while SME NPLs have been shrinking moderately.

Figure 1.28. Median growth rates for SME lending and SME NPLs

As a percentage

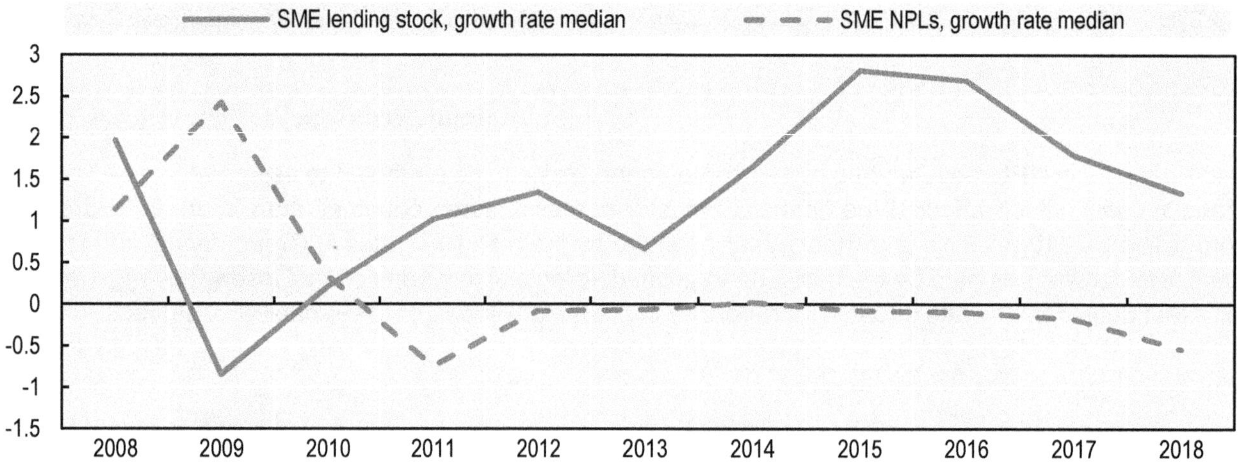

Source: Data compiled from the individual country profiles.

StatLink https://doi.org/10.1787/888934115939

Government policy responses in 2018-19

Table 1.2. summarises the government policies in place in 2018 and the first half of 2019 for participating countries. This is not a comprehensive overview of policy initiatives, but rather an overview of broad categories. More information about the policy landscape can be found in the individual country profiles. In addition, Chapter 2 provides an overview of policy trends since the crisis.

Table 1.2. Government policy instruments to foster SME access to finance, 2018-19

	Government loan guarantees	Direct lending to SMEs	Subsidised Interest rates	SME Banks	Support for start-up finance		
					Special guarantees and loans for start-ups	Venture capital funds	Business Angels co-investment
Australia		✓			✓	✓	✓**
Austria	✓	✓	✓	✓	✓	✓*	✓
Belarus	✓						
Belgium	✓	✓			✓	✓	✓
Brazil	✓	✓		✓		✓	
Canada	✓	✓		✓	✓	✓	✓**
Chile	✓		✓	✓	✓	✓	
China	✓		✓		✓	✓	
Colombia	✓			✓			
Czech	✓	✓	✓	✓	✓	✓*	
Denmark	✓	✓		✓	✓	✓	✓*
Estonia	✓		✓	✓	✓	✓	✓*
Finland	✓	✓	✓	✓	✓	✓	✓*
France	✓	✓	✓*	✓	✓	✓	✓
Georgia			✓	✓		✓	
Greece	✓	✓		✓	✓	✓	
Hungary	✓	✓	✓	✓		✓	✓*
Indonesia	✓	✓	✓				
Ireland	✓	✓		✓	✓	✓	✓*
Israel	✓	✓		✓	✓	✓	✓
Italy	✓	✓	✓	✓	✓	✓	✓
Japan	✓	✓		✓	✓	✓	
Kazakhstan	✓	✓	✓	✓	✓		
Korea	✓	✓		✓	✓	✓	✓
Latvia	✓	✓	✓	✓	✓	✓*	✓
Lithuania	✓	✓	✓*	✓	✓	✓	✓*
Luxembourg	✓	✓	✓	✓	✓	✓	✓*
Malaysia	✓	✓	✓	✓	✓	✓	
Mexico	✓	✓		✓	✓	✓	✓
Netherlands	✓	✓			✓	✓*	✓*
New Zealand	✓*					✓	✓
Norway	✓	✓		✓	✓	✓	
Peru	✓	✓		✓	✓	✓	✓
Poland	✓	✓*	✓*	✓	✓	✓*	✓*
Portugal	✓	✓	✓	✓	✓	✓*	✓*
Russia	✓	✓	✓	✓		✓	✓
Serbia	✓	✓	✓				
Slovak	✓	✓	✓	✓	✓	✓	
Slovenia	✓	✓	✓	✓	✓	✓*	✓
South Africa	✓	✓		✓	✓	✓	
Spain	✓	✓		✓	✓	✓*	✓*
Sweden	✓	✓		✓	✓	✓*	
Switzerland	✓						
Thailand	✓		✓	✓	✓	✓	
Ukraine		✓	✓	✓			
Turkey	✓	✓	✓	✓	✓	✓	✓
United	✓	✓		✓	✓	✓	✓
United States	✓	✓		✓		✓	
European	✓	✓		✓	✓	✓	✓
	* For exporting firms only	* In cooperation with the EU only				* In cooperation with the EU only	**At the regional level only

Based on information from participating countries, a number of broad emerging trends can be discerned and are presented along with recent policy examples in the following sections. Full country profiles provide more detailed information on policy initiatives. In addition, the thematic chapter of this publication highlights broad policy trends since the financial crisis. The following recent trends can be distinguished and are discussed in more detail below:

- Credit guarantee volumes continue to rise;
- Public support for equity finance instruments remains strong;
- Regulatory approaches and targeted policies to support Fintech developments are becoming more widespread;
- Initiatives to foster "open banking," whereby financial institutions are obliged to share their data with third-party financial service providers, are emerging;
- Financial support for internationalisation is gaining importance;
- Governments are implementing online tools for SMEs and entrepreneurs to find the appropriate financial support;
- The spread of the coronavirus led to liquidity shortages in many businesses, and many governments and supra-national institutions have taken action to dampen the impact.

Credit guarantee volumes continue to rise

Credit guarantee schemes have traditionally been the most widespread policy tool to enhance SMEs access to finance. For the sixth year in a row, credit guarantee volumes were up in a majority of Scoreboard countries, as evidenced by the median value, although with considerable cross-country variance. In 2018, volumes increased in 14 out of 23 countries with available data. After a strong expansion in middle-income countries such as Turkey and Brazil in 2017, these economies experienced a contraction of credit guarantee volumes in 2018 (respectively -64.63% and -20.42%).

As a share of SME loan stock, guaranteed loans remain significant in economies like Colombia, Turkey and Hungary, all with figures superior to 15%. Recent trends in government loan guarantees also involve digitisation and optimisation of processes, with a cost reduction which increased the attractiveness of these instruments (written exchanges with experts from the European Association of Guarantee Institutions – AECM).

Figure 1.29. Government guaranteed loan volumes as share of SME loan stock

As a percentage

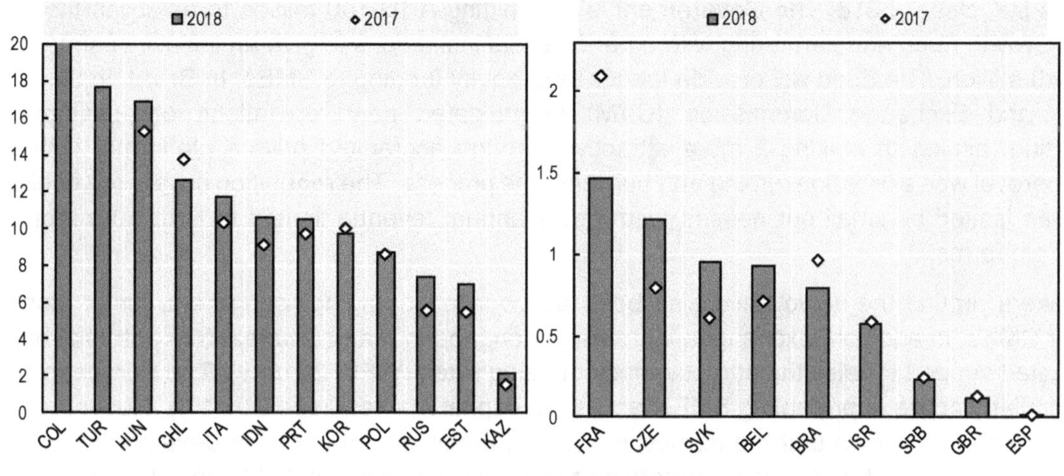

Note: The 2017 figure for Turkey is not represented in the graph (51.17%). All data are adjusted for inflation using the OECD GDP deflator. Data for non-OECD countries were extracted from the World Development Indicators from the World Bank.
Source: Data compiled from the individual country profiles.

StatLink https://doi.org/10.1787/888934115958

Support for equity finance instruments remains strong

A variety of measures have been implemented in recent years in order stimulate private equity, including the establishment of funds of funds, direct investment and co-investment, the setting up of networks and associations, new regulatory frameworks and tax incentives.

In the United Kingdom, for instance, various policy initiatives as well as direct government investments made through the British Business Bank (BBB) have had a clear effect on the diversification of supply, as shown in a recent report (UK Finance, 2018[15]). It has been estimated that BBB programmes supported 9% of equity deals in the UK between 2016 and 2018, representing approximately 13% of all investments in this period (British Business Bank, 2019[34]). In Portugal, the fund of funds that was established in 2017 in cooperation with the EIF (European Investment Fund) is yielding strong results, with more than a fourfold increase in venture and growth capital volumes in 2018.

There has also been a strong theoretical backlash against the idea that public intervention in equity markets "crowds out" private capital (Howell, 2017[35]). Nonetheless, equity financing remains concentrated in a few hubs and the offer remains insufficient in most countries to support strongly innovative firms. In 2018, the three Baltic states and the European Investment Fund (EIF) continued preparing for the launch of Baltic Innovation Fund II, with a planned volume of EUR 156 million. In Greece, 9 funds were chosen to provide equity to Greek SMEs EquiFund. The fund provides equity to enable high value-added investments, through an initial budget of EUR 320 million, funded jointly by ERDF, the EIF and the EIB.

In China, the regional equity trading market has played an important role in supporting direct financing for SMEs. By the end of 2018, there were 34 regional equity trading markets in China with over 24 808 listed companies and a total financing value of CNY 906.3 billion. The National SME Development Fund, focused on VC/PE investments to seed-stage and early-stage SMEs, completed 208 investment projects totalling CNY 6.05 billion in 2018 since its launch in 2015. Meanwhile, the National Guide Fund for Venture Investment in Emerging Industries, which aims to invest in venture phases of potential companies in high-tech fields accounted for an aggregate investment of over CNY 22.5 billion.

The Australian government has introduced a crowdsourced equity funding (CSEF) framework providing a new avenue of funding for early stage businesses, while still ensuring appropriate investor protection. The CSEF framework commenced in September 2017 for small public companies and was extended to private companies in October 2018. The Government is committing AUD 100 million to establish the Australian Business Growth Fund and partnering with other financial institutions to give an initial investment capacity of AUD 540 million. The Fund will provide longer term equity funding to SMEs. In Brazil, In July 2017, the Securities and Exchange Commission (CVM) promulgated new regulations on investment-based crowdfunding, aiming at making it more attractive through accredited private platforms. Until recently, gaining approval was a time consuming and burdensome process. The regulation covers the public offering of securities issued by small businesses (with gross annual revenue limited to BRL 10 million) through electronic platforms.

Policy makers around the world have also been active in encouraging listings and junior stock market activity for SMEs. In addition, exchanges increasingly engage in market outreach to potential businesses and dedicated support to raise the attractiveness of being listed (WFE, 2018[36]). The European Union has been particularly active in promoting SMEs' access to capital markets (see Box 1.3). Recent research on South-East Asia has shown that the domestic financial development (e.g. the development of domestic capital markets) that has taken place in emerging economies since the global financial crisis has benefited smaller businesses more than larger businesses. The study also shows that domestic markets have played a strong role in the region and have complemented international markets (Abraham, Cortina and Schmukler, 2019[37]). Crucially, domestic markets often open access to relatively smaller firms (Abraham, Cortina and Schmukler, 2019[37]).

Box 1.3. SME access to capital markets in the context of the European Union's capital markets union (CMU)

Junior stock markets in continental Europe were originally modelled on NASDAQ as part of the Euro New Markets alliance in the late 1980s (Granier, Revest and Sapio, 2019[21]). They were conceived mostly as means of exit for venture capitalists wishing to "cash out". Following the dot-com bubble in the early 2000s, most of these markets were closed down. Since then, markets have re-opened under different names, and in the context of a strong push from the European Commission (as part of its capital markets union agenda), these markets have expanded and listing requirements have become more accommodating for SMEs in order to enhance their access to capital (Granier, Revest and Sapio, 2019[21]). Recent developments in the EU since the Markets in Financial Instruments Directive – MiFID I (2004) and II (2014) – include the Prospectus Regulation (2017), which introduced lighter regulation for instruments issued by SMEs (European Parliament, 2019[38]). The results of a public consultation, published in May 2018, pointed towards three directions for future legislative action on this issue (European Parliament, 2019[38]):

- "reduce the administrative burden and the high compliance costs faced by SME growth market issuers while ensuring a high level of market integrity and investor protection"
- "foster the liquidity of publicly listed SME shares to make these markets more attractive for investors, issuers and intermediaries"
- "facilitate the registration of multilateral trading facilities as SME growth markets"

A political agreement between member states and the Parliament was reached in April 2019 on future technical amendments to the Market Abuse Regulation and to the Prospectus Regulation.

Regulatory approaches and targeted policies to support Fintech developments are becoming more widespread

Some countries have made their legislative framework more favourable to innovation in the financial sphere. In addition to new regulations concerning investment-based crowdfunding Fintechs implemented in 2017, Brazil decided to regulate credit Fintechs in 2018. Two specific business models have been authorised. The peer-to-peer lending model is regulated as a *Sociedade de Crédito entre Pessoas* (SEP) and the balance-sheet lending is regulated as a *Sociedade de Crédito Direto* (SCD).

In the United Kingdom, the Credit Referral Scheme is in place since November 2016, and by June 2018, nearly 19 000 small businesses which were rejected for finance from one of the 9 big banks in the country had been referred under the scheme. After information started being shared from the banks through the platforms and to alternative finance providers, more than GBP 15 million of funding was secured by 900 small businesses. Since the last quarter of 2017, the conversion rate for SMEs which make contact with one of the 4 platforms accredited in the scheme has been over 10%, falling in line with market expectations (UK HM Treasury, 2018[39]). The UK government has also supported digital challenger banks (See Box 1.2).

The first cross-border pilot for Fintech firms wishing to test innovative products, services or business models across multiple jurisdictions was put in place in 2019. The Global Financial Innovation Network (GFIN) was formally launched in January 2019 to support financial innovation while protecting the interests of consumers. An international group of 11 coordinating regulators, 20 members and 7 observers among national and subnational authorities as well as international organisations and fora gathered to create a platform for sharing experiences and approaches. The global sandbox selected 8 firms among 44 applicants and this first cohort will pilot their services in Australia, Bahrain, Bermuda, Canada (British

Columbia, Ontario and Québec), Hong Kong, Hungary, Kazakhstan (Astana), Lithuania, Singapore, United Arab Emirates (Abu Dhabi, Dubai), United Kingdom, Guernsey and Jersey (Global Financial Innovation Network and Financial Conduct Authority, 2019[40]).

Initiatives to foster "open banking" are emerging

As in previous years, many governments across the world are taking initiatives to foster financial innovation in a stable environment, mostly through the changes to legislation and supervisory oversight.

As part of this trend, some jurisdictions are moving towards open banking. Traditionally, banks have full control and ownership over the data they collect from their clients. Open banking legislation forces banks to allow third party access to consumers' bank data (with their consent) through application programming interfaces (APIs).

Policy makers around the world are encouraging open banking in the expectation that this will spur competition in the financial industry, as small business owners and entrepreneurs can share banking data securely and easily within a well-functioning open banking protocol. Such regulation could also encourage financial innovation by making banking data available to financial sector start-ups, as well as established actors.

The Australian government, for instance, agreed to the recommendations made in a review on open banking in May 2018. Over the 2019-22 period, open banking will be implemented in several phases in the country.

Similarly, the PSD2 (Revised Payment Service Directive) is being implemented in the European Union since 2018 (with certain provisions becoming mandatory only later, so as to allow the financial sector time to adapt). PSD2 obliges banks operating in the area to provide third-party financial providers access to their customers' accounts through open APIs.

In 2018, the United Kingdom initiated its own open banking initiative, under which the nine biggest banks have to release their data in a secure, standardised form, so that it can be shared more easily between authorised organisations online.

Japanese banks are encouraged to set up APIs since 2018, and most large banks in the country have plans to do so by 2020. Singapore and Hong Kong, China, are also encouraging financial institutions to share their APIs. Regulators in Canada and the United States are discussing open banking with financial institutions, some of which already have open APIs. In Canada, the discussion has taken the form of a consultation process that started in 2019.

Financial support for SME internationalisation is on the rise in some countries

Many governments have increased their (financial) support to enable small businesses to become active in foreign markets in recent years. With the aim of increasing the number of exporting companies, Brazil introduced modifications to its MSMEs Export Credit Insurance scheme in April 2018. The eligibility criteria, premium price and risk coverage among were all modified in order to increase the take-up.

Canada announced its Export Diversification Strategy in 2018. A total of CAD 1.1 billion will be invested over a period of six years to reach the objective to expand total exports by 50% or more by 2025. As part of the strategy, the Government of Canada will invest an additional CAD 100 million over six years in CanExport, the five-year, CAD 50 million program launched by the Government in January 2016 to provide direct financial assistance to eligible Canadians, and related funding programs to support businesses looking to reach new overseas markets. In addition, other non-financial support has been established and or expanded, such as awareness raising programmes and export capacity building activities for SMEs with potential to become active in foreign markets or to scale up activities. A key component of the strategy is to enhance trade services for exporters and ensure that Canadian businesses have enough resources to execute their export plans.

In Finland, one of the key focuses of Finnvera, its state-owned financing company, is on supporting small companies to export. To that aim, export credit activities rose by more than 50% between 2017 and 2018, standing at a post-crisis peak in 2018. Two-thirds of export guarantees were also accompanied with export credit to further address the financing needs of its beneficiaries.

The United Kingdom launched its export strategy in 2018. To reach the ambition of increasing exports from 30% of GDP to 35% of GDP, the government is deploying an awareness campaign to UK exporters most likely to benefit from export finance and insurance support, among other support measures such as providing information, advice and practical assistance on exporting.

Governments are implementing online tools for SMEs and entrepreneurs to find the appropriate (financial) support

Many entrepreneurs and small business owners find it hard to navigate the policy support landscape and therefore often do not apply for (financial and non-financial) assistance for which they could otherwise qualify. Governments across the world are increasingly putting into place online tools, sometimes based on artificial intelligence, to inform SMEs and guide them to appropriate support measures for their business.

In March 2019, the Irish government updated its site, Supportingsmes.gov.ie, designed to assist small businesses and entrepreneurs find information on over 170 government support instruments to which they may have access. Visitors can fill in a short questionnaire, after which the tool will generate a customised list of supports tailored to their business requirements with further information and contact details.

Also in 2019, the Hellenic Ministry for Economy & Development created a single online portal to inform SMEs about up to date available financial instruments currently available in Greece. The web page is client-oriented, provides information regarding each financial instrument, and guides SMEs to accredited organisations that provide these various financial instruments in Greece.

New Zealand aims to improve the user experience of its main online portal, https://www.business.govt.nz. In 2018, the government developed a "digital assistant, Tai." Its main purpose is to make it easier for businesses to navigate across several government agencies by using artificial intelligence (AI). Ten partner organisations, responsible for an estimated 83% of interactions between businesses and government bodies, strive to further improve the website and digital assistant under the umbrella of the "better for business initiative".

Policy makers are taking measures to address cash flow problems caused by the novel coronavirus pandemic

The COVID-19 pandemic is affecting the economy and SMEs in several ways. Among the many challenges, liquidity constraints represent a crucial concern for many firms, especially smaller ones. A recent survey in China, for example, highlights that one third of surveyed SMEs only had enough cash reserves to cover fixed expenses of one month and another third for two months (http://www.oecd.org/coronavirus/en/). Policy makers around the globe are taking action to prevent viable firms from going bankrupt because of temporary liquidity shortages. These measures take place in a financial context which was generally favourable for SMEs before the pandemic hit, but which was not sufficient to enable them to face the magnitude of the current shocks without government intervention.

The deferral of tax and social security payments, debt payments and rent and utility payments, are among the policy approaches that governments are increasingly adopting. Likewise, some government agencies, as well as commercial banks, have introduced debt repayment moratoria for SMEs facing liquidity shortages. Governments are also setting up or expanding financial instruments for small businesses which have been hit hard by the economic crisis. These include loan guarantees, direct lending facilities and grants and/or subsidies.

Policy makers are also employing different tax relief measures to cushion the blow of the crisis, as well as initiatives related to shortening of working time, temporary lay-offs and sick leave. Finally, some jurisdictions are also supporting SMEs with structural measures, for example to enable them to digitalise and facilitate teleworking[8].

Recommendations for data improvements

Data gaps on SME finance remain significant and further efforts to improve the collection of data and evidence on SME finance should be pursued. First, the SME population is very heterogeneous, and financing conditions and challenges differ substantially along parameters such as the age of the firm, its size, location, sector, growth potential as well as the characteristics of the principal business owner, such as their gender or business experience. Data from Canada's Survey on Financing and Growth of SMEs show pronounced differences in SME financing needs and outcomes based on different business characteristics, with the main sector of operation playing an important role. Indeed, owner characteristics appear to be less important when controlling for business characteristics.

Despite the widespread recognition of the need to tailor policies to the different needs of the enterprise population, data collection efforts do not always capture granular information along these parameters. This limits policy makers' ability to assess the impact and effectiveness of initiatives on these different segments. In addition, the absence of more granular data limits the analysis of the Scoreboard data. Recent research, for example, shows that financing patterns differ substantially between micro-enterprises and large SMEs, at least in Europe, with the former making more use of self-financing options, short term credit, and less of state subsidies, asset-based financing and trade credit (Masiak et al., 2019[42]).

The observed trends may mask very different developments among different segments of SMEs. Quantitative surveys, either directed to a representative group of SMEs or to senior loan officials, can provide valuable additional insights alongside more qualitative information. These surveys are not undertaken in all countries, however. In addition, there differences in terms of methodology, questions asked, coverage and scale of existing surveys are significant, hindering international comparisons. Analysis of Scoreboard data on credit rejections, credit applications and collateral requirements, for instance, is hampered by limitations in the number of countries with data on these indicators, as well as by limited cross-country comparability. Greater international harmonisation of demand-side survey methods in particular would enable more meaningful analysis of the drivers of trends in SMEs' access to finance and financial conditions. The OECD is supporting new efforts in this area.

In addition, the evidence base on most sources of finance other than straight bank debt continues to be weak. Often, data are not SME-specific, incomplete, hard to compare from one country to the other, and questions sometimes arise about the reliability and methodology of data collection efforts. Initiatives to promote the use of alternative sources of financing by SMEs have proliferated in recent years, but their impact often remains hard to gauge due to the lack of data. More systematic and harmonised efforts to collect data on alternative financing instruments and sources would be crucial in order to understand the trends and the potential of these instruments for SMEs.

The OECD will continue to advance and support national and international efforts in these areas. In this context, and to further strengthen the utility of the Scoreboard in the years ahead, work is being undertaken along several avenues:

- A stocktaking exercise on the availability of disaggregated data along a number of dimensions, including sector of operation, firm size, geographic location of the firm within countries, age of the firm and gender of the principal owner, with a view to include this type of data where they are available and encourage broader collection of disaggregated SME financing data;

- A mapping of current practices in demand-side surveys, with a view to improve the comparability and coverage of demand-side data in order to enable a better understanding of the drivers of SME financing trends, and to disentangle supply- and demand-side factors;
- Tracking of government policy responses towards SMEs in the context of the COVID-19 pandemic, analysis of its longer-term implications for SME access through the SME finance indicators of this publication.

Notes

[1] The distinction between high-income and middle-income countries is drawn by the World Bank, which assigns the world's economies into different income groups. This assignment is based on GNI per capita calculated using the Atlas method. More information on this classification can be found here: https://blogs.worldbank.org/opendata/new-country-classifications-income-level-2018-2019.

[2] The definition of short-term loans vary in some of the countries with available data for this variable. Some countries, like Denmark and Spain, include, as a proxy, loans with the rate fixation of 1 year or less. Others, like Austria and Spain, exclude overdrafts, credit lines and credit cards from the calculations.

[3] Small businesses are businesses with annual sales of less than USD 50 million.

[4] Senior loan officers are asked how the demand of small business loans changed over the last three months. Possible answers range from a "substantially stronger" demand to a "substantially weaker" demand. Subtracting the percentage of respondents who answered that demand was (substantially or moderately) weaker from the percentage who thought demand was (substantially or moderately) stronger, provides an indicator of overall demand for loans of small businesses.

[5] In order to provide an accurate picture of business trends, a representative and large-scale sample of the Japanese business population is asked to choose between different alternatives to best describe prevailing business conditions. One question pertains to the "lending attitude of financial institutions", where the respondents can choose between "accommodative," "not so severe" and "severe" as best describing their view of lending attitudes. A single indicator is derived on the basis of these answers.

[6] In the United Kingdom, the Bank of England surveys lenders about changes in trends. The survey covers secured and unsecured lending to households and small businesses; lending to non-financial corporations, as well as to non-bank financial firms.

[7] Data on factoring volumes are sourced from Factors Chain International (FCI), a sector organisation

[8] See https://read.oecd-ilibrary.org/view/?ref=119_119680-di6h3qgi4x&title=Covid-19_SME_Policy_Responses for an overview.

References

Abraham, F., J. Cortina and S. Schmukler (2019), *The Rise of Domestic Capital Markets for Corporate Financing*, World Bank Group, http://www.worldbank.org/prwp. [37]

Abraham, F. and S. Schmukler (2017), *Addressing the SME Finance Problem*, World Bank. [2]

Alternative Credit Council (2018), *Financing the Economy 2018: The role of private credit managers in supporting economic growth*, https://www.aima.org/educate/aima-research/fte-2018.html. [17]

Bank of Japan (2019), *Tankan Survey - June 2019*. [9]

Bank of Japan (2018), *Tankan Survey - June 2018*, http://www.boj.or.jp/en/statistics/tk/gaiyo/2016/tka1806.pdf (accessed on 25 July 2018). [43]

Borio, C. and L. Gambacorta (2017), "Monetary policy and bank lending in a low interest rate environment: Diminishing effectiveness?", *Journal of Macroeconomics*, Vol. 54, pp. 217-231, http://dx.doi.org/10.1016/J.JMACRO.2017.02.005. [3]

BPIFrance et al. (2016), *Building momentum in Venture Capital across Europe*, https://www.kfw.de/PDF/Download-Center/Konzernthemen/Research/PDF-Dokumente-Studien-und-Materialien/Building-Momentum-in-Venture-Capital-across-Europe.pdf. [13]

British Business Bank (2019), *Small Business Equity Tracker 2019*. [34]

British Business Bank (2017), *The benefits of diverse smaller business finance markets*, British Business Bank, Sheffield, https://www.british-business-bank.co.uk/wp-content/uploads/2017/10/291-Diversity-Report-2017-Final.pdf (accessed on 20 August 2019). [30]

Business Insider (2019), *Zendai has shuttered two P2P platforms worth $1.4 billion amidst Beijing's regulatory crackdown*, https://www.businessinsider.fr/us/zendai-latest-victim-of-china-p2p-crackdown-2019-8. [23]

Caplain, J. (2018), *Taking on the world. The rise of the challenger banks*, KPMG, https://assets.kpmg/content/dam/kpmg/xx/pdf/2018/02/kpmg-rise-of-challenger-banks.pdf (accessed on 20 August 2019). [31]

CBInsights (2018), *The Challenger Bank Playbook: How Six Challenger Bank Startups Are Taking On Retail Banking*, https://www.cbinsights.com/research/challenger-bank-strategy/ (accessed on 20 August 2019). [27]

Center for Venture Research (2019), *THE ANGEL MARKET IN 2018 MORE ANGELS INVESTING IN MORE DEALS AT LOWER VALUATIONS*, http://paulcollege.unh.edu/center-venture-research. [19]

Competition & Markets Authority (2016), *Retail banking market investigation Final report*, http://www.nationalarchives.gov.uk/doc/open-government- (accessed on 21 August 2019). [29]

Degryse, H., A. Karapetyan and S. Karmakar (2019), "To Ask or not to Ask: Collateral Vs. Screening in Lending Relationships", *Bank of England Working Paper* No. 778, 2019, http://dx.doi.org/10.2139/ssrn.3327304. [4]

Dunkelberg, W. and H. Wade (2018), *Small Business Economic Trends - June 2018*, NFIB Research Center, https://www.nfib.com/assets/SBET-June-2018.pdf (accessed on 25 July 2018). [7]

ECB (2019), *Survey on the Access to Finance of Enterprises in the euro area − April to September 2019*, https://www.ecb.europa.eu/stats/ecb_surveys/safe/html/ecb.safe201911~57720ae65f.en.html#toc1. [5]

European Central Bank (2019), *Survey on the access to finance of enterprises (SAFE)*, 2018/19, https://www.ecb.europa.eu/stats/ecb_surveys/safe/html/index.en.html (accessed on 22 July 2019). [6]

European Commission (2019), *EUROPEAN CENTRAL BANK Fourth Progress Report on the reduction of non-performing loans and further risk reduction in the Banking Union*, http://europa.eu/rapid/press-release_IP-16-. [33]

European Commission (2019), *Press Release: Capital Markets Union: Commission welcomes agreement on new rules to further improve access to capital markets for smaller businesses*, European Commission, https://europa.eu/rapid/press-release_IP-19-1568_en.htm. [41]

European Parliament (2019), *DEEPER AND FAIRER INTERNAL MARKET WITH A STRENGTHENED INDUSTRIAL BASE / FINANCIAL SERVICES*, European Parliament, http://www.europarl.europa.eu/legislative-train/theme-deeper-and-fairer-internal-market-with-a-strengthened-industrial-base-financial-services/file-sme-growth-markets-amendments-to-mar-and-prospectus. [38]

Florida, R. and I. Hathaway (2018), *The New Map of Entrepreneurship and Venture Capital*, Center for American Entrepreneurship, http://www.startupsusa.org/. [12]

Global Financial Innovation Network (2019), *GFIN One year on Report 2019*, Global Financial Innovation Network, http://dfsa.ae/Documents/Fintech/GFIN-One-year-on-FINAL-20190612.pdf (accessed on 26 August 2019). [45]

Global Financial Innovation Network and Financial Conduct Authority (2019), *GFIN cross-border testing pilot – next steps*, https://www.fca.org.uk/firms/gfin-cross-border-testing-pilot-next-steps (accessed on 26 August 2019). [40]

Granier, C., V. Revest and A. Sapio (2019), "SMEs and Junior Stock Markets: A Comparison between European and Japanese Markets", *Journal of Innovation Economics*, http://dx.doi.org/10.3917/jie.029.0043. [21]

Howell, S. (2017), "Financing innovation: Evidence from R&D grants", *American Economic Review*, http://dx.doi.org/10.1257/aer.20150808. [35]

Huang, L. et al. (2017), *The first in-depth report on the demographics and investing activity of individual American angel investors*, The American Angel, http://www.theamericanangel.org. [20]

IMF (2019), *IMF Data Mapper*, https://www.imf.org/external/datamapper/datasets. [26]

Masiak, C. et al. (2019), "How do micro firms differ in their financing patterns from larger SMEs?", *Venture Capital*, http://dx.doi.org/10.1080/13691066.2019.1569333. [42]

McKinsey (2019), *Private markets come of age: McKinsey Global Private Markets Review 2019*, https://www.mckinsey.com/~/media/McKinsey/Industries/Private%20Equity%20and%20Principal%20Investors/Our%20Insights/Private%20markets%20come%20of%20age/Private-markets-come-of-age-McKinsey-Global-Private-Markets-Review-2019-vF.ashx (accessed on 29 August 2019). [16]

Min-kyung, J. (2019), *Korean commercial bank apps struggle to stave off competition*, The Korean Herald, http://www.koreaherald.com/view.php?ud=20190618000501 (accessed on 21 August 2019). [32]

Moritz, A., J. Block and A. Heinz (2017), *Financing Patterns of European SMEs: An Updated Empirical Taxonomy and Determinants of SME Financing Clusters*, http://www.eif.org/news_centre/publications/eif_wp_40.pdf. [11]

OECD (2019), *OECD Economic Outlook, Volume 2019 Issue 2*, OECD Publishing, Paris, https://doi.org/10.1787/9b89401b-en. [1]

OECD (2019), *OECD SME and Entrepreneurship Outlook 2019*, OECD Publishing, Paris, https://doi.org/10.1787/34907e9c-en. [44]

OECD (2016), "The role of business angel investments in SME finance", in *Financing SMEs and Entrepreneurs 2016: An OECD Scoreboard*, OECD Publishing, Paris, http://dx.doi.org/10.1787/fin_sme_ent-2016-6-en. [18]

Paroma, S. and C. Mann (2010), *The Financial Structure of Startup Firms: The Role of Assets, Information, and Entrepreneur Characteristics.* [10]

Reuters (2019), *China gives P2P lenders two years to exit industry: document*, https://www.reuters.com/article/us-china-p2p/china-gives-p2p-lenders-two-years-to-exit-industry-document-idUSKBN1Y2039. [25]

Rogers, S. (2016), *Assessing the potential for EU investment in venture capital and other risk capital fund of funds*, European Commission, Brussels, http://dx.doi.org/10.2777/997836. [14]

South China Morning Post (2019), *China's P2P lending market could be decimated this year amid Beijing crackdown*, https://www.scmp.com/economy/china-economy/article/3006170/chinas-p2p-lending-market-could-be-decimated-year-amid. [24]

The Economist (2019), *Neobanks are changing Britain's banking landscape - Neobanks*, The Economist, https://www.economist.com/special-report/2019/05/02/neobanks-are-changing-britains-banking-landscape (accessed on 20 August 2019). [28]

UK Finance (2018), *SME finance in the UK: past, present and future*, UK Finance. [15]

UK HM Treasury (2018), *Bank Referral Scheme: Official Statistics*, https://assets.publishing.service.gov.uk/government/uploads/system/uploads/attachment_data/file/737136/Bank_Referral_Scheme_Official_Statistics_Publication_-_August_2018.pdf (accessed on 30 August 2019). [39]

United States Federal Reserve Board (2018), *Senior Loan Officer Opinion Survey on Bank Lending Practices - October 2018*, https://www.federalreserve.gov/data/sloos/sloos-201810.htm#aboutMenu (accessed on 25 July 2018). [8]

WFE (2018), *An overview of WFE SME markets*, https://www.world-exchanges.org/news/articles/world-federation-exchanges-publishes-report-global-sme-markets. [36]

World Federation of Exchanges & Milken Institute (2017), *Small and Medium-sized Enterprises and SME exchanges*, https://www.world-exchanges.org/home/index.php/news/world-exchange-news/world-federation-of-exchanges-publishes-joint-report-with-milken-institute-on-sme-exchanges. [22]

2 Policy developments in SME finance a decade after the global financial and economic crisis

This chapter provides an overview of the evolution of SME financing policies across Scoreboard countries over the last decade, focusing on the immediate post-crisis period (2008-11), the early recovery years (from 2012) and the most recent emerging policy trends. It also documents developments in the regulatory environment for SME financing. It draws heavily from information received for the Scoreboard exercise since its inception as well as other work on SME access to finance conducted for the OECD Working Party on SMEs and Entrepreneurship.

Overview

In the aftermath of the 2008 global financial and economic crisis, countries around the world took decisive action to counter the impact of the recession on a broad segment of the SME population. These measures were accompanied by financial reforms to strengthen banks' resilience, such as the Basel III framework, which introduced new minimal capital requirements and designed new rules for liquidity management. The crisis had a strong immediate impact: bankruptcies in Scoreboard countries grew strongly year-on-year from 2007, peaking at a 22.14% median growth in 2009. Only in 2012 did the median growth in bankruptcies start decreasing again.

Small businesses were hit particularly hard by the recession, with the share of SMEs in total business lending flows falling to 19.7% in 2009, against 25.6% in 2007 (in median terms). In Portugal, for instance, new lending in 2012, adjusted for inflation, stood at just 42% of 2007 volumes. In the United States, the Small Business Lending Index (SBLI), which measures the volume of new loans normalised to the base year of 2005, fell from 118.7 in 2007 to 73.7 in 2009. That same year, non-performing loans reached their highest mark for both SMEs and total business loans in the United States.

Venture capital investments also fell significantly in the aftermath of the crisis, reaching their lowest levels in 2011 at 0.025% of GDP (median value), against 0.043% of GDP in 2007 among participating countries (OECD, 2019[1]).

Recovery has come at a slow pace in many advanced economies. Pre-crisis levels of output have not yet been reached in a majority of high-income countries and investment levels are, on average, only at 75% of pre-crisis levels (Chen, Mrkaic and Nabar, 2019[2]).

These developments prompted national governments to take muscular action on many policy fronts, particularly regarding SME access to finance, which remains a policy priority to foster economic growth and well-being.

Policy responses to the crisis were significant. In the 2009-12 period, many governments set up or expanded direct lending and guarantee schemes, as well as credit mediation and other measures to ease SME access to credit, as a response to the drastic reduction in lending activities in the private financial sector.

While these measures largely remained in place in later years, the emphasis of policies as a whole shifted as the recovery took hold. Generally, equity instruments gained more attention as the crisis subsided, and credit measures (credit guarantees, direct loans) were increasingly targeted to specific subgroups of the SME population (innovative firms, women entrepreneurs, start-ups, etc.). This marked a shifting focus, from cyclical issues to more longstanding structural issues in SME access to finance.

Policy developments are increasingly shaped by megatrends such as globalisation, digitalisation and ageing. Digitalisation in particular offers new opportunities, but also challenges, both for policy makers and for SMEs seeking finance. Fintech, defined as technology-enabled innovation in financial services, is becoming more and more important in easing SMEs' access to finance. It is also ensuring financial inclusion for some segments of the SME population that are traditionally unserved or underserved by financial institutions and markets (OECD, 2019[3]).

Using technologies such as digital ID verification, distributed ledger technologies (DLT), big data and marketplace lending, new suppliers are offering an array of innovative services with the potential to revolutionise SME finance markets. Mobile banking, (international) mobile payments and the use of alternative data for credit risk assessment can significantly reduce information asymmetries and transaction costs, tackling structural barriers SMEs face when accessing finance. Fintech will likely become a more central feature in the range of SME financing options in the coming years.

Generally, incumbents in the financial sector are adopting techniques and instruments introduced by Fintech, blended models are emerging, and "Big tech firms" (such as Amazon or Alibaba) are entering the financial services realm (OECD, 2019[3]).

The Scoreboard has been mapping developments in SME finance since the pre-crisis benchmark year of 2007. The time series and yearly register of policy trends provide a reference for the analysis of governmental policy responses and their effects. More than ten years after the financial crisis, it is an opportune moment to take stock of the evolution in SME financing policies. Table 2.1 summarises general trends in SME finance policy that are analysed in this chapter and describes development in terms of the types of policies introduced to support debt and equity, target beneficiaries, and relevant regulatory measures and approaches.

Table 2.1. Overview of the evolution in SME finance policies

Characteristic	Aftermath of the crisis	Recent years
Target beneficiaries	Broad SME population	Subgroups of the SME population: innovative firms, start-ups, lagging regions, women
Support for debt financing	Strong increase in credit guarantee volumes Direct lending Credit mediation	More focus on the delivery and eligibility criteria of support measures Creation of SME banks
Support for equity financing	Equity instruments were kept largely in place	Tax incentives Establishment of funds/funds of funds SME bank activities
Regulatory measures	Emphasis on financial stability Supply-side regulation (bank capital requirements)	Regulation of Fintech industry Emergence of regulatory sandboxes

The chapter focuses on the major changes in the SME finance environment since the financial crisis, along with the principal policy responses. It first analyses the most important counter-cyclical instruments used in the immediate aftermath of the crisis, such as credit guarantees and direct lending. It then moves to the policy approaches that gained traction in the early recovery years and remained in the policy mix in most jurisdictions in later years. Initiatives related to equity and asset-based finance, digitalisation of financial services, tackling payment delays, and strengthening the financial acumen of entrepreneurs and business managers are analysed, drawing from policy cases from OECD Scoreboard countries and from the exercise undertaken to develop G20/OECD Effective Approaches for Implementing the High-Level Principles on SME Financing (Koreen, Laboul and Smaini, 2018[4]).

This overview of policy developments is timely, at a moment when SMEs around the world are once again facing mounting difficulties to access funding in the context of the coronavirus pandemic of 2020. Despite important differences between the 2008 financial crisis and the crisis brought on by the global pandemic, the policy experiences from the 2007-12 period may hold lessons for policy makers who want to cushion the impact on SMEs.

Policy action in the aftermath of the crisis (2008-2012)

The global financial crisis was one of the most severe crises to hit the global economy since the Great Depression. The underlying banking crisis resulted in a sovereign debt crisis and a recession across many countries, which prompted governments to take strong action.

As a result of the financial meltdown of 2008, 91 economies worth two-thirds of the global GDP in purchasing-power-parity faced a decline in output the following year (Chen, Mrkaic and Nabar, 2019[2]). GDP contracted 0.1% globally and 3.3% in advanced economies in 2009 (IMF, 2019[5]). The median loss in output in 2014 was estimated at 3.5% across all OECD countries (Ollivaud et al., 2015[6]). Moreover, the crisis gave rise to a "credit crunch", whereby credit became scarce and credit standards tightened significantly, making access to bank finance for SMEs more difficult (OECD, 2012[7]).

In 2008-09, loan rejection rates increased significantly in most countries, while application rates often decreased. The share of SME loans among all business loans dipped well below the SME contribution to national income and employment (OECD, 2012[7]). Meanwhile, insolvencies increased and SMEs' ability to self-finance shrank significantly.

Support to stimulate debt financing increased significantly in the immediate aftermath of the financial crisis.

As early as 2008, policy makers turned to different tools in order to counter the effects of the recession (WPSMEE, 2010[8]). This included primarily the creation and expansion of existing credit guarantee schemes (CGSs) and direct lending programmes. These policy instruments grew in importance immediately post-crisis, both in terms of the number of schemes in operation and in terms of guaranteed volumes of schemes already in place. The coverage rates of guarantees also increased. Guaranteed volumes continued to grow at moderate rates after 2009, sometimes evolving into more targeted programmes after 2012.

In the immediate years after the crisis, many measures were not targeted to a specific sector or firm segment, but concerned the bulk of the SME population, or even the business population at large.

For example, the United Kingdom launched the Enterprise Finance Guarantee (EFG) in 2009, replacing the Small Firm Loan Guarantee Scheme (SFLG), in operation since 1981. The new scheme enlarged the number of eligible firms and increased the upper limit of loans four-fold (to GBP 1 million). The upper limit of the turnover for beneficiaries increased from GBP 5.6 million to GBP 25 million and later to GBP 41 million to address the needs of larger SMEs that were facing increasing difficulties in obtaining finance. The number of loans that were granted under the scheme doubled between the first and the second quarter of 2009, from 1 202 to 2 339 (BBB, 2019[9]).

In OECD countries, there was a three-fold increase in the share of guaranteed loans in the total loan stock between the start of the crisis and 2010. Guarantees typically had the specific aim to support counter-cyclical lending to viable SMEs that were facing difficulties accessing credit because of the post-crisis environment, but would be able to secure lending from banks under normal circumstances (Cusmano, 2013[10]). The increase thus sought to satisfy an increased demand for government guarantees.

In addition, several countries increased the coverage rates of their guarantees, with the Czech Republic reporting a 10 percentage point increase (from 58% to 68%) for instance, and BpiFrance raising its coverage rate to 90% (written exchanges with experts from the European Association of Guarantee Associations – AECM).

In a few cases, the coverage rate reached 100%. Korea, for example, implemented an "Intensive Rescue Plan" via its credit guarantee fund (KODIT) in 2009. The Plan increased the coverage ratio to 100% and substantially reduced the screening of borrowers (Cusmano, 2013[10]). Members of CESGAR in Spain also increased the coverage rate to 100% (written exchanges with experts from the European Association of Guarantee Associations – AECM).

Figure 2.1. Trends in guaranteed loans and direct government loans for SMEs after the crisis

Year-on-year growth rate, Scoreboard median (%)

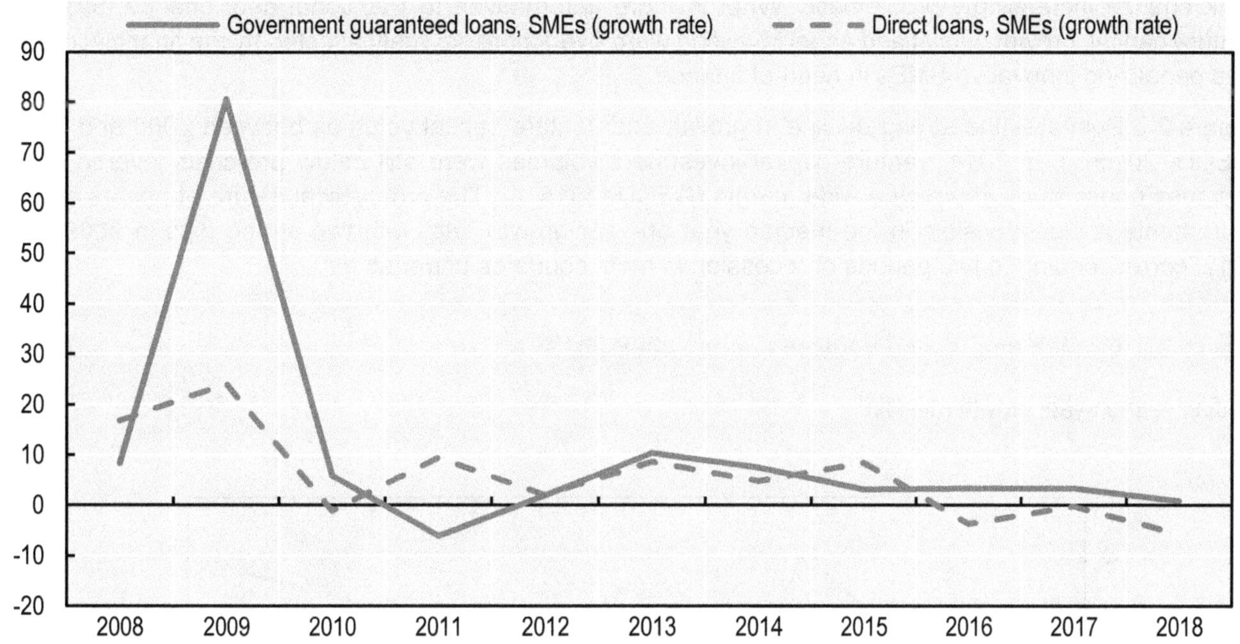

Source: OECD, Financing SMEs and Entrepreneurs: An OECD Scoreboard, 2012-2019.

StatLink https://stat.link/5298nd

Finnvera, Finland's state-owned financing company, was authorised to grant counter-cyclical loans and guarantees between 2008 and 2012. Finnvera loans were designed for working capital and catered to firms with less than 1 000 employees whose profitability or liquidity had declined because of the crisis. The SME applications grew by 12% in 2009 and SME loans and guarantees granted increased from EUR 801 million in 2007 to EUR 1 067 million in 2009, at its peak. The Finnish Government considers that the programme played an important role in safeguarding employment in SMEs during the years of the financial crisis. According to one estimation, job losses could have been twice as numerous in 2009 without the loans, which means over 20 000 positions were maintained with the help of the finance granted by public organisations (OECD, 2016[11]).

In European countries such as Belgium, France, Germany and Spain, various forms of credit mediation were introduced, with many SMEs eligible to benefit (Cusmano, 2013[10]). Credit mediation schemes were planned to be phased out within a few years but sometimes remained in place, evolving into a longer-term initiative to support SMEs in these countries (Wehinger, 2014[12]). In Germany, the programme was discontinued in 2011, as initially planned. Ireland created a Credit Review Office in 2010, and Spain and the United Kingdom implemented similar facilities in 2011 and 2012 respectively. The British facility is an independent credit review system that oversees the process of appeal to credit rejection in the largest UK banks.

Equity financing also suffered in the crisis aftermath, but was not the main focus of policy attention in the early post-crisis years

In the aftermath of the financial crisis, credit tightening in the financial sector made SMEs' dependence on bank finance increasingly problematic. What is more, alternatives to traditional debt finance, such as venture capital, growth capital and angel investing were even more severely affected by the financial crisis, thus penalising innovative SMEs in need of finance.

Figure 2.3 illustrates the strong decline in growth and venture capital volumes between 2008 and 2010 (OECD, 2015[13]). In 2014, venture capital investment volumes were still below pre-crisis level in most countries under study, often by a wide margin (OECD, 2015[13]). The pro-cyclical nature of private equity instruments is clearly visible in the median year-on-year growth rate, with two strong dips in 2009 and 2012, corresponding to two periods of recession in most countries under study.

Figure 2.2. Growth capital and venture capital, 2008-2018

Median year-on-year growth rate (%)

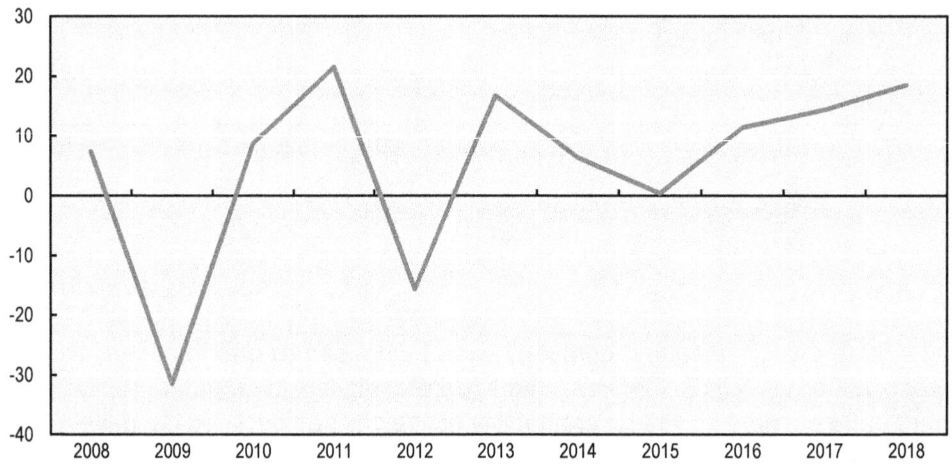

Note: Data is year-on-year change of current USD volumes, at the exception of Chile, Colombia, China, Indonesia, Malaysia, Mexico, Turkey and Ukraine for which the indicator captures variations of volumes in current local currencies.
Source: OECD Entrepreneurship at a Glance; based on the Entrepreneurship Finance Database, and data compiled from the individual country profiles of Financing SMEs and Entrepreneurs 2020 when the information was not otherwise provided.

StatLink https://doi.org/10.1787/888934115996

During this period, a number of governments maintained or created new equity support measures, although their focus continued to be on supporting SME access to debt. Sweden, for instance, created a public equity fund in 2009 (*Almi Invest*) and France launched the *Fonds d'investissement stratégique* in 2010. The Netherlands expanded its Growth Facility (GFAC), which offered banks, private equity enterprises and other financiers a 50% guarantee on newly issued equity or mezzanine loans. The total budget allocated to this scheme was raised from EUR 5 million to EUR 25 million during the crisis years. Canada, Chile, Denmark, Finland, Italy, New Zealand and the United Kingdom also provided assistance to equity financing throughout the crisis years (OECD, 2012[14]).

In Europe, national efforts were often supported at the regional level, with initiatives undertaken through the European Commission and European Investment Bank (EIB). These policy efforts sought to play a counter-cyclical role, but generally there was a decrease of capital available for investing in VC funds,[1] and there was a decrease in the valuation of VC-backed firms due to the recession, which in turn affected VC funds.

Box 2.1. Venture capital policy initiatives: Denmark and the United Kingdom

Denmark has high investment levels in venture capital when measured as a share of GDP, especially in early-stage investment. Venture and growth capital in Denmark have expanded significantly since 2016, with a 78% year-on-year growth rate over 2016-17, largely driven by growth capital, which stood at a record DKK 267 million in 2017 (OECD, 2019[15]). The Danish Growth Fund (DGF) is a state investment fund that has existed since 1992 and has funded 7 900 companies since its creation, with a total commitment of more than DKK 24.9 billion. Its instruments comprise direct investments, fund investments, fund-of-fund investments (through Danish Growth Capital, which is managed by DGC) and syndication loans (Rogers, 2016[16]). The rationale behind these instruments is the chronic underinvestment in innovative ventures in Denmark. There has been heavy public involvement in the development of the VC market, yet all investments are made on private terms with private investors (Rogers, 2016[16]) and DGC remains a highly independent structure. Overall, DGF has been showing strong performance and has experienced profitable exits.

A decrease in the importance of banks in the supply of financing for UK SMEs has been observed in recent years, in part due to the growth of private equity (UK Finance, 2018[17]). The UK Government has been involved in fostering this diversification, including through direct investments made through the British Business Bank. The need to encourage alternative instruments was recognised in the immediate aftermath of the crisis, in the 2012 Breedon Report and in the Young Reports (UK Finance, 2018[17]). The 2010 Taskforce review requested the creation of the Business Growth Fund (BGF), which serves an underserved segment of SMEs, namely SMEs requiring between GBP 2 million and GBP 10 million in equity funding. In addition to this, the United Kingdom implemented three tax incentive schemes for equity investors in SMEs between 1994 and 2012 (OECD, 2015[13]). While equity gaps remain, the equity market in the United Kingdom is now comprehensive and public resources have been strongly mobilised to foster alternative finance for SMEs.

Evolution of SME finance policies during the recovery period (2012 onwards)

SME financing has recovered at different paces in different countries, reflecting a number of factors in the domestic and global economy. Despite these cross-country differences, a visible shift in policies can be identified starting in 2012. As the crisis waned and recovery began to take hold, access to finance became a less pressing issue for many SMEs. In Europe, SMEs reporting access to finance as an extremely pressing problem steadily decreased from the first half of 2012 onwards (See Figure 2.4). In economies like Belarus, New Zealand, Ukraine, and the United States, the stock of outstanding business loans starting increasing again in 2012-13 following decreases or stagnations in the aftermath of the crisis. In Japan, the percentage of small businesses perceiving conditions as accommodative versus severe turned slightly positive in 2011 and the rise in the percentage of small firms with positive attitudes gained pace between the last quarter of 2012 and 2016 (Bank of Japan, 2019[18]).

Figure 2.3. Access to finance as a pressing problem for European SMEs

As a percentage of SMEs

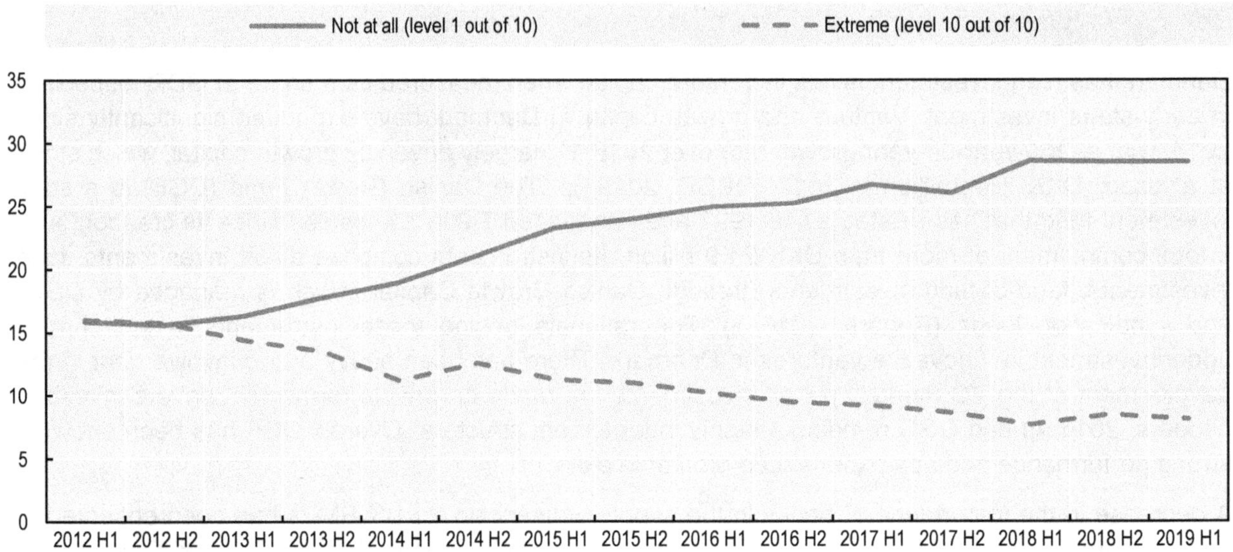

Source: (European Central Bank, 2019[19]).

StatLink https://doi.org/10.1787/888934116015

Nevertheless, SME financing remained a prominent policy priority in many countries in order to stimulate economic growth and well-being. In addition, international instances such as the G20 and the G7, as well as regional groupings such as Asia-Pacific Economic Cooperation (APEC), the European Union (EU) and the Association of Southeast Asian Nations (ASEAN), made SME finance a political priority in the years following the crisis.

In fact, the OECD developed this SME financing Scoreboard in part as a response to the crisis. Its first edition was published in 2012 following a pilot phase, in order to increase the evidence base and provide a tool to monitor the state of SME financing (see Box 2.2). In 2015, the OECD developed the G20/OECD High-Level Principles on SME Financing. The G20 Global Partnership on Financial Inclusion (GPFI) also developed the G20 Action Plan on SME Financing.[2] That same year, ASEAN included Access to Finance as a main goal in its Strategic Action Plan for SME development 2016-25, launched in November (ASEAN, 2015[20]).

Box 2.2. G20/OECD High-Level Principles on SME Financing

1. Identify SME financing needs and gaps and improve the evidence base
2. Strengthen SME access to traditional bank financing
3. Enable SMEs to access diverse non-traditional financing instruments and channels
4. Promote financial inclusion for SMEs and ease access to formal financial services, including for informal firms
5. Design regulation that supports a range of financing instruments for SMEs, while ensuring financial stability and investor protection
6. Improve transparency in SME finance markets
7. Enhance SME financial skills and strategic vision
8. Adopt principles of risk sharing for publicly supported SME finance instruments
9. Encourage timely payments in commercial transactions and public procurement
10. Design public programmes for SME finance which ensure additionality, cost effectiveness and user-friendliness
11. Monitor and evaluate public programmes to enhance SME finance

Source: (OECD, 2015[21]).

Despite marked improvements in SME access to finance since 2012, most policy instruments introduced during the crisis have largely been kept in place. Nonetheless, they have undergone transformation in their design, and in some instances, have been redirected to tackle structural problems concerning specific segments of the SME population.

Instruments to support SME lending were increasingly targeted to specific segments

Broadly, the trend towards segmentation can first be discerned in 2011, with the emergence of programmes that were more tailored to specific SME segments (OECD, 2013[22]). One objective of these changes was to ensure additionality, so that government support would reach firms that would not be able to access financing otherwise, and so as not to crowd out private sector initiatives.

Evidence indicates that some segments of the SME population face more difficulties to access appropriate sources of finance. These include fast-growing, innovative firms, micro-enterprises, start-ups, young SMEs, businesses located in remote and/or rural areas and women-owned enterprises (OECD, 2018[23]). With counter-cyclical policies becoming less relevant, the structural obstacles faced by these firms secured a place at the top of the policy agenda.

The rising number of countries that designed loan and guarantee programmes for start-ups is one example of this trend. Among Scoreboard participants, 2 countries out of 11 reported that this policy was in place in 2012, against 21 countries out of 46 in 2018.[3] Moreover, in 2017, around two-thirds of the countries surveyed for the implementation of the G20/OECD Principles were targeting either young entrepreneurs, SMEs located in remote areas or women entrepreneurs with specific policies (Koreen, Laboul and Smaini, 2018[4]).

Credit guarantee schemes were also increasingly tailored to disadvantaged segments of the SME population, such as innovative start-ups, women entrepreneurs, and SMEs in underserved regions. Several conditions need to be fulfilled in order to make CGSs accessible to disadvantaged or underserved entrepreneurs (OECD/European Commission, 2014[24]). These may include increasing the coverage ratio, making sure that the guarantee period is below five years, subsidising the price of the guarantee product, and offering non-financial support (OECD/European Commission, 2014[24]).

Turkey is a good example of this segmentation, with grants and loan guarantees applied with preferential rates to SMEs led by women entrepreneurs and combined with non-financial support. A recent partnership between the European Bank for Reconstruction and Business (EBRD) and the Turkish guarantee fund (KGF) unlocked EUR 300 million to support women's entrepreneurship (Rosca, 2018[25]). Korea represents another example, with certain policies aimed at innovative firms. KIBO (Korea Technology Finance Corporation), which offers guarantee products that are tailored for start-ups and innovative firms, was an early adopter of this strategy (OECD, 2013[22]).

It is important to note that the number of beneficiaries of loan guarantees continued to increase, if more slowly, after 2012. The role of guarantees thus shifted from a primarily counter-cyclical one to a tool to overcome market failures in a more stable economic context. Most programmes were maintained after the crisis (written exchanges with AECM). Segmentation and financial regulation also played a role in the continued demand for loan guarantees (see section 1.5).

Other efforts to target innovative SMEs in need of finance focus on providing support to enable them to collateralise their intangible assets. Indeed, these firms often possess little tangible collateral, and financial institutions are often reluctant to provide credit to them for this reason. Governments have recognised the importance of enabling fast-growing, intangible asset-rich firms to access appropriate sources of financing, and that market failures for these types of SMEs are at play.

A steadily increasing number of countries, particularly in Asia, have set up special schemes to address the challenges associated with collateralising intangible assets. Initiatives range from funds established by development banks, as well as the combination of subsidies and guarantees to encourage private sector engagement. Additional efforts to overcome the problems of valuation and high transaction costs are also being deployed (Brassell and Boschmans, 2018[26]).

In Japan, for example, recent efforts have focused on influencing lender behaviour by providing subsidised intellectual property (IP) evaluation reports to regional banks and credit unions. China is the most active market for state-backed IP financing, having first experimented with bank lending against intangible assets in 2006. It has a wide range of policy measures in support of IP. In Korea, the government has provided a range of support to knowledge-based SMEs in recent years. The Korea Development Bank (KDB) operates a "Techno Banking" initiative providing loans for purchasing, commercialising and collateralising IP. KODIT, the Korea Credit Guarantee Fund, offers underwriting of up to 95% of an IP valuation for lending or securitisation, while the valuation activity is subsidised by the Korean Intellectual Property Office (KIPO), and the valuation work itself is done by others such as the Korea Invention Promotion Association (KIPA) (Brassell and Boschmans, 2018[26]).

With the specialisation of programmes, governments gained increased awareness of the need to produce disaggregated data in order to strengthen the evidence base. Indeed, disaggregated data collection remains a challenge to support evidence-based policies in support of these targeted approaches (Alliance for Financial Inclusion, 2017[27]). Box 2.3 provides an overview of some of the issues and policy initiatives to leverage data for better policy targeting.

Box 2.3. The role of data for policy targeting

An increasing number of countries are reporting improvements and new initiatives in granular data to grasp the heterogeneity of SMEs. Nonetheless, much remains to be done in this area. The United Kingdom's British Business Bank developed a typology to support better targeting for its initiatives. It clusters SMEs based on attitudes and needs according to data from a UK demand-side survey. The characteristics taken into account to cluster SMEs include the need for and the use of finance as well as SMEs' openness to external information about finance and how they obtain it. With these categories, rather than focusing on the nature of "average" SMEs, policy makers and practitioners target SMEs with similar characteristics, especially separating those groups with high ambition and growth mind-sets from the others (OECD, 2019[15]).

Gender-disaggregation of data on SMEs has also been recognised as essential for fostering women's entrepreneurship, and most countries are behind on the collection and analysis of such data. Gender-disaggregated data started being produced by the Chilean financial sector regulator (SBIF - *Superintendencia de Bancos e Instituciones Financieras de Chile*) in a gradually expanded process that started in 2001. Supply-side data feeds into the annual report "Gender and the Financial System" and the information, made available for over a decade, has supported the creation of programmes targeting women as a distinct segment by Chilean financial institutions.

BancoEstado has put in place its *Crece Mujer Emprendedora* program, derived from the SBIF data set. The programme targets women entrepreneurs through access to capital, education and networking. The Chilean Financial Cooperative Sector started producing gender-disaggregated data for their operations and the Chilean Banking Association publishes research notes on women's banking trends aiming at highlighting growth opportunities such as increasing women's participation in credit markets and higher repayment rates (Data2X et al., 2016[28]). The OECD is also working to enhance the collection of more disaggregated SME finance data along a number of dimensions; ongoing work is outlined in Chapter 1 of the report.

Equity financing became a key focus of SME financing support policies

Government support for private equity markets continued following the immediate post-crisis years and often played a pivotal role in the development of these markets. In Europe, public funding bodies were found to support first-time investment funds more often than private investors, and their participation in venture capital (VC) funds generates positive signalling effect on private investors (Kraemer-Eis, Signore and Prencipe, 2016[29]).

The importance of first movers in the development of active VC environments is recognised and the experience of various countries shows that public support can play an important role as an initiator for a viable VC industry (Kraemer-Eis, Signore and Prencipe, 2016[29]).

In addition, VC markets in 2018 had often not recovered to pre-crisis levels. There are economic benefits of public support for equity instruments, hand in hand with market-led developments, as well as the potential for public investments in these markets to generate financial returns.For these reasons, instruments to stimulate equity markets for SMEs have increasingly attracted policy attention. Initiatives to stimulate private equity gained momentum following the growing recognition that overreliance on debt calls for a diversification of financing instruments (OECD: SME Ministerial Conference, 2018[30]).

In 2019, 40 out of 46 countries reported having policies in support of private equity financing for SMEs in place and 27 had specific programmes related to business angel investment. Policies have mainly consisted of supply-side measures (direct public investments, co-investment between the private and public sector, tax incentives and government support to networks and associations) (OECD, 2015[13]).

The creation of funds-of-funds also became more common. Funds-of-funds are pooled funds that invest in smaller VC funds instead of investing directly into firms. This helps bridging the gap between larger investors (including institutional investors) and firms in need of private equity. Funds-of-funds also offer an opportunity to diversify and mitigate risk for investors. While it is difficult to evaluate the success of these measures in general, it is clear that public actors play an important role in private equity markets in many economies, alongside private players.

Attention to venture and growth capital support policies grew as recovery began to take hold

As part of their initiatives to stimulate innovative start-ups and high-potential SMEs, many governments included equity finance support measures related to this group of SMEs from 2012, and many public investment vehicles and co-funding schemes were created.

In 2013, Canada announced the Venture Capital Action Plan, in which it pledged to invest CAD 400 million over the following 7 to 10 years to reinvigorate the VC sector. That same year, the governments of Estonia, Latvia and Lithuania, together with the European Investment Fund (EIF), set up the Baltic Innovation Fund. Greece launched the New Economic Development Fund (Taneo), which takes minority participations in venture capital funds. The Italian Fund for Sustainable Growth launched its first call for proposals that year, with 60% of its total volume of EUR 300 million directed to investments in SMEs. In 2014, Finland introduced a growth financing programme to co-fund investment in growth start-ups with private investors, and the Swedish Government also strengthened the budget for its venture capital programmes (OECD, 2015[31]).

In Chile, the Early-Stage Fund (*Fondo Etapas Tempranas*) is in place since 2013. This fund-of-funds supports new investment funds that provide high-growth SMEs with equity financing. In 2013, the Netherlands, in cooperation with the EIF, introduced a fund of funds for later stage venture capital investments as a new policy measure in support of SME equity finance. It included a demand-side element: together with banks, the government also promoted the diffusion of information to SMEs with regard to these types of instruments (OECD, 2017[32]).

In the United Kingdom, various policy initiatives as well as direct government investments made through the British Business Bank (BBB) since the crisis have had a clear effect on the diversification of supply (UK Finance, 2018[17]). Denmark has shown a similar trend with the Danish Growth Fund (DGF) (see Box 2.1). The European Investment Fund (EIF) noted that 2010 can be singled out at the starting year for the expansion of profitable EIF-backed investments (Prencipe, 2017[33]). Even though the causes of this trend are multiple, the counter-cyclical role of such institutions is clear. Some empirical studies have shown show that EIF-supported VC investments have a positive effect on start-up growth, leading to higher capitalisation, higher revenues and higher job creation, and higher investment and borrowing levels in the first five years after the VC investment (Pavlova and Signore, 2019[34]).

Policy support for business angel investments also expanded

Business angels (BAs) are financially independent, high net worth individuals who invest their private money in start-ups or seed companies, in return for ownership (OECD, 2015[13]). BAs, who are often entrepreneurs or former entrepreneurs, are known to be more involved in the firms that they finance, and often add value by getting involved in management and strategy themselves. While BA activity has existed for centuries, the sector has been receiving strong recognition and is increasingly structured by associations and networks. This is particularly the case in Europe, where awareness of this instrument was traditionally less widespread than in the United States, for example.

The activity slowed down significantly as a result of the recession, although not as dramatically as VC activity (OECD, 2015[13]). Like venture capital, business angel activity is increasingly supported by policy makers, who recognise its complementarity with venture capital in early-stage finance for high-growth and innovative firms. Policy attention generally increased a few years after the financial crisis, as the BA market recovered only slowly, and there was mounting evidence of a shortage of early-stage investment capital.

Tax incentives to boost innovation and the creation of fast-growing SMEs are commonly targeted at business angel investors. In Turkey, business angel investors are able to deduct up to 75% of capital invested in SMEs from the annual tax base since 2013. In December of that same year, Sweden introduced a tax break for private business angel investors, totalling SEK 800 million annually of tax relief (OECD, 2015[31]).

Progressively, more varied supply-side policies in favour of BAs have mainly taken the form of co-investment via dedicated funds (this is the case in the Netherlands and in the United Kingdom, for instance), alongside with tax exemption schemes like in Italy and Japan – see Box 3 (OECD, 2015[13]). In August 2014, the Austrian Government established its "aws Equity Finder", a contact platform which facilitates matchmaking between start-ups and SMEs and providers of risk capital, business angels, crowdfunding or other alternative financiers. Moreover, aws provides subsidies up to 50% (capped at EUR 50 000) to ease the external costs of publishing a capital market prospectus, one of the few demand-side policy support measures that explicitly targets SMEs by reducing the barrier to raise funds via capital markets above the regulatory threshold (OECD, 2016[11]).

Another important trend since the crisis is the strong formalisation of the BA sector, with the setting up of networks, associations and syndicates, sometimes with public support. Gaps in the evidence base remain to be filled, and survey tools as well as statistical instruments are expected to develop in the years to come.

Box 2.4. Fostering business angel activity through tax schemes: Italy and Japan

Tax incentives are part of the supply-side instruments that can be mobilised to encourage business angel activity. The objective of tax incentives is both to increase the number of active business angels and to encourage BAs to invest larger amounts. Italy put such a measure in place in 2008, in the form of a tax relief system. Capital gains on the sale of a start-up's undertakings are exempt from taxes, provided that certain conditions are met. Amongst other things, shares must be held for more than three years and the gains must be reinvested into another start-up within the next two years (OECD, 2014[35]).

Japan was a precursor in this field, with a similar business angel tax scheme being introduced as early as 1997 and being updated in later years to include an income exemption system. Under certain conditions, business angels can deduct a certain amount of money from their taxes, proportionate to the BA investments carried out in that year (OECD, 2015[13]). In addition, capital losses on BA investments can be carried forward for three years (European Commission, PwC and IHS, 2015[36]). The Japanese system is also one of the only tax incentive schemes to offer loss relief on such a favourable basis.

Governments have sought to consolidate their SME financing efforts and increase efficiency through dedicated national financial institutions

Public financial institutions (PFIs) are a common policy tool to address failures in the financial market and supply financial services to underserved groups. They have long existed in many OECD and non-OECD countries, often pre-dating the 2008-09 crisis, but they attracted increasing attention for the role they played in its aftermath. In many countries, PFIs increased the scale and scope of their activities.

PFIs may engage in first-tier lending, i.e. lending directly to end-consumers, in this case SMEs and entrepreneurs. This includes commercial public banks, often with an explicit mandate to provide funding to SMEs. PFIs can also act as second-tier lenders, providing funding to banks and other financial institutions, which then is lend on by these organisations to businesses. . Some PFIs combine first-tier and second-tier funding mechanisms, and may be active in other areas than debt products (direct loans, trade finance, guarantees), such as equity operations, hybrid instruments and grants .

PFIs also typically provide indirect support related to financial infrastructure (reverse factoring, market liquidity provision, insurance for exports, PPP arrangements, loan securitisation) and non-financial infrastructure, like consulting services.

In the early years of recovery, many governments restructured the PFIs providing these services. In the case of France, Portugal and the United Kingdom, centralised institutions were set up to coordinate and provide all these direct and indirect support facilities for small businesses.

France created a public development bank (Bpifrance) at the start of 2013 through the fusion of several public operators (OSEO, CDC Entreprises, Fonds stratégique d'investissement). Bpifrance offers businesses a local financing service supported by an extended portfolio of financial instruments and consultation options. It provides guarantees, co-financing, direct loans, and manages, on behalf of public authorities government support for innovation and services. It also guarantees venture capital funds. On the equity side, Bpifrance manages several investment funds, including funds-of-funds, mostly targeting SMEs needs (OECD, 2017[37]).

The British Business Bank became operationally independent in late 2014 with the aim to improve the structure of finance markets to the benefit of SMEs by increasing competition and diversity of supply (OECD, 2017[38]). Portugal's public development bank was created in October 2014 to complement the existing credit institutions. It focuses especially on SMEs and provide credit lines (through other banks), risk-sharing, guarantees, as well as capital to business angel and venture capital funds (Instituição Financeira de Desenvolvimento, 2019[39]).

In Russia, the Bank for Development was first established in 1999 and later became the Russian Bank for Small and Medium Enterprises Support as a subsidiary of Vnesheconombank, a state development corporation, in 2008. It provides low interest rate financing for innovation and modernisation as well as leasing for start-ups and microfinance.

Business development banks have also gathered through the Montreal Group, a global forum for development financial institutions created in 2012 and coordinated by the Business Development Bank of Canada. In 2019, the Group had eight member institutions from Brazil, Canada, China, Finland, France, Mexico, Morocco and Saudi Arabia (The Montreal Group, 2019[40]). The Group acts as a network for the exchange of knowledge and best policy practices for SMEs.

Recent and emerging policy developments

The focus of SME finance policies has transformed in recent years. Among other areas, Fintech and digital tools for SME finance, non-financial support targeting the financial acumen of entrepreneurs and payment delays are three major themes on policy makers' agenda. More information on each topic is provided below.

There is an increasing policy focus on Fintech developments and digital tools for SME financing

Digitalisation increasingly creates both new opportunities and new challenges for SME financing. This includes new approaches to credit risk assessment and new digital tools for SME financing. Governments have responded to these developments primarily through regulatory measures, which are discussed in section 1.5 below.

Credit instruments are increasingly being affected by digital transformations. New opportunities for data collection have led to new developments in data analytics for financial services. One of the applications of these methods is credit scoring, i.e. the statistical analysis of creditworthiness, on which the decision to grant credit is often based.

While the methods for credit scoring form part of the oldest applications of analytics, they have recently been transformed, not so much by an upheaval of the statistical methods, but by the diversification of data sources (Óskarsdóttir et al., 2019[41]). Most notably, there is a strong interest on the part of financial institutions in broadening their evidence base for credit risk assessment by using so-called "alternative data sources", i.e. non-credit data (transactional data, behavioural data, social media data) (ICCR, 2018[42]). Use of this data has raised legal and regulatory issues in certain jurisdictions, in particular linked to data protection (see section 1.5).

As recognised by the Financial Stability Board (FSB), the returns from enhanced quality and accessibility of information to financial system participants and regulators could be substantial (FSB, 2017[43]). Better credit scoring mechanisms lead to a reduction of information asymmetries and should lower default rates for firms (OECD: SME Ministerial Conference, 2018[30]). Both of these issues affect SMEs disproportionately. Nonetheless, it is difficult to assess these new models based on big data in the absence of a full credit cycle, and fears of pro-cyclicality and volatility as a result of new analytics are relatively widespread (FSB, 2017[43]).

Meanwhile, several countries have been involved in setting up and expanding information infrastructures for credit risk assessment, such as credit registries and credit bureaus (OECD: SME Ministerial Conference, 2018[30]) (GPFI, 2017[44]). This includes the Credit Risk Database established in Japan in 2001, for example, and the euro-Secured Notes Initiative established in France in 2014 (OECD, 2017[32]).

The growth of Fintech instruments has resulted in a growth in the access to, and convenience of, financial services, whether for households or for SMEs (FSB, 2017[43]). This is particularly the case in emerging markets, where instruments such as mobile payment have greatly facilitated daily payment needs for firms (FSB, 2017[43]). In line with the discussion above, Fintech has also contributed to decrease transaction costs for lenders wishing to reach out to underserved segments of the SME population, such as firms in rural and remote areas, micro-enterprises and informal ventures (OECD: SME Ministerial Conference, 2018[30]), all of which are more common in emerging markets. This trend fits well within the G20/OECD High Level Principles, which comprises financial inclusion, including for informal firms (Koreen, Laboul and Smaini, 2018[4]).

The digitalisation of financial services has also facilitated cross-border investments, although this remains incomplete in the face of regulatory discrepancies. The Financial Stability Board (FSB) has questioned the "cross-jurisdictional compatibility of national legal frameworks" (FSB, 2017[43]). More fundamentally, digitalisation prompts the question of the relevant level for regulation (see Box 3 below), as cross-border transactions often exist in legal grey zones (FSB, 2017[43]). Finally, policy makers are realising that as access to finance increases, so does the importance of financial literacy (FSB, 2017[43]): non-financial support is increasingly included in instruments that target SMEs and entrepreneurs.

Policy support increasingly includes efforts to enhance the financial acumen of business owners and entrepreneurs

Evidence suggests that financial support is most effective when it is provided alongside non-financial support, which includes mentoring, counselling, consulting, or general financial education (OECD, 2017[32]). This is because SMEs sometimes face not only a financing gap but also a skills gap (OECD, 2019[3]). Tackling this skills gap has moved up policy makers' agendas. An increasing number of countries, close to 60 in 2015, have adopted a national strategy for financial education with a nationally co-ordinated approach. Many of the approaches prioritise specific groups and SMEs are among the main target audiences for these strategies globally (OECD/INFE, 2015[45]). Box 2.5 puts a spotlight on the Portuguese model.

Box 2.5. Promoting financial literacy in Portugal

Since 2016, Portugal has set up its "Core Competencies for Financial Training" that provides guidelines to all actors in financial education for business in the country. The initiative aims at harmonising programmes and promoting good practices. It was submitted to public consultation and was later fine-tuned during a series of pilot training actions.

The document is the result of a joint effort between the financial sector supervisors, the Agency for Competitiveness and Innovation (IAPMEI) and the Agency for Tourism (TP). It is part of the "Portuguese National Action Plan for Financial Education", a broader government scheme for financial literacy. It was set up in 2011 and revised in 2016 and involves a large group of stakeholders including ministries, financial sector and consumer associations, trade unions, business associations and universities.

The ambition of the Portuguese action plan is not only to boost financial knowledge among business owners and managers, but also to restore confidence and trust between the business community and the financial sector, which was damaged considerably by the financial crisis.

In 2017, the cooperation protocol members delivered a series of courses in order to form a pool of trainers in the country. Participants were part of business associations, universities and polytechnic institutes. Out of the 34 participants, 10 were certified as trainers in the pool, coordinated by IAPMEI and TP.

In 2018, the pool of trainers began its activities, delivering 24 sessions to entrepreneurs and managers. These training sessions were held in different parts of Portugal, mainly in the premises of local business associations, town councils and business, tourism and hotel schools. They were attended by a total 382 trainees.

In addition to regular courses, IAPMEI and TP will maintain an annual conference to raise awareness of the importance of financial education in the management of SMEs.

Source: Written correspondence with experts from CMVM.

Non-financial support has emerged as a finance policy tool

The G20/OECD High-Level Principles on SME Financing called for the enhancement of SMEs financial skills and strategic vision, as part of the eleven policy priorities approved by G20 Finance Ministers in 2015 (Koreen, Laboul and Smaini, 2018[4]). A study commissioned by Canada's Business Development Bank in 2013 showed that consulting services, notably focusing on financial literacy, significantly enhanced business performance, as measured by the growth in sales, employment, productivity and profits, as well as the firms' survival rates (Boschmans and Pissareva, 2017[46]).

In 2018, twenty-seven Scoreboard countries reported that they had a non-financial support tool in place as part of their policy range for SME finance (OECD, 2018[47]). They vary greatly in their design, but a few categories can be drawn from the myriad of policy examples:

- Advisory support as part of the institutional mission of public financial services providers (e.g. Austria, Brazil, Colombia, Georgia, Israel, Malaysia, Sweden);
- Multiple advisory facilities, mainly through partnerships with the private and non-profit sector (e.g. Australia and New Zealand);
- Finance-specific Public Advisory Facilities (e.g. Finland, the Netherlands);

- Specific programmes combining debt finance products and advisory services (e.g. Belgium – Flanders region and the Czech Republic);
- Web-based advisory services (e.g. Belgium – Walloon region and France);
- Coaching and mentoring provided together with loan guarantees by guarantee institutions (e.g. Austria, Belgium and Finland) (written exchanges with experts from the European Association of Guarantee Institutions – AECM).

Non-financial support is also provided as part of business accelerators and incubators

There has been a proliferation of public-private business support provided through accelerators and incubators. Business accelerators are often associated with venture capital funds in the United States and stem from mixed public and private investments in Europe. Incubators and accelerators typically provide both financial and non-financial support to start-ups and SMEs with high growth potential. Their target populations, business models, and service portfolios differ greatly (see Table 2.2).

Incubators tend to provide more comprehensive but less specialised training and mentoring, while accelerators often provide targeted support with management skills and strategy. One common denominator is the opportunity for business owners and entrepreneurs to benefit from a local network. Different initiatives have arisen at different levels, whether local or national. One of the early adopters of the public-private model is Finland, which launched the VIGO accelerator programme in 2009 (see Box 5). Generally, there has been a trend for incubators and accelerators to target more specific populations like women, youth, migrant, or senior entrepreneurs and business owners (European Commission / OECD, 2019[48]).

Table 2.2. Differences and similarities between business accelerators and business incubators

	Business incubators	Business accelerators
Objective	**Support business creation and development**	**Accelerate business growth**
Service portfolio	Training: Entrepreneurship skills Mentoring: Focus on business model and initial business plan Networking: Other entrepreneurs and actors in the broader entrepreneurial eco-system Access to finance: Grants or seed capital Other: Managerial support (e.g. accounting), access to specialised equipment	Seminars: Management skills Mentoring: Intense, with a focus on growth strategy Networking: Other entrepreneurs and actors in the broader entrepreneurial eco-system Access to finance: Debt or equity
Service provision	On-demand	Mandatory and provided in a structured programme
Length of support	Often up to 3 or 4 years, or more	Usually 3 or 6 months
Business model	Mostly non-profit, with operating costs being largely covered by the rental fees collected	Mostly for-profit, associated with private venture capitalist funds (in the US) or a mix of private and public investors (in Europe)

Source: (OECD / European Commission, 2019[49]), adapted from other sources.

Box 2.6. Accelerators and incubators in Finland: from VIGO to Start-up Refugees

The VIGO venture accelerator programme (Finland) – 2009-15

The VIGO venture accelerator programme reflects the conviction that capital alone (supply-side measures) is not enough to help Finnish start-ups reach the global market, but rather must be complemented with know-how (demand-side measures). The programme was shaped by different groups of entrepreneurs who formed teams of "accelerators". It was up to these teams to invest their own private money into the start-ups and to coach them. Accelerator companies could apply for up to EUR 1 million from Finnvera in equity, and up to EUR 1 million from Tekes in the form of a grant. Both financing companies are state-owned. The VIGO programme is currently discontinued, but as of 2014 it had hosted 100 start-ups and was still hosting 80 more. The programme has been recognised for combining public and private investment in an innovative way and for catalysing the Finnish VC and accelerator market. It also led to the emergence of high-growth ventures (Halme et al., 2018[50]). As one of the first large-scale projects of this type, VIGO can be seen as a pioneering model that was later replicated in other jurisdictions

Startup Refugees – 2015-ongoing

Two Finnish entrepreneurs set up an initiative in November 2015 to encourage refugees to launch their businesses. They had observed that refugees were often highly skilled, which offered many untapped opportunities, but also that in a context of growing unemployment in Finland, entrepreneurial initiatives would be all the more welcome in order to create jobs (European Commission / OECD, 2019[48]). Startup Refugees started by mapping skills and employer needs with the help of volunteers, in order to match employers with potential employees. The second phase saw the launch of an incubator programme operating in various refugee reception centres (European Commission / OECD, 2019[48]). The incubator connects aspiring entrepreneurs with mentors and potential investors, including business angels. The initiative is partly funded by the Finnish Ministry of the Interior and the Finnish Immigration Service, and was complemented with a specific programme targeting women (European Commission / OECD, 2019[48]). While the initiative remains modest in size, it is a good example of the growing importance of policies geared towards specific segments of SMEs and entrepreneurs

Governments are taking action to tackle payment delays

Evidence shows that late or non-payments (whether B2B or government-to-business) are detrimental to the growth and even survival of enterprises. This is especially the case for small businesses, which often lack cash-flow management capacities and have limited options to smooth their cash flows. Moreover, SMEs suffer from a negotiation power asymmetry in B2B transactions, which may push them to agree to poor payment terms, especially when the survival of their business depends on securing the contract. The Federation of Small Businesses estimates that reducing or ending late payments could reduce the total number of business failures by up to 50 000 per year in the United Kingdom (Federation of Small Businesses, 2016[51]).

The EU, for its part, has estimated that one in four bankruptcies in the EU is due to late payments. As of 2019, the EU estimated that 6 out of 10 firms in B2B transactions are still being paid later than was agreed in the contract, with SMEs reporting an even higher rate. This has prompted a number of policy responses in different jurisdictions, with initiatives multiplying around the world in recent years.

As early as 2011, the EU passed the Late Payment Directive. The directive, which was transposed in national law by several Member States between 2012 and 2014, states that payments must be settled in under 60 days for B2B transactions and 30 days (exceptionally, 60 days) for government-to-business payments. The directive also provides automatic entitlement for interest and financial compensation. It enables member states to make conditions stricter (e.g. reduce the maximum payment time).

An evaluation of the directive published in 2015 showed that most firms were aware of the legislation concerning payment, and were also aware of the rights conferred to them. Nonetheless, this awareness is lower among SMEs, and usage of the provisions remains low, with 60% of firms reporting that they never claimed interests or compensation following a payment delay. Evidence on the effect of the directive on payment delays remains mixed (DG GROW et al., 2015[52]), even though the legislation put the issue of payment delays in the spotlight. A resolution adopted by the European Parliament in January 2019 called for a better enforcement of the legislation and a diversification of tools to tackle late payment.

Chile introduced the Bill of Timely Payment in June 2018 to encourage the timely payment of invoices. The bill seeks to limit payment terms to 30 days and agreed-upon terms to 60 days. For public procurements, payments to suppliers must be made within 30 calendar days following receipt of an invoice or the respective tax instrument issued, and terms of up to 60 calendar days may be established for a respective auction or public procurement instrument.

In Australia, public entities are required to pay invoices for contracts worth up to AUD 1 million within 20 calendar days since July 2019, compared to the previous policy and industry norm of 30 days. Furthermore, to increase transparency and accountability in complying with the new policy, the government is requiring large businesses to pay small businesses on time by developing an annual reporting framework on payment performance.

New-Zealand puts digitalisation at the centre of its efforts to tackle payment delays. The New Zealand Business Number (NZBN) initiative (first introduced in 2013 for registered companies) makes a globally unique identifier available to all New Zealand businesses, including unincorporated entities. Having a single identifier will make it faster to interact with other businesses and government agencies, as these entities will not have to update their information multiple times and all their primary business data will be kept online.

The government will also encourage the wider adoption of e-Invoicing among businesses in New Zealand through the NZBN. All invoices will be instantly sent to customers through their financial management systems, and manual errors will be minimised. In March 2019, New Zealand joined the Pan-European Public Procurement Online (PEPPOL) framework, and e-Invoicing is expected to be available by the end of 2019. The government also plans to introduce measures to prohibit “unconscionable” payment conduct in B2B transactions and extend the existing consumer protections (under the Fair Trading Act) against unfair contract terms to protect business contracts under NZD 25 000.

The evolution of regulatory approaches

The regulatory environment for SME financing has also faced major changes since the financial crisis. This section highlights the key areas of regulatory focus in the immediate aftermath of the crisis, which centred on financial stability through supply-side regulation, and which have evolved towards providing a framework for financial innovation, often driven by technological developments.

Basel III financial reforms and SME finance in the aftermath of the crisis

The Basel III framework was a central element of the policy response to the global financial crisis. Regulators identified and addressed shortcomings in the pre-crisis framework with the aim to bring more resilience to the banking system and to contain systemic vulnerabilities. A risk based capital ratio, liquidity coverage ratio, leverage ratio and additional macro-prudential requirements for systemically important banks were gradually introduced after the crisis. In this changing scenario, the overdependence of SMEs to banking finance made reforms an important issue for SME finance policy makers in the post-crisis years (OECD, 2012[53]).

One policy response to mitigate possible negative effects of the more stringent regulation on SME lending was the introduction of the SME Supporting Factor Article by European legislators in 2014. The Capital Requirements Regulation (CRR) allowed a capital reduction factor for exposures to SMEs at a discount factor of 0.7619 with the aim to provide stimulus for bank-firms to lend to SMEs (see Box 2.7). Across jurisdictions, non-regulatory measures were also put in place as counter-cyclical measures for SME financing.

Box 2.7. Capital requirements and SME financing: the case of the "Supporting factor"

Rising capital requirements in the wake of the crisis sparked fears that banks would be less willing to lend to SMEs. This is why the transposition of Basel III standards into EU law in 2014 saw the introduction of the "Supporting Factor" (SF) – a reduction of capital requirements associated with SME loans by 23.81%. The aim of this measure is to compensate for the loss in credit availability for SMEs, and to provide an incentive for banks to lend to eligible SMEs.

The authors of a recent study find that the SF has been effective in supporting bank lending to SMEs, with increasing strength over time. Comparing a group of firms that were affected by the reform with a group of similar non-affected firms, the authors find that the SF had a significant effect on lending to SMEs. This analysis suggests that capital requirements impact banks' decision to lend to SMEs.

In addition, the study also indicates that capital requirements for SME lending do not properly reflect their risk, especially at the portfolio level. In particular, SME exposures are either very weakly correlated or even negatively correlated with exposures for large firms. This means that banks with a diversified portfolio including both SME and large business loans are more resilient to economic cycles.

Source: (Dietsch et al., 2019[54]).

Nine years after the initial Basel III package was agreed upon, results of an ongoing evaluation of the effects of reforms on SME financing find that no material and persistent negative effects on SME financing occurred in general, despite some differentiation across jurisdictions.[4] Nonetheless, risk-based capital requirements may have temporarily affected growth and tightened the conditions of SME lending in some jurisdictions when considering the most exposed banks (the least capitalised). In addition, financial institutions have appeared to be more conservative in their decisions to grant credit, redirecting activities towards less risky segments (FSB, 2019[55]). This is in line with the observation that, in some jurisdictions, there has been an increase in demand for credit guarantees in recent years because of banks' stricter capital and reporting requirements (written exchanges with AECM).

It is noteworthy that anecdotal evidence from this evaluation suggests that macroeconomic conditions and factors other than financial regulation are the most important drivers of SME financing trends. In the aftermath of the crisis, public policies put in place and the positive financial conditions such as the low interest rate environment were important confounding factors that might have mitigated some of the negative effects of financial reforms (FSB, 2019[55]).

Furthermore, in addition to international reforms adopted after the crisis, many countries took measures to tighten bank supervision and regulation, and to tackle the fast expansion of non-performing loans. In Spain, for example, this included the creation of FROB (Fund for the Orderly Restructuring of the Banking Sector), which managed the restructuring process of credit institutions in financial distress, the recapitalisation of banks, resulting in some cases in partial or total nationalisation and the creation of asset protection schemes.

The country also took measures to strengthen safeguards to minimise the probability and severity of future financial crises. Notable measures are new capital requirements, requirements to improve credit transaction management policies and to reduce non-performance, increased liquidity risk assessment systems. Additional information requirements were put in place on restructured and refinanced loans, NPLs, asset quality across different parts of loan portfolios, the concentration by sector of portfolios, etc.

Following the recapitalisation of certain banks, Italy also strengthened supervisory controls and introduced new rules concerning bank loans to SMEs. This included the obligation to put reserves aside (reserve requirements), proportional to credit granted to SMEs, and was a direct attempt to tackle non-performing loans.

Regulation of online alternative finance for SMEs

Alternative finance instruments such as factoring, leasing and online alternative finance have shown sustained growth in recent years, often supported by the development of Fintech. In parallel with these evolutions, recent digitalisation dynamics are presenting new opportunities and challenges for SME finance (OECD, 2019[3]). Fintech, defined by the Financial Stability Board (FSB) as "[t]echnology-enabled innovation in financial services that could result in new business models, applications, processes or products with an associated material effect on the provision of financial services" (FSB, 2017[43]), spans a wide range of financial services, including debt and equity instruments.

Developments include online challenger banks, Fintech credit marketplaces, the digital transformation of private equity instruments, the diversification of potential borrowers and the possibilities offered by new data analytics and distributed ledger technologies.

Online alternative finance activity has been increasingly included in SME finance policy initiatives. Fintech presents potential for enhancing SME access to finance, offering more convenient and accessible services, more effective credit risk assessments and lower transaction costs. These instruments can be a unique opportunity for projects that are too small, too risky, or have a social purpose (OECD: SME Ministerial Conference, 2018[30]), and their strong expansion in particular in the early 2010s has prompted regulators to intervene.

Even though the share of firms that turn to online alternative finance remains relatively low in most markets, they have reached critical mass in others, most notably China, the United Kingdom and the United States. Moreover, recent operational failures highlight the challenges for regulators seeking to ensure adequate consumer and investor protection (Claessens et al., 2018[56]). The underlying question is whether intermediation platforms should have to conform to existing financial services regulation, or whether tailored regulation should be promoted (see Box 2.8).

In the context of the exercise to identify Effective Approaches for implementing the G20/OECD High Level Principles, a large majority of countries reported supporting the development of Fintech solutions as a way of increasing SME access to finance (27 out of 38). Regulatory initiatives comprised 19 out of these 27 measures. In addition, platforms to inform and connect SMEs to Fintech companies, workshops and the creation of Fintech association were also mentioned (Koreen, Laboul and Smaini, 2018[4]).

Regulatory efforts focused on this new industry seek to ensure consumer and investor protection, while at the same time taking care not to stifle innovation. For credit Fintech firms, since 2015, a number of countries have created specific regulation and licencing schemes. Brazil, China and Mexico are among the latest adopters. Finland, France, New Zealand, Spain and the United Kingdom also have frameworks in place. In other jurisdictions such as Germany and the United States, Fintech firms work jointly with a commercial bank to provide the loans channelled by the platform. In Brazil, many firms also work under this partnership models, even after regulation was in place allowing them to issue loans from their own balance sheets.

Regulatory sandboxes are a frequently adopted policy response to uncertainty related to innovative financial service providers. As part of these instruments, firms can test services and business models under the financial regulator's oversight and in a controlled environment. The Global Financial Innovation Network (GFIN) is a network of regulators committed to supporting financial innovation and protecting the interests of consumers. It was formally launched in January 2019 and comprises an international group of 11 coordinating authorities, 20 members and 7 observers among national and subnational authorities as well as international organisations and fora (see Table 3) (Global Financial Innovation Network, 2019[57]).

Beyond aiming to offer a platform for sharing different experiences and approaches, GFIN provides a more efficient way for innovative firms to interact with regulators. A cross-border pilot for firms wishing to test innovative products, services or business models across multiple jurisdictions is in place and 8 firms among 44 applicants were selected. This first cohort will pilot their services in Australia, Bahrain, Bermuda, Canada (British Columbia, Ontario and Québec), Hong Kong (China), Hungary, Kazakhstan (Astana), Lithuania, Singapore, United Arab Emirates (Abu Dhabi, Dubai), United Kingdom, Guernsey and Jersey (Global Financial Innovation Network and Financial Conduct Authority, 2019[58]).

Table 2.3. Global Financial Innovation Network (GFIN) members

Financial authorities' sandboxes and international fora, as of June 2019

Jurisdiction	Organisation
Australia	Australian Securities & Investments Commission (ASIC)
Bahrain	Central Bank of Bahrain (CBB)
Bermuda	Bermuda Monetary Authority (BMA)
Brazil	Securities and Exchange Commission of Brazil (CVM)
Canada (Alberta)	Alberta Securities Commission (ASC)
Canada (British Columbia)	British Columbia Securities Commission (BCSC)
Canada (Ontario)	Ontario Securities Commission (OSC)
Canada (Québec)	Autorité des marchés financiers (AMF)
China	Qianhai Financial Authority
Curaçao and Sint Maarten	Centrale Bank van Curaçao and Sint Maarten
Hong Kong, China	Hong Kong Monetary Authority (HKMA)
Hong Kong, China	Hong Kong Securities and Futures Commission (HKSFC)
Hong Kong, China	Hong Kong Insurance Authority (IA)
Hungary	Magyar Nemzeti Bank (Central Bank of Hungary)
Israel	Israel Securities Authority (ISA)
Israel	Capital Market, Insurance, and Savings Authority (CMISA)
Kazakhstan	Astana Financial Services Authority (AFSA)
Kenya	Capital Markets Authority (CMA, Kenya)
Lithuania	Bank of Lithuania (BL)
Luxembourg	Commission de Surveillance du Secteur Financier (CSSF)
Mauritius	Financial Services Commission Mauritius (FSC)
Qatar	Qatar Development Bank
Singapore	Monetary Authority of Singapore (MAS)
South Africa	South African Reserve Bank (SARB)
Swaziland (Eswatini)	Central Bank of Eswatini
Taiwan	Financial Supervisory Commission Taiwan
United Arab Emirates	Dubai Financial Services Authority (DFSA)
United Arab Emirates	Abu Dhabi Global Market (ADGM)
United Kingdom	Financial Conduct Authority (FCA)
British Crown: Guernsey	Guernsey Financial Services Commission (GFSC)
British Crown: Isle of Man	Isle of Man Financial Services Authority (IOMFSA)
British Crown: Jersey	Jersey Financial Services Commission (JFSC)

Jurisdiction	Organisation
United States	Consumer Financial Protection Bureau (CFPB)
IO and fora	Financial Sector Deepening Africa (FSD Africa)
IO and fora	European Bank for Reconstruction and Development (EBRD)
IO and fora	Consultative Group to Assist the Poor (CGAP)
IO and fora	International Monetary Fund (IMF)
IO and fora	World Bank Group

Source: (Global Financial Innovation Network and Financial Conduct Authority, 2019[58])

Box 2.8. Regulatory frameworks for Fintech: sandboxing and other measures

Many government programmes aim to support and regulate Fintech at the implementation stage, when ideas are tested on the market (OECD, 2018[59]). Sandboxing offers a regulatory perimeter for innovative business ideas to be tested in a controlled environment. The rationale behind such an approach is to allow for more flexibility and experimentation for innovative (and typically small-scale) financial activities. Certain conditions are imposed on the businesses in order to ensure consumer protection, and consumer feedback (concerning both the business idea and its regulation) is an essential component of this kind of framework.

Apart from the establishment of a regulatory sandbox, flexible regulation may take the form of reduced licencing requirements, like in the Netherlands and the United Kingdom (OECD, 2018[59]). In return, businesses which benefit from these schemes are sometimes obliged to remain under a certain number of customers or certain sales figures, like in Australia (OECD, 2018[59]). Under certain conditions, a business idea that has failed may also be exempt from certain legal requirements. Often, conditions regarding consumer protection are relatively strict, including the designation of a dedicated point of contact or advisor within the business, with whom regulators can remain in dialogue throughout the process.

Source: (Global Financial Innovation Network and Financial Conduct Authority, 2019[58]).

Conclusions

The decade following the global financial crisis saw pronounced changes in the policy landscape for SME and entrepreneurship finance. Direct lending activities and credit guarantee schemes were often expanded and broadened in its immediate aftermath. The aim was to counter the cyclical impact of the crisis and mitigate potential unintended consequences of tighter bank regulation. As credit conditions eased, these policies were largely maintained and often targeted more explicitly to certain segments of the SME population. SME access to finance became recognised as a continuing policy priority in many countries, as illustrated by the G20/OECD High-Level Principles on SME Financing and the G20 Action Plan on SME Financing, welcomed by G20 Leaders in November 2015.

In more recent years, the focus in many jurisdictions shifted to addressing SME overdependence on traditional bank debt, in order to enhance SME access to the financial instruments most suited to their needs at different stages of their business cycle, and to increase SME resilience in the face of potential future downturns. Programmes to support private equity became the second most common SME finance policy approach among Scoreboard countries.

Immediate post-crisis financial regulation focused on reforming the banking sector in order to contain systemic risk. The widespread adoption of Fintech and online alternative finance instruments in the second half of the decade prompted regulators to change their focus. Tools also evolved from general macro-prudential measures to new regulatory measures such as sandboxing and relaxing licensing schemes.

While many governments have taken action in recent years to harness the potential of financial innovation, further initiatives can be expected, and the next decade may well witness a profound transformation in how many SMEs access finance. In addition, the experience from the financial crisis provide insights for government responses to current and future crises affecting SME access to finance. This includes the economic fallout caused by the outbreak and spread of the coronavirus (COVID-19) in the first half of 2020. This Scoreboard will continue to monitor financing trends and policy developments closely, building on its rich network of experts.

Notes

[1] Institutional investors, especially, displayed risk-averse behaviour.

[2] The G20 Investment and Infrastructure Working Group (IIWG) and the G20 Global Partnership for Financial Inclusion (GPFI) SME finance Sub-group coordinated efforts related to the promotion of SME financing and compiled a set of priority actions, endorsed by G20 leaders in 2015. The actions encompassed priority reforms in financial market infrastructures as well as a continued knowledge agenda that covered data gaps on SME finance data, innovation in SME finance policies and long-term finance instruments for SMEs (GPFI, 2015[67]).

[3] This data refers to the number of countries in the Scoreboard that declared policies under various categories throughout the Scoreboard editions. The list of countries is presented in the Trends Chapters in each edition. Categories varied slightly over time. The complete list includes: (i) Government loan guarantees; (ii) Special guarantees and loans for start-ups; (iii) Government export guarantees, trade credit; (iv) Government co-financing/Pension fund co-finance; (v) Direct lending to SMEs; (vi) Subsidised interest rates; (vii) Venture capital, equity funding, business angels; (viii) Business angel co-investment (added in 2019); (ix) SME Banks; (x) Business advice, consultancy; (xi) Tax exemptions, deferments; (xii) Credit mediation/Review/Code of Conduct; (xiii) Bank targets for SME lending, negative. Interest rates for Central Bank deposits; (xiv) CB funding to banks dependent on net lending rate.

[4] The report has been released for consultation from June-August 2019. In November 2019, a final version will be published.

References

Alliance for Financial Inclusion (2017), *Sex-disaggregated data toolkit: how to leverage sex-disaggregated financial inclusion data to accelerate women's financial inclusion*, http://info.worldbank.org/etools/docs/library/192862/introductorymaterials/Glossary. [27]

ASEAN (2015), *ASEAN Strategic Action Plan for SME Development 2016-2025*, ASEAN, http://www.asean.org (accessed on 4 September 2019). [20]

Banco de España (2017), "Report on the financial and banking crisis in Spain, 2008-2014". [68]

Bank of Japan (2019), *Tankan Survey - June 2019.* [18]

BBB (2019), *Enterprise Finance Guarantee: Quarterly Statistics for Q2 FY 2019-20.* [9]

Boschmans, K. and L. Pissareva (2017), "Fostering Markets for SME Finance: Matching Business and Investor Needs", *OECD SME and Entrepreneurship Papers*, No. 6, OECD Publishing, Paris, https://dx.doi.org/10.1787/0bd38639-en. [46]

Brassell, M. and K. Boschmans (2018), *OECD SME and Entrepreneurship Paper Fostering the use of intangibles to strengthen SME access to finance*, http://www.oecd-ilibrary.org/papers (accessed on 4 September 2019). [26]

Chen, W., M. Mrkaic and M. Nabar (2019), "The Global Economic Recovery 10 Years After the 2008 Financial Crisis", *IMF Working Paper*, No. 19/83, IMF, Washington, https://www.imf.org/en/Publications/WP/Issues/2019/04/26/The-Global-Economic-Recovery-10-Years-After-the-2008-Financial-Crisis-46711 (accessed on 19 July 2019). [2]

Claessens, S. et al. (2018), "Fintech credit markets around the world: size, drivers and policy issues", https://www.bis.org/publ/qtrpdf/r_qt1809e.htm (accessed on 25 July 2019). [56]

Cusmano, L. (2013), "SME and Entrepreneurship Financing: The Role of Credit Guarantee Schemes and Mutual Guarantee Societies in supporting finance for small and medium-sized enterprises", *OECD SME and Entrepreneurship Papers*, No. 1, OECD Publishing, Paris, https://dx.doi.org/10.1787/35b8fece-en. [10]

Data2X et al. (2016), *Catalyzing Inclusive Financial Systems: Chile's Commitment to Women's Data*, https://data2x.org/wp-content/uploads/2019/05/Chile-Case-study_English_Final.pdf. [28]

DG GROW et al. (2015), *Ex-post evaluation of the Late Payment Directive*, European Commission, http://dx.doi.org/10.2873/016503. [52]

Dietsch, M. et al. (2019), "Lower bank capital requirements as a policy tool to support credit to SMEs: evidence from a policy experiment", *EconomiX*, https://economix.fr/pdf/dt/2019/WP_EcoX_2019-12.pdf (accessed on 17 September 2019). [54]

European Banking Authority (2016), *EBA Report on SMES and SME supporting factor*, https://eba.europa.eu/documents/10180/1359456/EBA-Op-2016-04++Report+on+SMEs+and+SME+supporting+factor.pdf (accessed on 27 August 2019). [63]

European Central Bank (2019), *Survey on the access to finance of enterprises (SAFE)*, 2018/19, https://www.ecb.europa.eu/stats/ecb_surveys/safe/html/index.en.html (accessed on 22 July 2019). [19]

European Commission / OECD (2019), *Policy Brief on Incubators and Accelerators that Support Inclusive Entrepreneurship*, http://dx.doi.org/10.2767/092345. [48]

European Commission, PwC and IHS (2015), *Effectiveness of tax incentives for venture capital and business angels to foster the investment of SMEs and start-ups*, http://dx.doi.org/10.2778/51300. [36]

Federation of Small Businesses (2016), "Time to Act: the Economic Impact of Poor Payment Practices". [51]

FSB (2019), *Evaluation of the effects of financial regulatory reforms on small and medium-sized enterprise (SME) financing*, https://www.fsb.org/wp-content/uploads/P291119-1.pdf. [55]

FSB (2017), *Financial Stability Implications from FinTech: Supervisory and Regulatory Issues that Merit Authorities' Attention*, http://www.fsb.org/emailalert. [43]

Global Financial Innovation Network (2019), *GFIN One year on Report 2019*, Global Financial Innovation Network, http://dfsa.ae/Documents/Fintech/GFIN-One-year-on-FINAL-20190612.pdf (accessed on 26 August 2019). [57]

Global Financial Innovation Network and Financial Conduct Authority (2019), *GFIN cross-border testing pilot – next steps*, https://www.fca.org.uk/firms/gfin-cross-border-testing-pilot-next-steps (accessed on 26 August 2019). [66]

Global Financial Innovation Network and Financial Conduct Authority (2019), *Global Financial Innovation Network (GFIN)*, https://www.fca.org.uk/firms/global-financial-innovation-network (accessed on 26 August 2019). [58]

GPFI (2017), *G20 Action Plan on SME Financing: Credit Infrastructure Country Self-Assessment Consolidated Report*, World Bank Group, Washington, http://www.gpfi.org/sites/gpfi/files/documents/GPFI%20-%20G20%20AP%20SME%20Financing%20Self%20Assessment%20Consolidated%20Report.pdf (accessed on 19 July 2019). [44]

GPFI (2015), *G20 Action Plan on SME Financing*. [67]

Halme, K. et al. (2018), *Startups, accelerators and the role of Tekes - Evaluation Report TEKES – EVALUATION REPORT*, Tekes, https://www.businessfinland.fi/globalassets/julkaisut/startups_accelerators_and_role_of_tekes_1_2008.pdf. [50]

ICCR (2018), *Use of Alternative Data to Enhance Credit Reporting to Enable Access to Digital Financial Services by Individuals and SMEs operating in the Informal Economy*, https://www.gpfi.org/sites/gpfi/files/documents/Use_of_Alternative_Data_to_Enhance_Credit_Reporting_to_Enable_Access_to_Digital_Financial_Services_ICCR.pdf. [42]

IMF (2019), *World Economic Outlook (April 2019) - Real GDP growth*, https://www.imf.org/external/datamapper/NGDP_RPCH@WEO/OEMDC/ADVEC/WEOWORLD. [5]

IMF (n.d.), *World Economic Outlook (April 2019) - Real GDP growth*, 2019, https://www.imf.org/external/datamapper/NGDP_RPCH@WEO/OEMDC/ADVEC/WEOWORLD (accessed on 22 July 2019). [60]

Instituição Financeira de Desenvolvimento (2019), *Sobre a IFD - Instituição Financeira de Desenvolvimento*, http://www.ifd.pt/pt/ (accessed on 3 September 2019). [39]

Koreen, M., A. Laboul and N. Smaini (2018), "G20/OECD Effective Approaches for Implementing the G20/OECD High-Level Principles on SME Financing", *OECD SME and Entrepreneurship Papers*, No. 9, OECD Publishing, Paris, https://dx.doi.org/10.1787/329168b6-en. [4]

Kraemer-Eis, H., S. Signore and D. Prencipe (2016), "The European venture capital landscape: an EIF perspective Volume I: The impact of EIF on the VC ecosystem", *EIF Research & Market Analysis*, No. 2016/34, European Investment Fund (EIF), Luxembourg, http://www.eif.org/news_centre/research/index.htm (accessed on 27 August 2019). [29]

NEFI (2019), *NEFI - Network of European Financial Institutions for SMEs: NEFI*, http://www.nefi.eu/nefi/ (accessed on 3 September 2019). [61]

OECD (2019), *Entrepreneurship at a Glance*, https://stats.oecd.org/Index.aspx?DataSetCode=VC_INVEST. [1]

OECD (2019), *Financing SMEs and Entrepreneurs 2019: An OECD Scoreboard*, OECD Publishing, Paris, https://doi.org/10.1787/23065265. [15]

OECD (2019), *OECD SME and Entrepreneurship Outlook 2019*, OECD Publishing, Paris, https://doi.org/10.1787/34907e9c-en. [3]

OECD (2018), *Enhancing SME access to diversified financial instruments*, https://www.oecd.org/cfe/smes/ministerial/documents/2018-SME-Ministerial-Conference-Plenary-Session-2.pdf. [23]

OECD (2018), *Financial Markets, Insurance and Private Pensions: Digitalisation and Finance*, OECD. [59]

OECD (2018), *Financing SMEs and Entrepreneurs 2018: An OECD Scoreboard*, OECD Publishing, Paris, https://dx.doi.org/10.1787/fin_sme_ent-2018-en. [47]

OECD (2017), ""France", in Financing SMEs and Entrepreneurs 2017: An OECD Scoreboard", in OECD Publishing (ed.), , http://dx.doi.org/10.1787/fin_sme_ent-2017-23-en. [37]

OECD (2017), *Financing SMEs and Entrepreneurs 2017: An OECD Scoreboard*, OECD Publishing, Paris, https://dx.doi.org/10.1787/fin_sme_ent-2017-en. [32]

OECD (2017), "United Kingdom", in *Financing SMEs and Entrepreneurs 2017: An OECD Scoreboard*, OECD Publishing, Paris, https://dx.doi.org/10.1787/fin_sme_ent-2017-48-en. [38]

OECD (2016), *Financing SMEs and Entrepreneurs 2016. An OECD Scoreboard*, OECD Publishing, Paris, https://doi.org/10.1787/fin_sme_ent-2016-en. [11]

OECD (2015), *Financing SMEs and entrepreneurs 2015 : an OECD scoreboard.*, OECD Publishing, Paris, https://dx.doi.org/10.1787/fin_sme_ent-2015-en. (accessed on 28 August 2019). [31]

OECD (2015), *G20/OECD High-Level Principles on SME Financing*, https://www.oecd.org/finance/G20-OECD-High-Level-Principles-on-SME-Financing.pdf (accessed on 4 September 2019). [21]

OECD (2015), *New Approaches to SME and Entrepreneurship Financing: Broadening the Range of Instruments*, OECD Publishing, Paris, https://dx.doi.org/10.1787/9789264240957-en. [13]

OECD (2014), *Financing SMEs and Entrepreneurs 2014 : an OECD scoreboard.*, OECD Publishing. [65]

OECD (2014), *Italy: Key Issues and Policies*, OECD Studies on SMEs and Entrepreneurship, OECD Publishing, Paris, https://dx.doi.org/10.1787/9789264213951-en. [35]

OECD (2013), *Financing SMEs and Entrepreneurs 2013: An OECD Scoreboard*, OECD Publishing, Paris, https://dx.doi.org/10.1787/fin_sme_ent-2013-en. [22]

OECD (2012), "Basel III and SME Lending: Thematic Focus", *Financing SMEs and Entrepreneurs 2012: An OECD Scoreboard.* [53]

OECD (2012), *Financing SMEs and Entrepreneurs 2012: An OECD Scoreboard*, OECD Publishing. [14]

OECD (2012), *Financing SMEs and Entrepreneurs 2012: An OECD Scoreboard*, OECD Publishing, Paris, https://dx.doi.org/10.1787/9789264166769-en. [7]

OECD / European Commission (2019), "Policy Brief on Incubators and Accelerators that Support Inclusive Entrepreneurship", http://dx.doi.org/10.2767/092345. [49]

OECD WORKING PARTY ON SMES AND ENTREPRENEURSHIP (WPSMEE) (2010), *Assessment of Government Support Programmes for SMEs' and Entrepreneurs' Access to Finance in the Global Crisis*, http://www.oecd.org/cfe/smes/Assessment_Government_Support_Programmes.pdf. [64]

OECD/European Commission (2014), *Policy Brief on Access to Business Start-up Finance for Inclusive Entrepreneurship Entrepreneurial Activities in Europe*, http://europa.eu. [24]

OECD/INFE (2015), *OECD/INFE Policy Handbook: National Strategies For Financial Education*, http://www.oecd.org/finance/National-Strategies-Financial-Education-Policy-Handbook.pdf (accessed on 18 July 2019). [45]

OECD: SME Ministerial Conference (2018), *Enhancing SME access to diversified financing instruments: Plenary session 2*, OECD, Mexico City, https://www.oecd.org/cfe/smes/ministerial/documents/2018-SME-Ministerial-Conference-Plenary-Session-2.pdf. [30]

Ollivaud, P. et al. (2015), "The effect of the global financial crisis on OECD potential output", *OECD Journal: Economic Studies*, No. Volume 2014, OECD Publishing, Paris, https://www.oecd.org/eco/growth/The-effect-of-the-global-financial-crisis-on-OECD-potential-output-OECD-Journal-Economic-Studies-2014.pdf (accessed on 22 July 2019). [6]

Óskarsdóttir, M. et al. (2019), "The value of big data for credit scoring: Enhancing financial inclusion using mobile phone data and social network analytics", *Applied Soft Computing Journal*, Vol. 74, pp. 26-39, http://dx.doi.org/10.1016/j.asoc.2018.10.004. [41]

Pavlova, E. and S. Signore (2019), *EIF Research and Market Analysis Working Paper 2019/55: The European venture capital landscape: an EIF perspective Volume V: The economic impact of VC investments supported by the EIF*, EIF, http://www.eif.org/news_centre/research/index.htm. [34]

Prencipe, D. (2017), *EIF Research & Market Analysis Working Paper*, European Investment Fund, Luxembourg, http://www.eif.org/news_centre/research/index.htm. [33]

Rogers, S. (2016), *Assessing the potential for EU investment in venture capital and other risk capital fund of funds*, European Commission, Brussels, http://dx.doi.org/10.2777/997836. [16]

Rosca, O. (2018), *EBRD partners with Turkey's credit guarantee fund to expand financing for women-led firms*, https://www.ebrd.com/news/2018/ebrd-partners-with-turkeys-credit-guarantee-fund-to-expand-financing-for-womenled-firms-.html. [25]

The Montreal Group (2019), *The Montreal Group: Small and medium entreprise development banks*, http://www.themontrealgroup.org/en/about-us.html (accessed on 4 September 2019). [40]

UK Finance (2018), *SME finance in the UK: past, present and future*, UK Finance. [17]

Wehinger, G. (2014), *SMEs and the credit crunch: Current financing difficulties, policy measures and a review of literature*, https://www.oecd.org/finance/SMEs-Credit-Crunch-Financing-Difficulties.pdf (accessed on 24 July 2019). [12]

World Economic Forum (2014), *The Competitiveness Repository Finland-The VIGO Venture Accelerator Programme*, http://www.weforum.org/gcr. [62]

WPSMEE (2010), *Assessment of Government Support Programmes for SMEs' and Entrepreneurs' Access to Finance in the Global Crisis*, http://www.oecd.org/cfe/smes/Assessment_Government_Support_Programmes.pdf. [8]

Part I. Country snapshots

This chapter contains a snapshot view of SME and entrepreneurship finance developments, as well as the scoreboard with core indicators, for countries covered in this report. A more comprehensive discussion is provided in the full country profiles published online.

3. Australia

According to the Bureau of Statistics (ABS), there were 2 309 436 small and medium sized enterprises (SMEs) in Australia in 2017-18. SMEs account for 99.8% of all enterprises in Australia and employ more than 7.6 million people, which equates to around 68% of employment in the private sector.

The Australian economy has completed its 27th consecutive year of economic growth, and has performed remarkably well in adjusting from the investment phase of the mining boom towards broader-based sources of growth. Real GDP grew by 2.9% in 2017-18.

Interest rates are historically low for both SMEs and large businesses. SME interest rates in Australia have gradually declined from 8.6% in 2007 to 5.29% in 2018. The interest rate spread between SME loans and large enterprise loans increased from 96 basis points in 2007 to 183 basis points in 2008, and remained high at 200 basis points in 2017. However, the interest rate spread declined to 173 basis points in 2018.

New lending to SMEs declined in two consecutive years since 2015 (4.9% in 2016 and 8.1% in 2017) after a period of growth, having risen by 7.4% (2013), 7.9% (2014) and 6.7% (2015). Total outstanding SME loans increased by 3.8% in 2016 and 3.7% in 2017. In 2018, the share of SME outstanding loans stood at 29.48% of total outstanding business loans.

Total valuations of all investments by Venture Capital and Later Stage Private Equity (VC&LSPE) investment vehicles rose by 4.7% in 2015-16 and by 14.8% in 2016-17, from AUD 8 802 million reported as at 30 June 2015 to AUD 11 001 million as at 30 June 2018. Leasing and hire purchase volumes dropped from AUD 9 546 million in 2007 to a low of AUD 6 904 million in 2009. Leasing and hire purchase volumes have recovered since, rising to AUD 12 529 million in 2018, an increase of about 9% over the previous year.

The number of bankruptcies per 10 000 businesses increased from 45 in 2007 to 54 in 2013. It has since reached a ten-year low of 32 in 2018.

The Australian Government has a comprehensive SME agenda aimed at promoting growth, employment and opportunities across the economy. Its policies for promoting SMEs focus on reducing red tape, improving the operating environment for businesses, increasing incentives for investment, and enhancing rewards and opportunities for private endeavour. Policies aiming to increase long-term opportunities for SMEs include innovative finance and crowd-sourced equity funding; competition and consumer policies; taxation and business incentives; export financing; and small business assistance.

Table 3.1. Scoreboard for Australia

Indicator	Unit	2007	2008	2009	2010	2011	2012	2013	2014	2015	2016	2017	2018
Debt													
Outstanding business loans, SMEs	AUD billion	188.7	203.9	203.6	223.6	234.3	238.3	241.4	250.0	260.4	270.4	280.3	285.4
Outstanding business loans, total	AUD billion	710.3	771.3	720.7	705.1	713.8	736.8	748.6	783.3	833.6	879.6	907.3	968.1
Share of SME outstanding loans	% of total outstanding business loans	26.57	26.43	28.25	31.71	32.82	32.34	32.24	31.91	31.24	30.74	30.90	29.48
New business lending, total	AUD billion	375.0	336.1	265.5	265.8	310.7	273.8	292.4	360.5	391.7	341.8	346.0	346.9
New business lending, SMEs	AUD billion	77.5	79.9	69.6	82.5	81.6	73.7	79.1	85.4	91.2	86.7	79.7	76.7
Share of new SME lending	% of total new lending	20.67	23.77	26.20	31.04	26.25	26.91	27.06	23.69	23.27	25.37	23.03	22.11
Non-performing loans, total	% of all business loans	0.50	2.07	3.27	3.55	3.16	2.68	2.03	1.39	1.01	1.13	0.78	0.81
Interest rate, SMEs	%	8.56	7.99	7.56	8.29	7.94	7.07	6.43	6.18	5.58	5.29	5.23	5.29
Interest rate, large firms	%	7.60	6.16	5.85	6.67	6.37	5.29	4.29	4.15	3.59	3.20	3.23	3.56
Interest rate spread	% points	0.96	1.83	1.71	1.62	1.57	1.78	2.14	2.03	1.99	2.09	2.00	1.73
Non-bank finance													
Venture and growth capital	AUD billion	6.94	8.32	7.90	8.91	8.70	7.65	8.35	7.91	8.80	9.21	10.58	11.00
Venture and growth capital (growth rate)	%, Year-on-year growth rate	..	19.83	-4.95	12.77	-2.38	-12.05	9.10	-5.28	11.32	4.67	14.78	4.03
Leasing and hire purchases	AUD billion	9.55	9.34	6.90	7.14	7.58	8.69	7.55	8.69	10.37	9.47	11.52	12.53
Factoring and invoicing	AUD billion	54.76	64.99	63.10	58.66	61.42	63.36	63.27	62.39	64.40	..	..	..
Other indicators													
Payment delays, B2B	Number of days	..	..	..	..	22	20	20	15	13	14	12	10
Bankruptcies, Unincorporated	Number	5 045	4 427	4 426	5 616	5 266	5 858	4 761	4 007	4 088	4 350	4 168	4 291
Bankruptcies, Unincorporated	Per 10 000 enterprises	42	36	36	45	43	50	42	35	34	36	34	36
Bankruptcies, Corporates	Number	7 489	9 067	9 465	9 605	10 439	10 583	10 854	8 822	10 093	8 511	7 819	8 052
Bankruptcies, Corporates	Per 10 000 companies	48	55	56	54	57	55	54	41	45	36	31	31
Bankruptcies, Total	Per 10 000 businesses	45	47	47	50	51	53	49	39	41	36	32	32
Invoice payment days, average	Number of days	53	56	54	53	54	53	54	53	47	..	..	..
Outstanding business credit, Unincorporated business	AUD billion	111	117	119	122	125	131	136	142	150	157	164	165
Outstanding business credit, Private trading corporations	AUD billion	500	555	514	500	514	524	531	556	592	626	636	663

The full country profile is available at

https://doi.org/10.1787/061fe03d-en

4. Austria

As in many EU countries, SMEs contribute substantially to Austria's economy. In 2017, 99.6% of all firms were SMEs employing approximately 67.4% of the labour force.

The capital structure of SMEs in Austria is traditionally biased towards debt financing, whereas limitations on access to risk-finance are still apparent. Bank lending is therefore an important factor affecting the availability of external financing for SMEs. However, access to finance is generally not a major concern for Austrian SMEs.

Since 2014, new loans for SMEs have been relatively stable, with a short setback in 2016. As new loans to all enterprises have recovered since 2016, reaching EUR 64.4 billion in 2018, the share of new SME loans in all new business loans decreased slightly to 12.7%. This development is followed by a significant decline in short-term loans (less than 6 months) since 2009. Overall, the annual growth rate of business loans to non-financial corporations has been positive and outperformed the Euro Area.

In Austria, the public sector has established various credit guarantee programmes (e.g. via public promotional banks such as the aws) to increase the willingness of banks to provide loans to SMEs as they transfer the associated risk. Therefore, bank lending to SMEs has been much more resilient and had already recovered pre-crisis levels in 2016. In the light of historically low bank lending rates, debt financing continued to be attractive, supporting lending to the corporate sector. The average base rate on new loans to non-financial corporations up to EUR 1 million, which serves as a proxy for SME interest rates, is declining since the end of 2011 and amounted to 1.82% end of 2018.

In Austria, limitations on access to risk-finance (e.g. Venture Capital) are still apparent and have always been considered to be a particular weakness of the Austrian innovation system. Official data reported by Invest Europe regularly show ups and downs and no clear trend toward an ever increasing risk-capital market size. Due to the relatively small total market volume, large single investments - mostly in the Buyout segment - have disproportional effects. In 2018, the total venture and growth capital volume was EUR 123.4 million.

In terms of bankruptcies per 1 000 firms, a stable development is recorded since 2015, with a total of 11 cases in 2018. The continuous decline of insolvencies is, however, not only a result of the current favourable economic performance of Austria, but also attributed to the low interest rates, which disproportionally benefit weak-performing, highly indebted companies.

According to the European Payment Index, the general payment behaviour in Austria - B2B as well as B2C - is better than the EU average. In 2018, the average B2B payment delay decreased slightly by 1 day and is now at +1 day. The average B2C payment delay remained unchanged at +1 day.

Recent initiatives of the Austrian Government aim at fostering access to finance for innovative, young SMEs and reducing administrative barriers to improve the start-up ecosystem:

The aws Digital and Growth Fund will be initiated as a new boost for the non-dynamic Austrian Venture Capital Market to mobilise private venture capital and trigger investments for innovative tech-startups and scale-ups. The digitalisation of various administrative procedures (e.g. e-foundation of companies) was successfully implemented to reduce the administrative burden for companies and startups in particular. The implementation of regulatory sandboxes will reduce the administrative burden for startups and SMEs, so they can try new concepts and products under market conditions within a limited period.

Table 4.1. Scoreboard for Austria, 2010-18

Indicator	Unit	2010	2011	2012	2013	2014	2015	2016	2017	2018
					Debt					
Outstanding business loans, total	EUR billion	135.5	138.8	140.4	140.3	136.6	137.2	135.6	143.8	153.0
New business loans, total (flows)	EUR million	74 896	73 041	80 867	73 460	73 126	61 711	55 543	64 418	64 438
New business loans, SMEs (flows)	EUR million	9 414	9 476	9 347	8 884	8 237	8 116	7 499	8 304	8 182
Share of new SME loans	% of total business loans	12.57	12.97	11.56	12.09	11.26	13.15	13.50	12.89	12.70
short-term loans, SMEs (flow)	EUR million	5 139	4 944	4 901	4 536	4 016	3 345	3 010	2 539	1 998
long-term loans, SMEs (flow)	EUR million	4 275	4 532	4 446	4 348	4 221	4 771	4 489	5 765	6 184
Share of short-term SME lending	in %	54.59	52.17	52.43	51.06	48.76	41.21	40.14	30.58	24.42
Government loan guarantees, SMEs	EUR million	173	143	158	167	172	204	192	279	301
Government guaranteed loans, SMEs	EUR million	226	185	207	211	225	258	282	456	441
Government direct loans, SMEs	EUR million	607	633	539	594	490	543	454	649	545
Interest rate, SME, loans up to EUR 1m	in %	2.43	2.92	2.46	2.28	2.27	2.02	1.92	1.80	1.82
Interest rate, large firms, loans over EUR 1m	in %	1.96	2.55	1.98	1.77	1.74	1.61	1.54	1.45	1.38
Interest rate spread	in %	0.47	0.37	0.48	0.51	0.53	0.41	0.38	0.35	0.44
Non-performing loans, total	In %	..	2.71	2.81	2.87	3.74	3.39	2.67	2.37	1.88
					Equity					
Venture and growth capital (seed, start-up, later stage)	EUR million	43	97	44	59	60	112	57	108	78
Venture and growth capital (growth capital)	EUR million	34	118	29	26	45	85	29	179	46
Venture and growth capital (total)	EUR million	78	216	73	86	105	197	85	287	123
Venture and growth capital (growth rate)	In %	-31.53	177.61	-66.31	17.76	22.56	87.97	-56.63	235.47	-56.94
					Other					
Payment delays, B2B	Days	11	12	11	12	13	4	4	2	1
Payment delays, B2C	Days	11	11	9	9	9	1	4	1	1
Bankruptcies, total	Number	6 657	6 194	6 266	5 626	5 600	5 422	5 534	5 318	5 224
Bankruptcies, per 1 000 firms	Number	18	17	17	15	15	11	12	11	11

The full country profile is available at

https://doi.org/10.1787/061fe03d-en

5. Belarus

According to the National Statistical Committee, the Belarusian SME sector consists of 111 214 legal entities (including SOEs and companies in mixed ownership with fewer than 250 employees), which amounts to 78.3% of total businesses as of January 1 2019.

Micro, small and medium enterprises, as well as individual entrepreneurs and their employees, account for 30.7% of total employment (30.4% in 2014).

Gross value added produced by SMEs amounts to 28.8% (28.4% in 2017) and their share of GDP remains at the last year's level, which was 24.6%.

Outstanding SME loans (in both national and foreign currencies) increased by 19%, as compared with the beginning of 2018. As of January 1, 2019, total outstanding SME loans stood at BYN 9.88 billion.

Ensuring SME access to finance is an essential component of the general business support policies of the Belarusian government.

Financial support for SMEs has two basic dimensions. First, there is state support, i.e. public funding provided by central and local budgets and by the Development Bank of the Republic of Belarus (DBRB). The second dimension of financial support for SMEs involves non-governmental support provided by commercial and non-profit entities using various forms and methods of financing.

Table 5.1. Scoreboard for Belarus

Indicator	Unit	2007	2008	2009	2010	2011	2012	2013	2014	2015	2016	2017	2018
Debt													
Outstanding business loans, SMEs	BYN billion	..	..	..	..	..	..	..	7.74	8.49	7.59	8.30	9.88
Outstanding business loans, total	BYN billion	2.10	3.22	4.77	6.61	11.59	16.18	20.54	25.11	30.90	28.70	29.73	32.46
Share of SME outstanding loans	%	..							30.83	27.46	26.46	27.91	30.42
New business lending, total	BYN billion	4.11	5.95	7.43	10.96	16.63	27.07	29.23	33.03	38.31	45.10	56.99	69.33
New business lending, SMEs	BYN billion	..	..	..	..	..	..	..	10.77	12.10	13.13	18.29	26.59
Share of new SME lending	%	..							32.62	31.57	29.11	32.09	38.36
Outstanding short-term loans, SMEs	BYN billion	..	..	..	..	..	..	..	2.07	2.00	1.81	2.17	2.97
Outstanding long-term loans, SMEs	BYN billion	..	..	..	..	..	..	..	5.67	6.49	5.78	6.13	6.90
Share of short-term SME lending	%	..							26.76	23.55	23.88	26.14	30.11
Direct government loans, SMEs	BYN million	..	..	..	..	..	..	5.43	4.76	6.45	5.05	5.98	7.09
Non-performing loans, total	%	0.82	0.80	1.05	0.84	0.35	0.51	1.04	1.65	2.60	4.78	4.81	1.39
Non-performing loans, SMEs	%	..	..	..	..	..	..	..	2.06	5.18	6.95	3.34	1.71
Interest rate, SMEs	%	..	..	..	..	..	..	..	..	..	20.20	12.17	9.92
Non-bank finance													
Leasing and hire purchases	BYN billion	..	..	..	..	..	..	..	..	1.05	1.11	2.10	3.39
Factoring and invoice discounting	BYN thousand	..	..	..	..	..	..	..	..	..	..	..	126.8
Other indicators													
Bankruptcies, SMEs	Number	..	..	..	..	..	1725	1850	2047	2364	2410	1919	1970
Bankruptcies, SMEs (growth rate)	%							7.25	10.65	15.49	1.95	-20.37	2.66

The full country profile is available at

https://doi.org/10.1787/061fe03d-en

6. Belgium

In 2016, SMEs dominated the business enterprise landscape in Belgium, accounting for 99.85% of all firms.

The outstanding stock of SME loans expanded 4.5% in 2018, 2.6 percentage points down from its growth rate the previous year.

SME interest rates continued to decrease, and averaged 1.6% in 2018. The interest rate spread between loans charged to large enterprises and loans charged to SMEs was 25 basis points in 2018.

Survey data illustrates that lending conditions eased between 2013 and the end of 2015, and have remained relatively stable until the end of 2018. A deterioration of credit conditions has been reported for the fourth quarter of 2018 and the first quarter of 2019.

After having receded moderately in 2017 (-3.49%), leasing volumes expanded 4.62% in 2018. Overall, factoring continues to be more widely used by Belgian companies. Factoring expanded strongly in 2018, growing 9.62% during the year and achieving rates of more than 10% every year between 2012 and 2017 (with the exception of 2016, where the factoring growth rate was 2.74%). Factoring contributed to almost 17% of GDP in 2018, as opposed to only 6.3% of GDP in 2008.

Venture and growth capital investments continue to show considerable variation due to the small number of deals conducted every year. Total venture and growth capital investments decreased 5.38% in 2018, after having decreased 9% in 2017.

Average payment delays for business to business transactions decreased steadily during the last ten years. After having decreased from a 17-day average in 2009 to an 8-day average in 2017, payment delays expanded to a 9-day average in 2018.

After a steady decrease of bankruptcies during the 2014-2016 period, the number of registered failures rose to 9 968 (+8.7%) in 2017 before receding again in 2018 to 9 860 (-1.08%).

Policy initiatives to ease SMEs' access to finance are taken at the federal and regional level.

The Flemish region launched the Co-financing+ initiative, allowing companies to borrow up to four times their own contribution with a minimum of EUR 350 000 and a maximum of EUR 700 000.

The Brussels-Capital region launched the Bruseed initiative. Bruseed is a capital raising tool for innovative early-stage companies who provide loans, equity participations and convertible loans up to EUR 250 000.

The Federal government supported the signing of a new Code of Conduct for SME Financing. This code of conduct will contribute to improve the information provided to entrepreneurs contracting loans and limit funding loss indemnity to EUR 2 million.

Table 6.1. Scoreboard for Belgium

Indicator	Unit	2007	2008	2009	2010	2011	2012	2013	2014	2015	2016	2017	2018
						Debt							
Outstanding business loans, SMEs	EUR billion	82.8	89.1	88.9	93.9	100.0	109.6	109.5	100.7	104.4	108.0	115.7	121.0
Outstanding business loans, total	EUR billion	134.2	149.4	141.8	150.6	153.7	167.6	162.0	151.7	164.6	163.4	173.6	180.3
Share of SME outstanding loans	% of total outstanding business loans	61.72	59.62	62.73	62.35	65.07	65.43	67.60	66.39	63.44	66.12	66.66	67.09
Outstanding short-term loans, total	EUR billion	37.4	40.4	34.1	35.4	36.5	34.5	33.8	31.4	30.9	32.0	33.6	36.4
Outstanding long-term loans, total	EUR billion	59.7	66.1	72.2	77.2	79.3	82.5	83.9	80.3	84.8	90.8	97.8	103.8
Share of short-term lending, total	% of total business lending	38.52	37.91	32.08	31.45	31.50	29.48	28.74	28.08	26.71	26.05	25.58	25.95
Government loan guarantees, SMEs	EUR million	..	156.5	411.9	553.9	317.5	266.0	480.2	265.6	448.2	398.3	458.4	612.2
Government guaranteed loans, SMEs	EUR million	..	312.7	832.7	888.4	561.7	484.3	826.1	476.7	805.6	735.9	828.3	1130.3
Direct government loans, SMEs	EUR million	..	113.7	142.2	141.9	148.3	170.5	235.6	..	..	..	..	..
Interest rate, SMEs	%	5.45	5.70	3.01	2.51	2.88	2.32	2.06	2.09	1.83	1.72	1.66	1.60
Interest rate, large firms	%	4.72	5.05	2.09	1.70	2.22	1.74	1.76	1.77	1.60	1.34	1.40	1.35
Interest rate spread	% points	0.73	0.65	0.92	0.81	0.66	0.58	0.30	0.32	0.23	0.38	0.26	0.25
Collateral, SMEs	% of SMEs needing collateral to obtain bank lending	..	..	..	74.30	71.90	78.60	..	..	..	..	..	..
Percentage of SME loan applications	SME loan applications/ total number of SMEs	..	..	22.22	26.46	30.20	29.33	29.36	39.33	36.61	36.71	37.18	35.38
Rejection rate	1-(SME loans authorised/ requested)	..	..	0.52	5.13	6.44	10.40	10.91	5.88	5.71	6.13	5.07	5.51
Utilisation rate	SME loans used/ authorised	77.80	79.05	80.69	80.07	80.16	77.45	77.79	79.76	79.62	80.11	79.63	80.48
						Non-bank finance							
Venture and growth capital	EUR million	502.26	507.83	618.05	363.60	411.11	445.36	438.09	580.86	548.18	843.14	767.18	725.89
Venture and growth capital (growth rate)	%, year-on-year growth rate	..	1.11	21.70	-41.17	13.07	8.33	-1.63	32.59	-5.63	53.81	-9.01	-5.38
Leasing and hire purchases	EUR million	4405.9	4856.4	3756.4	4005.5	4439.0	4450.2	4121.7	4356.9	4800.5	6009.6	5800.1	6 068.4
Factoring and invoicing	EUR million	19.2	22.5	23.9	32.2	36.9	42.4	47.7	55.4	61.2	62.8	69.6	76.3
						Other indicators							
Payment delays, B2B	Number of days	..	..	17	17	15	19	18	19	13	10	8	9
Bankruptcies, total	Number	7 680	8 476	9 420	9 570	10 224	10 587	11 740	10 736	9 762	9 170	9 968	9878
Bankruptcies, total (growth rate)	%, year-on-year growth rate	..	10.36	11.14	1.59	6.83	3.55	10.89	-8.55	-9.07	-6.06	8.77	-0.90
Bankruptcies, SMEs	Number	7 652	8 443	9 391	9 531	10 187	10 526	11 680	10 675	9 728	9 134	9 935	9 860
Bankruptcies, SMEs (growth rate)	%, year-on-year growth rate		10.34	11.23	1.49	6.88	3.33	10.96	-8.60	-8.87	-6.11	8.77	-0.75

The full country profile is available at

https://doi.org/10.1787/061fe03d-en

7. Brazil

Micro and small-sized enterprises (MSEs) form an essential part of the Brazilian economy, accounting for 98.5% of all legally constituted companies (11.5 million), for 27% of GDP, and for 41% of the total payroll.

The reference interest rate of *Banco Central do Brasil* (Special Clearance and Escrow System - SELIC) has been gradually declining, from 14.15% per annum in December 2015, to 13.65% in December 2016, 6.9% in December 2017 and 6.4% in December 2018. The previous period of rate hike (from 7.25% in March 2013 to 14.25% in September 2016) led to high interest rates on loans for large corporate borrowers (14.8%) and SMEs (30.6%), leading to a shrinking demand for new SME loans. Interest rates have increased more for micro-enterprises and SMEs than for large businesses. However, this trend was reversed when the central bank decreased its rate at the end of 2016, thus decreasing interest rates for SMEs.

The stock of SME loans fell in 2015 and new lending to SMEs declined in 2014 and 2015. Both observations are in contrast with lending to large businesses, where the outstanding stock of loans, as well as new lending was up in 2014 and 2015.

Since 2008, large companies have been receiving a larger share of the business loans granted compared to SMEs. The government has taken on a more active role in this area, often with the aim to provide financial services to small businesses, excluded from classic financial institutions. Developments include a micro-credit programme, a quota to use 2% of demand deposits of the National Financial System to finance loans to low-income individuals and micro entrepreneurs, and a strong increase in the number of agencies where financial services are provided.

The regulatory framework for angel investors has been revised in 2016 and further adjusted in 2017, removing some long-standing barriers for investors in SME markets, most notably by offering more legal protection in the case of company closures, more latitude to investment and more information sharing between recipients and investors. In addition, new regulations concerning investment-based crowdfunding and Fintech were introduced in 2017 and 2018.

SEMPE, the Under-Secretariat for Micro and Small Enterprises (Ministry of Economy - ME) is the main body of the Brazilian government responsible for formulating, coordinating, articulating and defining public policy guidelines aimed at strengthening, expanding and formalising artisans, individual entrepreneurs and micro and small enterprises. In addition, SEMPE/ME leads the articulation of actions aimed at improving the business environment and at contributing to the expansion and sustainability of micro and small enterprises, with the aim to contribute to employment and income generation.

Table 7.1. Scoreboard for Brazil

Indicator	Unit	2007	2008	2009	2010	2011	2012	2013	2014	2015	2016	2017	2018
Outstanding business loans, SMEs	BRL billion	281.13	347.21	388.58	476.96	564.12	629.56	681.31	692.26	656.25	578.29	523.36	524.68
Outstanding business loans, total	BRL billion	506.61	689.55	780.83	935.86	1 114.03	1 286.53	1 460.03	1 623.01	1 734.61	1 565.18	1 436.38	1 440.78
Share of SME outstanding loans	% of total outstanding business loans	55.49	50.35	49.76	50.97	50.64	48.93	46.66	42.65	37.84	36.95	36.44	36.42
New business lending, total	BRL billion	..	..	..	..	..	917.83	948.01	992.11	1 027.21	817.48	735.23	813.87
New business lending, SMEs	BRL billion	..	..	..	..	..	566.88	562.21	532.2	490.9	408.98	398.48	429.13
Share of new SME lending	% of total business lending	..	..	..	..	..	61.76	59.3	53.64	47.79	50.03	54.20	52.73
Outstanding short-term loans, SMEs	BRL billion	105.57	109.37	104.07	119.57	150.72	158.58	161.9	155.96	141.47	122.28	116.75	125.36
Outstanding long-term loans, SMEs	BRL billion	160.04	200.91	240.04	309.64	386.91	469.35	518.06	534.8	513.04	454.62	403.23	396.71
Share of short-term SME lending	%	39.75	35.25	30.24	27.86	28.03	25.25	23.81	22.58	21.61	21.20	22.45	24.01
Government guaranteed loans, SMEs	BRL billion	0.07	0.08	0.11	0.05	2.21	2.01	1.74	2.02	2.84	3.27	5.05	4.14
Direct government loans, SMEs	BRL billion	10.09	11.76	13.85	14.47	17.16	18.93	22.12	24.12	27.21	29.06	30.46	29.18
Non-performing loans, total	% of all business loans	1.51	1.53	2.65	1.82	2.01	2.21	1.84	1.88	2.39	3.15	2.99	2.45
Non-performing loans, SMEs	% of SME loans	2.64	2.79	4.68	3.39	3.63	4.18	3.56	3.9	5.43	6.7	5.67	4.29
Interest rate, SMEs	%	..	..	..	..	..	19.7	23.7	25.2	34.8	31.7	25.1	21.50
Interest rate, large firms	%	..	..	..	..	..	9.0	12.0	13.3	16.4	17.4	9.0	8.60
Interest rate spread	% points	..	..	..	..	..	10.7	11.7	11.9	18.4	14.3	16.1	12.90

The full country profile is available at

https://doi.org/10.1787/061fe03d-en

8. Canada

In 2018, Canadian small businesses (1-99 employees) constituted 98.0% of all businesses and employed 8.4 million individuals, or 69.8% of the private sector labour force.

Supply-side survey data show that outstanding debt held by all businesses increased in 2018 to CAD 898 billion. Lending to small businesses increased to CAD 105.1 billion. Small businesses' share of total outstanding business loans was 11.7%.

Small business credit conditions have remained relatively stable since 2011. The average interest rate charged to small businesses in 2018 increased to 5.7% with an average business prime rate of 3.6%. The business risk premium reverted to its 2014 level of 2.1%, the lowest level since the 2009 recession reflecting an easing in access to financing for small businesses in Canada.

The small business 90-day loan delinquency rate has returned to pre-recession levels. In 2018, the 90-day loan delinquency rate reached 0.55%.

Total venture capital (VC) investment levels in Canada has had over eight straight years of growth reaching CAD 3.8 billion in 2017 followed by a modest decline in 2018 to CAD 3.7 billion. These are the highest levels of VC investment recorded in Canada since 2001.

In 2018-19, the Government of Canada continued its commitment to support entrepreneurship and the growth of SMEs.

The Business Development Bank of Canada (BDC), a crown corporation, with its mandate to support Canadian entrepreneurship had CAD 31 billion in financing, as of March 31, 2018, committed to 56 000 clients operating across Canada.

The government of Canada has also made CAD 450 million available for the Venture Capital Catalyst Initiative (VCCI) to increase late-stage venture capital available to Canadian entrepreneurs. VCCI will inject more than CAD 1.5 billion into the Canadian innovation capital market by leveraging funds from the public sector and private sector.

Futurpreneur Canada, a not-for-profit organisation, which provides financing, mentoring, and business support tools to young entrepreneurs, also received CAD 38 million in funding over five years, starting in 2019-20 to continue its support of Canada's next generation of entrepreneurs.

Supporting women entrepreneurs continues to be one of the key focus areas for the government of Canada. In Budget 2018, the government announced approximately CAD 2 billion investment in the first Women Entrepreneurship Strategy. It provides support by increasing access to financing, talent, networks, and expertise to encourage more women to start and grow their businesses, as well as to work with them to move into exporting.

Table 8.1. Scoreboard for Canada

Indicator	Unit	2007	2008	2009	2010	2011	2012	2013	2014	2015	2016	2017	2018
Debt													
Outstanding business loans, SMEs	CAD billion	83.4	83.4	86.4	85.7	89.1	87.2	91.1	94.0	96.1	99.2	102.5	105.1
Outstanding business loans, total	CAD billion	479.8	534.0	482.3	489.5	503.2	548.0	592.6	642.9	716.2	772.4	823.7	897.5
Share of SME outstanding loans	% of total outstanding business loans	17.39	15.61	17.92	17.50	17.71	15.90	15.38	14.62	13.42	12.84	12.45	11.71
New business lending, total	CAD billion	..	..	..	..	126.2	141.6	151.0	168.7	188.4	204.0	233.9	269.7
New business lending, SMEs	CAD billion	..	..	..	..	20.2	21.7	22.8	23.2	24.0	22.8	25.2	27.2
Share of new SME lending	% of total new lending	..	..	..	..	15.99	15.30	15.10	13.74	12.73	11.16	10.78	10.1
Outstanding short-term loans, SMEs	CAD billion	15.1	..			6.9	..	..	15.6	..	..	24.2	..
Outstanding long-term loans, SMEs	CAD billion	21.1	..	..	..	12.8	..	..	12.4	..	..	32.4	..
Share of short-term SME lending	% of total SME lending	41.62	..	43.40	36.30	35.13	39.00	46.00	55.71	47.20	36.20	42.8	30.10
Government loan guarantees, SMEs	CAD billion	1.20	1.30	1.20	1.30	1.30	1.10	1.10	1.50	1.20	1.3	1.4	1.8
Direct government loans, SMEs	CAD billion	4.40	4.10	5.50	4.70	6.00	5.80	4.60	6.50	6.70	7.9	8.0	8.4
Interest rate, SMEs	%	7.50	..	6.20	5.80	5.30	5.40	5.60	5.10	5.10	5.30	5.20	5.70
Interest rate, large firms	%	6.10	..	3.10	2.60	3.00	3.00	3.00	3.00	2.80	2.70	2.90	3.64
Interest rate spread	% points	1.40	..	3.10	3.20	2.30	2.40	2.60	2.10	2.30	2.60	2.30	2.06
Collateral, SMEs	% of SMEs needing collateral to obtain bank lending	47.7	..	56.1	66.7	64.8	76.0	56.0	66.6	80.0	74.0	64.1	70.0
Percentage of SME loan applications	SME loan applications/ total number of SMEs	17.0	..	14.0	18.0	24.0	26.0	30.0	27.0	23.0	26.0	26.0	27.0
Rejection rate	1-(SME loans authorised/ requested)	..	..	..	9.0	8.0	7.0	9.0	12.8	7.0	9.0	9.5	9.0
Non-bank finance													
Venture and growth capital	CAD billion	..	..	..	..	..	..	1.88	2.06	2.24	3.19	3.78	3.69
Venture and growth capital (growth rate)	%, Year-on-year growth rate	..	..	..	..	..	..	..	9.7	8.7	42.3	18.4	-2.4
Other indicators													
90-Day Delinquency Rate Small business	%	0.71	1.13	1.52	0.87	0.62	0.55	0.41	0.41	0.60	0.55	0.52	0.55
90-Day Delinquency Rate Medium business	%	0.03	0.05	0.3	0.13	0.02	0.01	0.01	0.03	0.03	0.03	0.03	0.07
Leasing request rate	%	20.8	..	1.00	2.00	7.00	8.00	11.0	7.90	8.00	9.00	7.2	9.00
Leasing approval rate	%	93	..	76	97	97.3	95	95	98.6	94	94	97.6	96.0
Bankruptcies, SMEs	Per 1 000 firms with employees	7.00	6.60	5.90	4.60	4.30	3.80	3.60	3.40	3.30	3.10	2.84	2.79
Bankruptcies, SMEs (growth rate)	%, Year-on-year growth rate	..	-5.71	-10.6	-22.0	-6.52	-11.6	-5.26	-5.56	-2.94	-6.06	-8.39	-1.76

The full country profile is available at https://doi.org/10.1787/061fe03d-en

9. Chile

After 4 years of negative growth in Chile, the year 2018 saw an increase in GDP by 4%, driven mainly by domestic demand (4.7% increase). According to the Central Bank of Chile, growth expectations for 2019 are between 2.75% and 3.5%.

According to the Commission for the Financial Market (CMF), credit activity, measured as the growth of credit placements, grew by 9.35% in 2017-2018. However, the participation of SMEs in outstanding commercial loans decreased in 2018 to 19.9%. Microenterprises and small businesses are responsible for the increase of outstanding SME loans, and Banco Estado has been the key financial institution working to improve access of SMEs to financing, together with the Corporation for the Promotion of Production (CORFO).

According to the bank credit survey of the Central Bank of Chile, credit conditions were more restrictive for SMEs during 2018 and relatively stable throughout the year. This contrasts with large companies, for which credit conditions showed very favourable levels compared to other periods. According to the Central Bank, the demand for credit is weaker, due mostly to large companies. Indeed, SMEs maintained their levels of credit demand. On the other hand, the interest rate differential between large companies and SMEs was reduced from 4.7% in 2017 to 4.5% in 2018, its lowest level since 2013.

According to the data of the fifth Longitudinal Enterprises Survey (ELE), which surveyed more than 339 022 companies between 2016 and 2017, the rejection rates of loans to SMEs decreased significantly from 12.4% in 2015 to 9.4% in 2017. The utilisation rate for SMEs was 89.3%, the second highest rate since 2007. On the other hand, the rate of application for credit by SMEs decreased from 30.4% in 2015 to 26.7% in 2017.

With respect to venture capital funds, Production Development Corporation (CORFO) and Start-Up Chile's programmes are the main instruments of SME capital financing, although other private and public initiatives have also developed. Venture capital investments increased again in 2018, reaching an investment of more than CLP 39 billion.

A novelty concerning SME financing is the development of the Fintech industry in Chile, which has grown by 34% in 2017 and 29% in the last year. This rapid growth highlights a thriving ecosystem comprised of more than 84 companies that offer a wide range of financial services for SMEs, ranging from payments and remittances to loans and crowdfunding and scoring services. This was taken into account by the Ministry of Finance, which announced in April 2019 the sending to Congress of a Bill that will regulate and strengthen this industry.

Although the average payment delays for SMEs have decreased in recent years, they continue to be high and unfavourable for SMEs, considering one of the main reasons (declared by these companies) for applying for financing is the availability of capital. The Government has made progress in this area through the promulgation of the Law of Payment in 30 Days, which seeks to obtain certainty in the terms and amounts of the invoices, along with the right to compensation in the case of a breach of deadlines. At the beginning of 2020, a report will be issued that will reflect the impact of this practice on the average term of payment for large companies and SMEs.

Table 9.1. Scoreboard for Chile

Indicator	Unit	2007	2008	2009	2010	2011	2012	2013	2014	2015	2016	2017	2018
Debt													
Outstanding business loans. SMEs	CLP trillion	6.8	7.6	8.1	9.3	10.1	11.5	11.8	13.7	15.8	17.3	18.7	19.8
Outstanding business loans. total	CLP trillion	40.9	49.9	46.3	48.1	57.2	64.6	69.8	76.4	84.9	88.7	90.3	99.5
Share of SME outstanding loans	% of total outstanding business loans	16.7	15.2	17.5	19.3	17.7	17.9	16.9	18.0	18.6	19.5	20.7	19.9
New business lending. total	CLP trillion	..	..	..	53.3	58.0	58.0	58.1	63.9	67.8	67.4	67.7	71.4
New business lending. SMEs	CLP trillion	..	..	..	2.6	3.1	3.8	3.8	4.4	5.1	5.1	5.6	5.63
Share of new SME lending	% of total new lending	..	..	..	4.9	5.3	6.5	6.6	6.8	7.5	7.6	8.2	7.8
Outstanding Short-term loans. SMEs	CLP trillion	..	..	..	1.6	2.0	2.3	1.8	1.8	1.9	1.8	1.8	1.9
Outstanding Long-term loans. SMEs	CLP trillion	..	..	..	1.0	1.1	1.5	2.0	2.5	3.2	3.3	3.8	3.8
Share of short-term SME lending	% of total SME lending	..	..	..	60.2	63.3	60.3	47.8	41.9	36.9	35.8	32.8	33.3
Government loan guarantees. SMEs	CLP trillion	0.2	0.3	0.8	1.1	1.3	1.9	1.9	1.6	1.7	1.8	1.7	1.6
Government guaranteed loans. SME	CLP trillion	0.3	0.5	1.3	1.8	2.0	2.9	3.1	2.3	2.4	2.6	2.6	2.5
Non-performing loans. total	% of all business loans	...	...	2.5	2.2	2.1	2.2	2.4	2.6	2.4	2.1	2.3	2.5
Non-performing loans. SMEs	% of all SME loans	..	..	5.9	6.1	5.5	5.4	6.1	6.1	5.9	5.3	5.2	5.9
Interest rate. SMEs	%	..	..	..	..	..	..	11.8	10.3	9.3	9.3	8.4	8.3
Interest rate. large firms	%	..	..	..	..	..	..	4.7	4.0	3.8	4.0	3.7	3.8
Interest rate spread	% points	..	..	..	..	..	..	7.1	6.3	5.5	5.3	4.7	4.5
Collateral. SMEs	% of SMEs needing collateral to obtain bank lending	44.0	..	49.8	..	..	..	72.8	..	68.1	..	59.9	..
Percentage of SME loan applications	SME loan applications/total number of SMEs	32.9	..	32.4	..	..	..	26.4	..	24.6	..	26.2	..
Rejection rate	1-(SME loans authorized/ requested)	41.4	..	15.0	..	..	..	12.3	..	14.7	..	9.4	..
Utilisation rate	SME loans used/ authorized	86.6	..	91.0	..	..	..	87.9	..	96.7	..	89.3	..
Non-bank finance													
Venture and growth capital	CLP billion	26.7	19.3	22.2	27.1	33.9	43.1	30.8	43.2	34.7	40.0	21.9	39.2
Venture and growth capital (growth rate)	%. year-on-year growth rate	..	-27.8	15.3	22.0	25.1	27.0	-28.5	40.1	-19.6	-100	-45.3	79
Leasing and hire purchases	CLP billion	3.0	3.6	3.5	3.8	4.5	5.0	5.6	6.2	6.6	6.7	7.8	8.2
Factoring and invoicing	CLP billion	2.0	2.0	1.4	1.9	2.4	2.6	2.6	2.6	2.8	3.0	3.8	4.4
Other indicators													
Payment delays. B2B	Number of days	..	..	..	75.8	74.9	56.7	52.7	55.2	58.0	54.9	56.0	51.8
Bankruptcies. SMEs	Number	122	127	125	136	146	146	164	6	154	295	285	397
Bankruptcies. SMEs (growth rate)	% year-on-year growth rate	..	4.1	-1.6	8.8	7.4	0.0	12.3	-96.3	2 467	91.6	-3.4	39.0

The full country profile is available at

https://doi.org/10.1787/061fe03d-en

10. Colombia

Access to finance is one of the main conditions for strengthening entrepreneurship and growth of SMEs. It allows them to prosper and make investments in order to increase their productivity and competitiveness. It is more difficult for these companies to invest, to modernise their operations, and to innovate or cope with crises when they do not have sufficient access to formal financing.

Since 2006, the National Association of Financial Institutions (ANIF) has been running the Great SME Survey (Anif - Asociación Nacional de Instituciones Financieras, 2019[1]), which gathers the opinion of a sample of SME entrepreneurs from the largest sectors, namely industry, trade and services.

The SME indicator Anif – IPA is constructed with the results of this survey. The indicator constitutes the main thermometer for the economic climate for formal and informal SMES. It compares the evolution of the following variables: economic situation, sales volumes, general performance expectations and sales expectations.

It is estimated that two out of three SMEs are informal in Colombia, according to the study "Demand for Financial Inclusion in Colombia" (Superintendencia Financiera de Colombia, 2015[2]). Having made this clarification, results from the Great SME Survey – GEP, which is conducted on a sample of the business fabric that is considered to be formal, are presented.

According to the results of the last survey round, bank credit has remained the main source of financing for formal SMEs. On average and in the three largest sectors, 40% of SMEs companies requested credit to the financial system. This percentage amounted to 39% in the industrial sector, 41% in the commerce sector and 40% in the services sector. Loan applications remained stable during the last year.

Moreover, 45% of SMEs did not have recourse to alternative sources of financing during the second half of 2018. For the remaining 55%, external providers were the most important source of alternative funding, followed by own resources. Leasing, reinvestment of profits, factoring and the non-banking market did not exceed 8% for any macro sector. In addition, the survey reveals that resources from private equity funds or entrepreneurial support have marginal importance.

During the first half of 2018, resources were allocated by SMEs as follows: working capital (63%), consolidation of liabilities (22%), purchase or leasing of machinery (11%) and remodelling or adjustments (9%).

With a business fabric such as that made up of SMEs in Colombia, it is important to highlight the benefits of access to credit. These include greater growth in sales, greater margins of production and investment in machinery and equipment compared to the companies that do not have access to credit. SMEs that cannot enter the financial system are often forced to resort to informal sources of financing, such as non-bank loans that do not adapt to their needs and have high costs.

The Great SME Survey showed that SMEs are not requesting credit for several reasons. The main reason put forward is that they do not need it; next, SMEs invoke the high costs associated with interest and commissions; and third, they mention the number of procedures for obtaining it, coupled with their distrust in the financial system. SMEs' lack of recourse to credit is considered a problem of self-exclusion associated with different factors, including the belief that the loan application will be rejected and the ignorance of the importance of financial products for the development of their activity. SMEs often do not perceive financing as a necessity despite the fact that this business segment has a high financial dependence. All these factors are highly correlated with the weak financial education of SMEs.

Table 10.1. Scoreboard for Colombia

Indicator	Unit	2007	2008	2009	2010	2011	2012	2013	2014	2015	2016	2017	2018
Debt													
Outstanding business loans, SMEs	COP billion	25.61	28.59	26.58	29.12	39.97	46.76	51.6	55.23	58.17	62.09	64.88	68.50
Outstanding business loans, total	COP billion	78.4	94.7	95.9	113.8	134.8	152.8	171.3	197.2	226.3	243.2	251.8	253.6
Share of SME outstanding loans	% of total outstanding business loans	32.67	30.19	27.70	25.58	29.66	30.61	30.11	28.01	25.70	25.53	25.77	27.01
New business lending, total	COP billion	67.7	76.0	77.2	79.0	77.7	95.4	104.0	117.0	117.7	117.3	153.3	160.09
New business lending, SMEs	COP billion	13.2	13.5	15.22	16.91	21.09	23.53	23.57	24.69	25.53	25.3	34.11	35.48
Share of new SME lending	% of total new lending	19.50	17.76	19.71	21.39	27.13	24.67	22.65	21.10	21.70	21.57	22.25	22.05
Outstanding short-term loans, SMEs	COP billion	4.98	7.52	6.14	6.41	10	11.55	12.36	12.93	13.8	13.59	14.44	12.86
Outstanding long-term loans, SMEs	COP billion	20.63	21.07	20.44	22.71	29.97	35.22	39.24	42.3	44.37	48.5	50.44	55.63
Share of short-term SME lending	% of total SME lending	19.45	26.30	23.10	22.01	25.02	24.70	23.95	23.41	23.72	21.89	22.26	18.78
Government loan guarantees, SMEs	COP billion	0.56	1.39	1.82	1.94	5.46	6.19	7.14	7.51	7.72	10.52	11.53	9.40
Government guaranteed loans, SMEs	COP billion	2.23	2.59	2.98	3.16	7.26	9.12	10.81	11.96	12.69	15.37	16.51	15.22
Non-performing loans, total	% of all business loans	0.95	1.27	1.59	1.07	1.00	1.03	1.08	1.33	1.34	1.51	2.36	2.61
Non-performing loans, SMEs	% of all SME loans	2.52	3.66	5.05	3.68	1.76	1.81	1.99	2.45	2.25	3.12	3.71	3.84
Interest rate, SMEs	%	20.09	23.13	20.43	18.66	14.34	14.68	13.24	13.54	14.69	16.87	15.37	18.17
Interest rate, large firms	%	12.53	14.24	10.09	7.23	9.28	9.25	7.98	8.33	8.78	11.00	9.16	13.57
Interest rate spread	% points	7.56	8.89	10.34	11.43	5.06	5.43	5.26	5.21	5.91	5.86	6.21	4.60
Collateral, SMEs	% of SMEs needing collateral to obtain bank lending	79.25	87.54	86.28	87.31	90.04	90.12	90.02	89.30	91.04	91.71	92.15	91.75
Percentage of SME loan applications	SME loan applications/ total number of SMEs	49	53	44.6	49.6	47	44	43.3	39.6	42.6	34	40	40
Rejection rate	1-(SME loans authorised/ requested)	2	4	9	5	3	4	7	3	7.5	4	8	7
Utilisation rate	SME loans used/ authorised	98	96	91	95	97	96	93	97	92.5	96	92	93
Non-bank finance													
Venture and growth capital	COP billion	..	..	..	..	..	..	..	..	1.83	2.91	4.23	5.61
Venture and growth capital (growth rate)	%, Year-on-year growth rate	..	..	..	..	..	..	..	..	..	59 .3	45 .5	32.69

Indicator	Unit	2007	2008	2009	2010	2011	2012	2013	2014	2015	2016	2017	2018
Leasing and hire purchases	COP billion	..	..	..	..	..	..	..	..	33.34	39.45	41.98	50.17
Factoring and invoice discounting	COP billion	5.77	6.04	7.15	7.01	12.85	10.55	17.56	23.75	31.47	25.77	25.53	26.58
Other indicators													
Payment delays, B2B	Number of days	49	50	61	62	59	55	56	65	66	85	95	101
Bankruptcies, SMEs	Number	33	95	149	159	178	116	156	141	164	200	246	198
Bankruptcies, SMEs (growth rate)	%, Year-on-year growth rate	..	187.9	56.84	6.71	11.95	-34.8	34.48	-9.62	16.31	21.95	23.00	-19.51

The full country profile is available at

https://doi.org/10.1787/061fe03d-en

11. Czech Republic

In 2018, there were roughly 1.155 million active enterprises in the Czech Republic. 99.83% of these firms were SMEs with less than 250 employees each. Together, they employed almost 1.88 million people, or 57.68% of the Czech Republic's workforce. Micro-firms dominated the business landscape, comprising 96.4% of all SMEs in 2018 (roughly stable from 2017).

SME interest rates increased by 25.6 % in 2018 vis-à-vis 2017. It is the first year of increasing after the period 2008-17, when SME interest rates continued dropping year-on-year (by 55.1% in total). The recent development in interest rates was likely caused by tightening a monetary policy by the Czech National Bank (CNB) from 2017 onwards, which decided to increase interest rates from 0.50 to 0.75 percentage points in 2018.

Venture capital investments peaked in 2008, and then declined dramatically to 2017. This trend changed in 2018, with VC investments amounting to EUR13.9 million, 33.6% of their 2008 value. Growth capital fell even more steeply, from EUR 191.9 million in 2009, to EUR 4.9 million in 2016. In 2018, it dropped to 3.5 million.

Government support for enterprises and entrepreneurs primarily comprises measures with respect to developmental and operational financing, export support, support of the energy sector, development of entrepreneurial skills and financial literacy of entrepreneurs, technical education and research, as well as development and innovation.

In December 2012, the Czech government adopted a Small and Medium Sized Enterprises Support Strategy 2014-20 (SME 2014+), which represents the key strategic document for the preparation of the European Union (EU) cohesion policies over the 2014–20 programming period in the area of enterprise development. This includes the Operational Programme Enterprise and Innovations for Competitiveness (OPEIC), and similarly important national SME support programmes.

SME 2014+ also acknowledges the need to support social enterprises and strengthen social entrepreneurs' education. The SME 2014+ is implemented through national programmes that support enterprises, such as the GUARANTEE, ENERG, VADIUM or Inostart programmes; and via the OPEIC.

SME 2014+ aims to motivate entrepreneurs to utilise available funding for the development of their businesses through national and EU programmes. This includes several tools, such as government loan guarantees (Czech-Moravian Guarantee and Development Bank), financing schemes for exporting SMEs (Czech Export Bank) and innovative businesses (INOSTART programme), as well as a programme to draw financial resources from the EU structural fund (OPEIC), which provides support to SMEs through grants, preferential loans and guarantees.

The Czech-Moravian Guarantee and Development Bank (CMGDB) is a specialised state-owned banking entity with a primarily mission of facilitating SME access to financing. Next to the programmes GUARANTEE and EXPANSION, the CMGDB launched two new programmes – ENERG and VADIUM, financed by the national budget. In June 2017, the CMGDB launched a new programme ENERG, earmarked for SMEs located in the capital of Prague. Entrepreneurs can obtain an investment loan of up to CZK 20 million for investment projects that spur energy savings in the company. In July 2018, the Bank launched a new programme VADIUM, which provides small entrepreneurs with guarantees (of up to CZK 50 million) for bids in public tenders. In 2018, the Bank also became an intermediary for equity investments from the Central Europe Fund of Funds (CEFoF), administered by the European Investment Fund. CEFoF will invest into innovative SMEs and small mid-caps in a later stage venture and growth phase, with a volume of financial resources of at least EUR 80 million.

Table 11.1. Scoreboard for the Czech Republic

Indicator	Unit	2008	2009	2010	2011	2012	2013	2014	2015	2016	2017	2018
Debt												
Outstanding business loans, SMEs	CZK billion	555.03	527.55	550.08	587.91	589.68	610.79	621.39	652.59	702.81	725.63	762.99
Outstanding business loans, total	CZK billion	850.76	784.07	783.54	831.21	840.59	871.58	890.23	935.36	994.86	1036.1	1097.39
Share of SME outstanding loans	% of total outstanding business loans	65.24	67.28	70.20	70.73	70.15	70.08	69.80	69.77	70.64	70.03	69.53
New business lending, total	CZK billion	866.11	780.87	667.98	599.09	694.94	500.50	544.73	607.59	510.58	457.94	461.84
New business lending, SMEs	CZK billion	207.24	147.74	123.40	124.12	129.83	86.66	97.76	118.28	100.46	101.24	97.92
Share of new SME lending	% of total new lending	23.93	18.92	18.47	20.72	18.68	17.31	17.95	19.46	19.68	22.11	21.20
Outstanding short-term loans, SMEs	CZK million	..	..	73 626	72 433	77 853	45 531	40 360	41 742	36 974	33 918	29 835
Outstanding long-term loans, SMEs	CZK million	..	..	49 772	51 684	51 977	41 129	57 404	76 475	63 490	67 325	68 090
Share of short-term SME lending	% of total SME lending	..	..	59.67	58.36	59.97	52.54	41.28	35.31	36.80	33.50	30.47
Government loan guarantees, SMEs	CZK million	3 529	6 369	6 593	472	1 534	3 251	4 010	6 913	3 530	4 014	6 485
Government guaranteed loans, SMEs	CZK million	5 094	9 550	10 070	630	2 215	4 616	5 771	9 947	5 055	5 758	9 287
Direct government loans, SMEs	CZK million	286	209	629	1 090	782	101	86	65	7	291	1 440
Non-performing loans, total	CZK million	35 340	61 904	70 166	67 876	61 480	62 032	58 694	52 677	50 307	43 225	39 999 (P)
Interest rate, SMEs	%	5.57	4.64	4.01	3.73	3.48	3.13	3.76	2.70	2.50	2.50	3.14
Interest rate, large firms	%	4.84	3.46	3.34	2.63	2.43	1.89	2.00	1.80	1.80	1.90	2.62
Interest rate spread	% points	0.73	1.18	0.67	1.10	1.05	1.24	1.76	0.90	0.70	0.60	0.52
Non-bank finance												
Venture and growth capital	EUR million	104.0	219.7	153.8	18.3	9.5	23.3	34.6	12.4	9.4	16.3	17.4
Venture and growth capital (growth rate)	%, Year-on-year growth rate	..	111.2	-30.0	-88.1	-48.1	145.4	48.3	-64.0	-24.6	73.9	6.7
Other indicators												
Payment delays, B2B	Number of days	18.00	19.00	14.00	14.00	15.00	14.00	14.00	14.00	19.00	16.00	15.00
Bankruptcies, SMEs	Number	873	1 280	1 301	1263	1345	1379	1228	1001	904	769	649
Bankruptcies, SMEs (growth rate)	%, Year-on-year growth rate	..	46.62	1.64	-2.92	6.49	2.53	-10.95	-18.49	-9.69	-14.93	-15.60

The full country profile is available at

https://doi.org/10.1787/061fe03d-en

12. Denmark

In 2016, not counting non-employer enterprises, SMEs accounted for 98.2% of all enterprises in Denmark.

The share of new business lending directed towards SMEs has decreased since 2015 and stood at 8.6% in 2018, which is low by international standards. However, this is mainly the result of an increase in loans to large businesses, as new lending to SMEs remained stable between 2016 and 2018.

Survey data illustrates that credit conditions in Denmark have become much more favourable since 2011, when almost 40% of SMEs described their financial conditions as poor. Between December 2017 and December 2018, the share of SMEs describing their financial conditions as poor decreased from 17.2% to 16.3%. For new small enterprises, the demand for loans increased and credit standards were relaxed between the first quarter of 2015 and the third quarter of 2018. However, in the last quarter of 2018 and the first quarter of 2019, demand has decreased and credit standards have tightened.

SME interest rates have decreased from an average of 6.6% in 2008, to 2.3% in 2018. Since interest rates for large enterprises declined even more during this period, the interest rate spread between small and large firms widened from 0.9% in 2008 to 2% in 2013. Since then, however, the spread has consistently decreased, reaching 1.3% in 2018.

Due to an increase in the venture capital investments of Danish private equity firms, total venture and growth capital investments increased by 29% between 2017 and 2018, reaching their highest level to date. This is the net effect of a sharp increase in venture capital investments in the later stages but a decrease in growth capital investments compared to 2017.

Average payment delays remained at an all-time low of 2 days in 2018, after a decline from 4 to 2 days in 2017, continuing their downward trend since 2012.

Vækstfonden (The Danish Growth Fund) is a government backed investment fund created in 1992. Vækstfonden offers guarantees and loans to established SMEs and entrepreneurs, invests equity in young companies with growth potential, and engages in fund-of-funds activities by investing in venture and small/mid-cap funds.

The amount of government loan guarantees and government-guaranteed loans developed in opposite directions between 2012 and 2017. The issuance of government loan guarantees in most years decreased while a continuously higher proportion was accounted for by government-guaranteed loans. However, the trend reversed between 2017 and 2018. Government loan guarantees issued to SMEs increased from a total loan amount of DKK 514 million in 2017 to DKK 529 million in 2018, while the amount of government guaranteed loans on the other hand decreased from DKK 1 377 million in 2017 to DKK 1 225 million 2018.

Table 12.1. Scoreboard of Denmark

Indicator	Unit	2007	2008	2009	2010	2011	2012	2013	2014	2015	2016	2017	2018
Debt													
Outstanding business loans, total	DKK billion	732	809	814	812	809	830	860	914	940	989	1 033	1 080
New business lending, total	DKK billion	332	385	318	313	292	241	303	474	519	508	521	568
New business lending, SMEs	DKK billion	41	35	28	35	34	39	37	55	73	51	52	49
Share of new SME lending	% of total new lending	12.29	9.15	8.96	11.21	11.70	16.25	12.07	11.51	14.10	10.12	10.08	8.62
New short-term loans, SMEs	DKK billion	26	26	22	23	24	20	22	34	35	31	29	27
New long-term loans, SMEs	DKK billion	14	9	6	23	10	19	15	21	38	21	23	22
Share of short-term SME lending	% of total SME lending	64.70	74.57	78.79	50.00	70.53	51.49	60.25	62.38	48.48	60.00	55.63	55.09
Government loan guarantees, SMEs	DKK million	210	178	209	769	1 192	1 222	783	658	668	620	514	529
Government guaranteed loans, SMEs	DKK million	..	..	..	..	17	61	286	746	1 076	1 257	1 377	1 225
Interest rate, SMEs	%	5.97	6.59	5.33	4.39	4.38	3.91	3.78	3.44	2.99	2.74	2.36	2.27
Interest rate, large firms	%	5.23	5.68	3.63	2.49	2.40	2.14	1.73	1.65	1.53	1.34	1.23	0.98
Interest rate spread	% points	0.75	0.91	1.70	1.90	1.97	1.77	2.04	1.79	1.45	1.40	1.12	1.29
Non-bank finance													
Venture and growth capital	DKK million	263	205	159	280	186	270	241	230	339	554	532	684
Venture and growth capital (growth rate)	%. Year-on-year growth rate	..	-22.34	-22.45	76.57	-33.49	45.13	-10.81	-4.73	47.66	63.33	-4.03	28.65
Other indicators													
Payment delays, B2B	Number of days	7.2	6.1	12.0	12.0	13.0	12.0	10.0	9.0	4.0	4.0	2.0	2.0
Bankruptcies, SMEs	Number	..	..	2 563	2 583	1 938	1 958	1 698	1 328	1 584	1 853	1 888	2 013
Bankruptcies, SMEs (growth rate)	%. Year-on-year growth rate	..	..	..	0.78	-24.97	1.03	-13.28	-21.79	19.28	16.98	1.89	6.62

The full country profile is available at

https://doi.org/10.1787/061fe03d-en

13. Estonia

In 2017, Estonian SMEs employed 79% of the workforce and accounted for 79.2% of total value added. 91.6% of all firms were micro-enterprises, i.e. firms with less than 10 employees, employing 34% of the workforce and accounting for 29.9% of total value added in 2017.

Lending to Estonian SMEs contracted significantly in the aftermath of the financial crisis, with new SME loans almost halving from EUR 3.6 billion in 2007 to EUR 1.9 billion in 2010. Following the rebound of the Estonian economy, new SME lending began to slowly pick up again after 2011, but remained below pre-crisis levels in 2018, as was the case for outstanding SME loans.

Under the Estonian corporate income tax system, all reinvested profits are tax-free. Thus, companies have incentives to reinvest their profits, which may be an explanation for the low demand for loans. Loans under EUR 1 million, which are used as a proxy to describe SME loans, may have become unreliable to depict SME activities. This is because the high inflation rates in recent years may have pushed SMEs to contract larger loans.

The base interest rate on SME loans up to EUR 1 million decreased steadily from 4% in 2012 to slightly below 3% in 2016. After that, interest rates started to increase again reaching 3.28% in 2018. For larger loans, the interest rate has risen for the last three years in a row to 2.12%.

Venture and growth capital has been growing steadily on recent years. Estonia has a well-developed start-up community that has good potential for raising venture capital. The year of 2018 was a record year, with companies raising EUR 329 million, a 21% year-on-year growth.

Leasing and hire purchases turnover declined sharply between 2008 and 2009, and only recovered somewhat in 2011. After that, recovery was stronger and total turnover grew by 13% in 2018. Factoring was also much more important in 2018 than in previous years, reaching EUR 3 billion. This is close to EUR 700 million more than the year before.

Payment delays, bankruptcies and non-performing loans increased sharply in the aftermath of the financial crisis, peaking in 2009-10, but began to level off post-2010. In 2017, non-performing loans amounted to a 1.99% share of total SME loans (slightly higher than the previous year), while SME bankruptcies decreased by 20% year-on-year. The share of non-performing loans in total loans decreased strongly to 0.81%, with SME NPLs slightly increasing from 1.94% to 1.99% in 2018.

The Estonian government provides loan guarantees to all types of companies. Government loan guarantee volumes have been much higher in recent years than in the past (especially over 2007-08), but have overall followed an erratic pattern since 2009. In 2018, government loan guarantees to SMEs increased by 18.5%, and so did total guaranteed loans. Higher economic activity also improves demand for guarantees.

KredEx, a state owned financing institution, remains an investor in several fund- of-funds. The Baltic Innovation Fund, which has been running since 2012, in the EstFund, since 2016, offering private and venture capital. KredEx also provides the management of the fund-of-funds Early Fund II via the subsidiary AS SmartCap. With the support of these funds, a total of nearly EUR 700 million is being invested in the rapidly developing companies of the region.

Table 13.1. Scoreboard for Estonia

Indicator	Unit	2007	2008	2009	2010	2011	2012	2013	2014	2015	2016	2017	2018
Debt													
Outstanding business loans, SMEs	EUR billion	2.44	2.49	2.13	1.90	1.68	1.61	1.65	1.70	1.67	1.71	1.81	1.70
Outstanding business loans, total	EUR billion	6.80	7.20	6.86	6.46	5.95	6.15	6.25	6.44	6.80	7.34	6.93	7.17
Share of SME outstanding loans	% of total outstanding business loans	35.83	34.55	31.01	29.37	28.28	26.24	26.45	26.40	24.56	23.23	26.1	23.7
New business lending, total	EUR billion	8.55	7.31	4.46	4.26	5.06	5.61	6.17	6.41	6.68	6.99	7.19	7.92
New business lending, SMEs	EUR billion	3.60	3.52	2.13	1.87	1.96	2.12	2.37	2.46	2.25	2.37	2.55	2.63
Share of new SME lending	% of total new lending	42.09	48.21	47.70	43.82	38.63	37.80	38.43	38.42	33.73	33.84	35.5	33.26
Short-term loans, SMEs	EUR million	480.53	475.13	377.13	317.84	325.92	302.35	317.41	333.41	300.81	314.86	320.18	299
Long-term loans, SMEs	EUR billion	1.96	2.01	1.75	1.58	1.36	1.31	1.34	1.37	1.37	1.39	1.49	1.40
Share of short-term SME lending	% of total SME lending	19.73	19.09	17.74	16.76	19.39	18.74	19.20	19.62	18.00	18.46	17.7	17.63
Government loan guarantees, SMEs	EUR million	15	23	52	66	53	60	52	66	66	93	61	72
Government guaranteed loans, SMEs	EUR million	27	39	86	122	116	122	100	111	112	171	100	118
Non-performing loans, total	% of all business loans	0.61	3.71	8.76	8.53	5.91	3.79	2.01	1.97	1.56	1.62	1.35	0.81
Non-performing loans, SMEs	% of all SME loans	0.95	3.59	7.36	8.17	6.31	5.18	3.27	2.96	2.79	2.88	1.94	1.99
Interest rate, SMEs	%	6.11	6.71	5.34	5.06	4.92	4.02	3.41	3.36	3.04	2.96	2.99	3.28
Interest rate, large firms	%	5.68	6.13	4.21	3.90	3.76	3.05	2.86	2.68	2.05	2.08	2.12	2.13
Interest rate spread	% points	0.43	0.58	1.14	1.16	1.16	0.98	0.56	0.68	0.99	0.88	0.87	1.15
Non-bank finance													
Venture and growth capital	EUR million	..	4.74	4.51	17.8	5.53	16.6	10.9	68.7	96. 6	105.7	272.6	329
Venture and growth capital (growth rate)	%, Year-on-year growth rate	..	..	- 5.00	293.72	- 68.84	200.24	- 34.34	530	40.6	9.4	157.9	20.7
Leasing and hire purchases	EUR million	891.17	709.63	222.77	281.29	519.37	649.60	545.75	537.16	543	676	718	811
Factoring and invoicing	EUR billion	1.29	1.41	0.99	0.91	1.13	1.92	1.98	2.09	2.239	2.09	2.29	3 034
Other indicators													
Payment delays, B2B	Number of days	9	8.1	12.7	12.8	10.2	10.1	9.4	7	6.9	6	5.5	..
Bankruptcies, SMEs	Number	202	423	1055	1028	623	495	459	428	376	335	343	273
Bankruptcies, SMEs (growth rate)	%, Year-on-year growth rate	..	109.41	149.41	- 2.56	- 39.40	- 20.55	- 7.27	- 6.75	- 12.15	- 10.90	2.39	-20.41

The full country profile is available at

https://doi.org/10.1787/061fe03d-en

14. Finland

The Finnish economy continued to grow in 2018. The uncertainty in the global economy, however, slowed down exports and corporate investments. Low interest rates supported investments and the availability of SME financing.

In Finland, 99.3% of all employer firms were SMEs in 2017 (84 043 SMEs), employing 66.6% of the labour force. The vast majority of them (76.5%) were micro-enterprises with less than 10 employees. The decline in the number of employer firms levelled off in 2017 after a few years of downswing, whereas the number of self-employed has been increasing.

The volume of new lending to SMEs continued to increase in 2018, almost approaching the pre-crisis level. New business lending to SMEs grew by 5.5% in 2018 in comparison to the previous year. Meanwhile, total new lending to all enterprises declined by 2.2%. SMEs' strong demand for loans was supported by the bright economic situation and positive expectations regarding economic growth in Finland in 2018.

The base rate on small loans of up to EUR 1 million, which is used as an interest rate proxy for loans to SME, remained quite stable during 2010–2017, with the average interest rate at around 2.8%. In 2018, the interest rate on small loans increased to 3.9%. On the other hand, the interest rate charged on loans over EUR 1 million has remained at around 1.3% for three consecutive years. The widening of credit spread between small and large business loans indicates a tightening of credit terms for SMEs compared to large enterprises.

A record-high figure of EUR 479 million was invested into start-ups and early stage growth companies in Finland in 2018. Of the total sum, foreign investments accounted for EUR 291 million. Finnish Venture Capital (VC) funds invested EUR 101 million and business angels invested EUR 36 million. Foreign VC funds allocated EUR 103 million of direct investments into Finnish companies. The amounts of investments from both Finnish and foreign VC funds has grown significantly from the previous year.

Ample availability of bank financing lowered the demand for public sector financing from Finnvera. Finnvera is a financing company owned by the government of Finland and the country's official export credit agency. The volume of direct government loans to SMEs has decreased yearly since 2015 from EUR 385 million to EUR 203 million. Moreover, the introduction of EU guarantee programmes targeted at SMEs has increased availability of SME loans intermediated by banks and reduced the demand for loans provided by Finnvera.

Table 14.1. Scoreboard for Finland

Indicator	Unit	2007	2008	2009	2010	2011	2012	2013	2014	2015	2016	2017	2018
Debt													
Outstanding business loans, total	EUR billion	48.4	57.6	54.1	56.5	60.4	63.3	66.7	68.4	72.5	76.0	78.1	85.3
New business lending, total	EUR billion	42.7	54.4	50.9	54.4	37.4	34.9	39.5	35.6	35.0	36.4	37.1	36.3
New business lending, SMEs	EUR billion	11.6	11.9	9.9	8.3	7.9	7.7	7.3	6.8	8.4	9.1	9.6	10.1
Share of new SME lending	% of total new lending	27.11	21.85	19.56	15.25	21.11	22.23	18.55	19.21	24.14	24.92	25.90	29.95
Short-term loans, SMEs	EUR million	..	..	..	839	1 615	1 613	1 312	1 250	1 655	1 864	2 046	2 384
Long-term loans, SMEs	EUR million	..	..	..	3 314	6 287	6 136	6 018	5 583	6 789	7 219	7 561	7 747
Share of short-term SME lending	% of total SME lending	..	..	..	20.20	20.44	20.82	17.90	18.29	19.60	20.52	21.30	23.53
Government loan guarantees, SMEs	EUR million	416	438	474	447	497	408	379	476	522	570	540	563
Direct government loans, SMEs	EUR million	385	468	593	397	369	342	284	287	385	275	241	203
Non-performing loans, total	% of all business loans	..	..	..	..	..	..	..	..	4.07	3.07	2.68	3.72
Non-performing loans, total (amount)	EUR million	..	..	..	..	..	..	..	..	1 423	1 119	994	3 170
Interest rate, SMEs	%	5.39	5.58	3.02	2.66	3.23	2.86	2.81	2.94	2.96	2.76	2.75	3.92
Interest rate, large firms	%	4.83	5.08	2.24	1.86	2.59	2.07	1.91	1.92	1.46	1.33	1.35	1.34
Interest rate spread	% points	0.56	0.50	0.78	0.80	0.64	0.79	0.90	1.02	1.50	1.43	1.40	2.58
Collateral, SMEs	% of SMEs needing collateral to obtain bank lending	..	..	..	33	34	35	41	41	38	35	34	31
Percentage of SME loan applications	SME loan applications/ total number of SMEs	..	..	13.85	18.42	20.79	21.50	21.85	27.70	21.97	23.89	19.99	20.35
Rejection rate	1-(SME loans authorised/ requested)	..	..	6.98	4.92	3.12	8.08	7.06	6.71	6.24	5.59	6.76	4.15
Non-bank finance													
Venture and growth capital	EUR million	144	191	119	319	120	149	133	134	175	203	207	315
Venture and growth capital (growth rate)	%, year-on-year growth rate	..	32.6	-37.7	168.1	-62.4	25.0	-10.7	1.0	30.6	16.0	2.0	52.2
Leasing and hire purchases	EUR million	..	..	1 067	1 361	1 566	1 765	1 658	1 858	..	..	..	..
Other indicators													
Payment delays, B2B	Number of days	6	5	7	7	7	7	6	6	5	5	5	5
Bankruptcies, SMEs	Number	2 254	2 612	3 275	2 864	2 947	2 961	3 131	2 986	2 574	2 408	2 160	2 534
Bankruptcies, SMEs (growth rate)	%, year-on-year growth rate	..	15.9	25.4	-12.5	2.9	0.5	5.7	-4.6	-13.8	-6.4	-10.3	17.3

The full country profile is available at

https://doi.org/10.1787/061fe03d-en

15. France

France has approximately 4 million small and medium enterprises (SMEs). They account for 99.9% of all enterprises.

Outstanding SME loans increased by more than 4.3% between 2017 and 2018, reaching EUR 254 135 million in 2018. After having decreased between 2014 and 2017, the spread between interest rates charged to SMEs and to large firms increased in 2018, reaching 0.45 percentage points. Furthermore, SMEs' access to bank lending remains high: 88% of SMEs' requests for cash credits were fully or almost fully granted as of Q4 2018.

Private equity investments in French firms have continued to increase in 2018 to EUR 14.7 billion, up 2.8% compared to 2017. The average yearly growth rate over 2013-2018 is around 16.4%.

Factoring volumes have continuously increased in France since 2009.

Payment delays reached 13.3 days in 2015, the highest since the crisis, and have been steadily decreasing since 2015 to just under 11 days in 2018.

For the third year since recovery, the number of SME bankruptcies has remained under 60 000, staying stable over 2017-2018 at around 54 000.

In terms of government policies responding to the financing constraints faced by SMEs, in 2018, credit mediation continued to assist French enterprises via an online platform. In line with the trend from 2017, the number of requests has continued to decrease in comparison with previous years, partly due to the better dynamism of economic growth, as well as to the overall global easing of access to bank financing. The share of mediation applications that are accepted stabilised at around 66% in 2018.

The Government is also involved in reducing business-to-business payment delays. The transparency, anti-corruption and economic modernisation law enacted in December 2016 strengthened the legislative framework to fight against business-to-business payment delays. The maximum fine for firms that do not respect legal payment delays was raised to two million. Moreover, a "name and shame" procedure was introduced. Henceforth, there is a systematic advertising of decisions on fines on the website of the Ministry of Economy and Finance. As a result, three firms were required to pay record fines of more than EUR 500 000 in 2018. It remains the case that the largest firms are responsible for the largest payment delays. While the longest delays (superior to 30 days) have decreased in number since 2017, the share of firms with timely payments has decreased from 44% to 41.8%.

Better access to financing for very small firms has also been the focus of public policy. Since 2016, Bpifrance has distributed online development loans to address the investment financing needs of firms from 3 to 50 employees with tangible and intangible investment projects. This measure, implemented in some regions, is being expanded and diversified in certain regions. In addition, the Banque de France set up a network of correspondents in every region since 2016 to break the isolation of entrepreneurs and to solve financing issues.

Table 15.1. Scoreboard for France

Indicator	Unit	2007	2008	2009	2010	2011	2012	2013	2014	2015	2016	2017	2018
Debt													
Outstanding business loans, SMEs	EUR Billion	180.5	189.1	189.6	199.7	210.3	214.0	216.5	219.2	224.2	232.8	243.7	254.1
Outstanding business loans, total	EUR Billion	868.5	927.1	938.4	974.0	1012.2	1009.6	1025.9	1036.0	1078.2	1130.0	1193.7	1257.2
Share of SME outstanding loans	% of total outstanding business loans	20.78	20.40	20.21	20.50	20.77	21.20	21.11	21.16	20.80	20.60	20.41	20.21
New business lending, total	EUR Billion	86.4	67.6	-9.5	9.1	34.6	7.8	1.6	18.9	35.0	43.8	56.1	58.7
Outstanding short-term loans, SMEs	EUR Billion	43.1	42.7	37.5	38.1	40.3	41.1	42.8	43.3	43.5	43.9	44.7	44.9
Outstanding long-term loans, SMEs	EUR Billion	115.2	123.3	127.8	134.4	142.6	146.5	146.3	148.6	151.9	158.6	166.7	175.8
Share of short-term SME lending	% of total SME lending	27.20	25.70	22.70	22.09	22.05	21.91	22.65	22.55	22.27	21.66	21.15	20.33
Government loan guarantees, SMEs	EUR Billion	5.9	6.9	11.3	11.9	9.8	8.5	8.9	7.8	8.0	8.4	8.9	8.7
Government guaranteed loans, SMEs	EUR Billion	2.7	3.2	5.8	5.3	4.2	4.2	4.4	4.8	5.0	5.2	5.1	3.7
Non-performing loans, total	% of all business loans	3.70	3.66	4.71	4.56	3.96	4.06	4.25	4.14	4.05	3.90	3.62	3.28
Interest rate, SMEs	%	5.10	5.42	2.86	2.48	3.11	2.43	2.16	2.08	1.78	1.50	1.40	1.48
Interest rate, large firms	%	4.52	4.76	1.96	1.57	2.23	1.72	1.46	1.30	1.19	1.14	1.10	1.03
Interest rate spread	% points	0.58	0.66	0.90	0.91	0.89	0.71	0.70	0.78	0.59	0.35	0.30	0.45
Collateral, SMEs	% of SMEs needing collateral to obtain bank lending	..	..	..	..	..	9.42	8.52	7.28	6.33	5.17	4.34	4.22
Percentage of SME loan applications	SME loan applications/ total number of SMEs	..	..	..	..	..	38.42	35.64	35.73	37.88	37.90	37.17	36.72
Rejection rate	1-(SME loans authorised/ requested)	..	..	..	..	..	11.12	8.00	6.61	7.55	6.21	5.14	4.36
Utilisation rate	SME loans used/ authorised	87.69	87.77	87.17	86.37	87.03	87.64	87.32	87.49	87.17	86.98	86.76	86.85
Non-bank finance													
Venture and growth capital	EUR Billion	2.0	2.4	2.4	2.9	3.5	2.4	2.5	3.2	4.6	4.7	4.4	5.1
Venture and growth capital (growth rate)	%, Year-on-year growth rate	24.73	21.34	-1.08	22.22	21.34	-32.46	3.35	30.98	42.55	2.54	-7.38	15.87
Leasing and hire purchases	EUR Billion	9.3	9.5	9.0	8.5	8.1	6.6	6.1	5.7	7.1	7.7	7.8	8.1
Factoring and invoice discounting	EUR Billion	21.2	22.5	18.8	20.7	22.5	22.6	24.8	25.6	28.0	31.0	36.1	37.6
Other indicators													
Payment delays, B2B	Number of days	12.18	11.90	11.80	11.98	12.18	11.83	12.08	12.21	13.28	11.90	11.12	10.79
Bankruptcies, SMEs	Number (thousands)	51.3	55.5	63.2	60.3	59.4	61.1	62.5	62.4	63.0	58.0	54.4	54.0
Bankruptcies, SMEs (growth rate)	%, Year-on-year growth rate	..	8.23	13.75	-4.53	-1.39	2.71	2.37	-0.22	0.99	-7.90	-6.14	-0.81

The full country profile is available at

https://doi.org/10.1787/061fe03d-en

16. Georgia

In 2016, pursuant to the National Strategy of SME Development, the Georgian National Statistics office introduced a new methodology and new definitions to gather statistics on the country's SMEs. According to the new methodology, as of 2018, 99.70% of active enterprises in Georgia are SMEs. In total, SMEs account for 63.3% of total private employment and contribute to 53.0% of total business sector turnover and 59.1% (GEL 24.1 million) of value of all production in the business sector (GEL 40.9 million).

In line with the recent economic expansion, credit to SMEs rose significantly year over year, amounting to a staggering 242.1% increase from GEL 938 million in 2010 to GEL 3 211 million in 2018. Throughout this period, total business loans grew more than 176%, and the proportion of SME loans as a percentage of total business loans grew from 36.4% to 45.1%, the highest point over the period.

The average interest rate charged to SMEs in Georgia is high by OECD standards, but has significantly declined over the decade, from 16.5% in 2010 to 12.3% in 2018. However, the interest rate charged to SMEs has been increasing over the last two years, from 9.7% in 2016, to 10.36% in 2017, and finally to 12.3% this year. As a result, the interest rate spread between large enterprises and SMEs grew to 3%, from 1.06% in 2017.

Although precise data on the availability and use of alternative financial instruments is lacking, available evidence strongly suggests that Georgian SMEs are very dependent on the banking sector for meeting their financing needs and that non-bank instruments still play a very marginal role. However, the rapid growth of micro-financing organisations should not be neglected.

According to the World Bank Group's Doing Business indicator, Georgia improved its "ease of doing business" rank to 9th in 2018, and to 6th in 2019. The Ease of Doing Business 2019 report shows that by allowing voluntary value added tax registration at the time of business registration, Georgia reduced its relative gap to the best regulatory performance the most in 2017/18. Previously, entrepreneurs had to make a separate visit to the Revenue Service for value added tax registration after company registration. Georgia also enhanced its existing one-stop shop for business incorporation, allowing entrepreneurs to start a company through a single procedure. Currently, the country has the lowest number of procedures required to start a business and to register a property. In addition to the business registration procedures, Georgia simplified the tax system, and the enforcement of contracts. Paying taxes was made easier by levying income tax on distributed profits rather than on taxable profits.

Georgia facilitated the enforcement of contracts by introducing random and automatic assignment of cases to judges across courts. Most notably, the country improved its insolvency framework by making insolvency proceedings more accessible for debtors and creditors, improving provisions on the treatment of contracts during insolvency, and granting creditors greater participation in important decisions during the proceedings. According to the information from the Public Registry Agency, after a 28% growth in the number of liquidation procedures in 2017, the indicator saw a 47.78% decrease in 2018, reaching 153 cases total.

In 2018, the overall volume of non-performing SME loans exceeded GEL 407 million, the highest level since 2010, and the share of non-performing SMEs loans is now at 6.1%. The lowest level was reached in 2014 when the share of non-performing SMEs loans was 4.2%. Over the past year, the volume of non-performing SME loans increased by 84%, amounting to a 1.8% increase in the share of all SME loans.

Georgia ranks 48th among the 129 economies featured in the Global Innovation Index 2019. Georgia ranks 3rd among the 26 lower middle-income economies and 4th among the 19 economies in Northern Africa and Western Asia. Between 2018 and 2019, the rank increase for Georgia is a mix of improved performance and new availability of innovation-related data. Its most notable gains this year include indicators such as Patent families in two or more offices, High-technology imports, Exports of Information and communication (ICT) services, and Industrial designs by origin.

Government of Georgia has prioritised SME development as the main source of private sector growth, jobs creation and innovation. Among the successful reforms Georgian Government has conducted are the Innovation and Entrepreneurship Policy. Through the budgetary support, in 2014, the Ministry of Economy and Sustainable Development of Georgia established two sister agencies, Georgia's Innovation and Technology Agency (GITA) and Enterprise Georgia, with the main aim of promoting SME development and strengthening SME competitiveness. Both agencies provide financial support to SMEs, as well as a broader range of services that includes access to special infrastructure, mentoring, trainings and various advisory services. In addition to the establishment of these two agencies, the government of Georgia has introduced several private sector development programmes, which include financial and technical assistance components to support small and medium-sized enterprises at different stages of development.

The Global Competitiveness Report 2018 ranks Georgia at 66th place out of 140 economies. Venture capital availability, lack of workforce diversity and low quality of vocational training remain as problematic factors for the Georgian economy. Despite the low global ranking, Georgia tops Eastern Partnership countries in terms of SME access to finance according to the 2016 SME Policy Development Index Dimensions, and is increasing government efforts in this regard. Government initiatives have thus far focused on decreasing entry barriers to SMEs by simplifying business registration, reducing taxes for small businesses and introducing robust regulatory initiatives.

Table 16.1. Scoreboard for Georgia

Indicators	Units	2009	2010	2011	2012	2013	2014	2015	2016	2017	2018
Business loans, SME	GEL million	..	1 400	1 548	1 738	2 051	2 422	3 621	3 992	5 176	6 620
Business loans, total	GEL million	3 097	3 843	4 501	4 989	5 663	6 715	8 433	10 500	12 000	14 687
Business loans, SMEs	% of total business loans	..	36.4	34.4	34.8	36.2	36.1	42.9	38.0	43.1	45.1
Non-Performing Loans, total	GEL million	926	784	667	810	791	988	1 200	1 380	1 337	1 480
Non-performing loans, SMEs	GEL million	..	144	134	111	102	101	161	206	221	407
Non-performing loans, total	% of all business loans	..	16.1	11.5	12.2	10.7	10.6	9.8	10.1	7.7	6.6
Non-performing loans, SMEs	% of total SME loans	..	10.3	8.7	6.4	5	4.2	4.4	5.2	4.3	6.1
Interest rate, SME	%	..	16.50	15.50	14.50	11.60	10.70	12.70	9.70	10.36	12.3
Interest rate, large firms	%	..	13.60	14.10	12.80	11.20	10.00	11.40	9.90	9.30	9.3
Interest rate spread		..	2.90	1.40	1.70	0.40	0.70	1.30	-0.20	1.06	3.0
Collateral, SMEs	%	..	..	..	..	95.6	..	..	..	..	..
Rejection rate	%	..	..	..	..	4.6	..	..	..	..	..
Utilization rate	%	..	..	..	..	95.4	..	..	..	..	..
Procedures of enterprises' liquidation (incl. bankruptcy)	Number	52	2 094	3 176	2 524	1 775	1 785	1 560	229	293	153
Procedures of enterprises' liquidation (incl. bankruptcy)	Year-on-year growth rate (%)	-14.75	3 926.92	51.67	-20.53	-29.68	0.56	-12.61	-85.3	28	-47.78

The full country profile is available at

https://doi.org/10.1787/061fe03d-en

17. Germany

Policy developments

In general, SMEs' access to finance is currently very good in Germany. The continued period of low interest rates has led to favourable conditions for bank finance, which is still the most important source of financing for German SMEs. Thus, the majority of SMEs report no or few difficulties to finance their investments through bank loans. However, where the market supply is not sufficient, the Federal Government provides a wide range of financial instruments to support SMEs, potential entrepreneurs and innovative start-ups so that they can implement new projects, products, processes and services.

A key area of support is broad-based support for start-up and growth projects. The focus in recent years has been on the politically important area of financing innovation and supporting venture capital for start-ups, which has greatly expanded over the last legislative period.

As a result, the German venture capital market has considerably developed over the last years. Thanks to numerous public funding programmes at the federal and the state level, Germany's VC market has observed a very positive development, especially in the early-stage financing of start-ups. In international comparison, however, the German VC market is still relatively small. Particularly in the second and third growth phase (with financing volumes of EUR 50 to 150 million), German start-ups often face a lack of financing opportunities. One reasons for this is that there are still relatively few venture capital funds in Germany that invest in the growth phase. However, an increasing number of funds are emerging with a volume of EUR 500 million or more, which allows for larger financing rounds.

Programmes

Credit-based financing for start-ups

The ERP Special Fund provides for a differentiated and well-established system of promotional loan instruments for different start-up phases. The loan programmes [ERP-Gründerkredit Startgeld] # ERP Start-Up Loan - Start-Up Money, [Gründerkredit Universell] # ERP Start-Up Loan - Universal and [ERP-Kapital für Gründung] # ERP Capital for Start-Ups provide low-interest loans with a long maturity for start-ups as well as business succession. In some of these programmes, banks providing the financing are relieved from a portion of the credit default risk. ERP-Capital for Start-Ups provides subordinated loans with favourable interest rates in order to strengthen the company's equity base and thereby to facilitate further external financing.

ERP-Innovationsfinanzierung # ERP innovation financing

ERP Innovation financing was restructured as of 1 July 2017 with the aim to promote the digital transformation of SMEs by providing an expanded range of innovation financing, with an explicit focus on digitisation projects.

The ERP Digitisation and Innovation Loan serves to finance digitisation and innovation projects as well as investments and working capital for innovative companies. Funding goes to established commercial companies and to professional service providers. The programme has been refined further over the last year and is now also available to business starters and young companies. The funding takes the form of a low-interest loan of up to EUR 25 million per project and up to EUR 7.5 million per financing need of innovative companies. Funding is provided both for investments and for working capital. The bank processing the application can be relieved of up to 70% of its liability.

High-Tech Gründerfonds (HTGF) # High-tech Start-up Fund

The High-tech Start-Up Fund (HTGF) is an early-phase funding programme for highly innovative and technology-oriented companies whose operative business activities started less than three years ago. To be eligible for financing, projects must have shown promising research findings, be based on innovative technology, and the market situation for the product must be bright. In addition to providing capital, the fund ensures that the management of young start-ups receives the necessary help and support. An initial funding amount of up to EUR 1 000 000 is provided, with a total of up to EUR 3 million usually being available per company. In the first phase of the fund (up to November 2011), a total of EUR 272 million was available. The follow-up fund (HTGF II) provides total funding of EUR 304 million. A third fund, HTGF III, was launched in autumn 2017. In addition to the support from the Economic Affairs Ministry and the German Promotional Bank (KfW), more than 30% of the EUR 319.5 million fund has been provided by 33 private investors – either well-established SMEs or large corporations.

Mikromezzaninfonds # Micro-Mezzanine Fund

The Micro-Mezzanine Fund was launched in 2013 and provides dormant equity of up to EUR 50 000 for small companies and business starters and of up to EUR 150 000 for companies within the special target group. The fund's special target group are companies that provide training, are operated by women or people with a migrant background, or were founded by persons who were formerly unemployed. Social enterprises operating commercially are also eligible to apply for financing on the terms of the special target group, as are companies with a focus on environmentally-compatible production. Both the European Social Fund (ESF) and the European Recovery Programme (ERP) finance the fund. The volume of the first fund was EUR 74.5 million. The current fund (MMF II) has a volume of EUR 153.2 million.

KfW Capital (German Promotional Bank Capital)

On the basis of a decision by the Bundestag, the Ministry for Economic Affairs, the Ministry of Finance and the KfW have drafted an overall concept for an organisationally independent, growth-oriented venture capital company; it started operations as "KfW Capital" in October 2018. KfW plans to double the annual amount of funding provided by KfW Capital to EUR 200 million by 2020. This initially takes place primarily via investments in venture capital funds, particularly as part of the ERP-VC Fund Investments programme, which has been in place since 2015. In addition, KfW Capital is a partner in the High-tech Start-up Fund and coparion. Finally, KfW Capital aims to improve the quality of the venture capital funding. The aim is to develop a product structure in which the individual financing phases are coordinated throughout the entire company lifecycle. In total, the expansion should result in funding commitments of around EUR 2 billion in the next ten years or so.

Venture Tech Growth Financing

At the end of 2018, the KfW programme Venture Tech Growth Financing commenced operations. As part of this programme, the German Promotional Bank (KfW) can issue EUR 50 million of venture capital loans to innovative fast-growing tech companies each year. Over the entire funding period, EUR 500 million in funding will be made available together with private-sector investors to start-ups in the growth phase.

INVEST–Zuschuss für Wagniskapital # INVEST – Grant for Venture Capital

INVEST is a grant programme run by the Federal Ministry for Economic Affairs and Energy. It has been set up in 2013 and was further developed in 2017 to support private investors who want to acquire a stake in young and innovative companies. Under this programme, business angels that invest in innovative start-ups receive an acquisition grant worth 20% of the sum invested. In addition, natural persons can receive an exit grant if they sell their shares. The amount provided is equivalent to 25% of the capital gains from the sale and thus more or less covers the tax imposed on the profit from the sale. The shares must be held for a minimum of three years. Both grants are tax-free for the investor. Funding can be provided for a maximum of EUR 500 000 of investment per investor and per year. The maximum amount eligible for funding that can be invested in a single company per year is EUR 3 million.

18. Greece

99.9% (almost 100%) of Greek enterprises are SMEs, and the majority of SMEs are micro-enterprises. On average, micro-enterprises contribute more to employment and add more value in Greece than in other European countries.

The financial crisis and the ensuing sovereign debt crisis has had a profound impact on the Greek economy since 2010.

Bank funding dried up for Greek SMEs in the aftermath of the financial crisis. In 2009, new lending shrank more than a tenfold from 2007 and 2008 levels. Although lending to SMEs recovered somewhat in 2010, data show a clear downward path in SME lending over the 2011-16 period. In 2016, new loans to SMEs more than halved compared to 2014. In 2017, however, SME lending slightly increased, following a 7-year period of consistent decline. The same trend further continued in 2018. Nevertheless, SME lending volumes were still far below their 2008-09 levels.

The SME interest rate has decreased in recent years, but remains much higher compared to other Eurozone economies, illustrating that the accommodative stance of the European Central Bank (ECB) has had relatively little impact on Greek SMEs. The interest rate spread between SMEs and large firms remained stable in 2017 compared to 2016 but increased in 2018, as the reduction of large firms' interest rate was higher than the reduction of SME interest rates during this period (2014-2018).

Leasing and hire purchases also decreased severely as a result of the economic crisis and remained well below pre-crisis levels in 2017. By contrast, factoring and invoice discounting activities have remained relatively stable over 2008-17. They increased strongly in 2018, following a more moderate increase over 2014-2017.

The Greek government operates a number of loan guarantee programmes. These programmes gained pace between 2010 and 2011, but the sovereign debt crisis prevented Greece from continuing such support in 2012. As a result, loan guarantees declined 50% that year, and have continued to decline ever since. The Greek government announced various actions in 2017, such as the establishment of the Intermediate Entrepreneurship Fund and the Western Macedonian's Regional Development Fund. These funds complement The Entrepreneurship Fund II and The Energy Saving Fund II established in 2016 and started to provide loans in 2018. Both finds use European Structural Investment Funds and national financial sources, as well as programmes for the provision of short-term and long-term export credit insurance to SMEs.

The government also supports equity financing through minority participation in venture capital funds, venture capital companies, and similar vehicles. Additionally, the Greek Government, with the cooperation of the European Investment Fund, announced the launch of EquiFund in 2016, a private equity fund since 2018 invests in high value-added and innovative early and growth stage companies.

Furthermore, various legislative tools continue to be used by the Government with the cooperation of the Central Bank of Greece to address the serious increase of non-performing loans (NPLs) among Greek SMEs.

In 2019 and according to Law 4608/2019, the Greek government established the Hellenic Development Bank (HDB), which took place through the transformation and administrative capacity building of two existing entities, the Hellenic Fund for Entrepreneurship and Development S.A. (ETEAN S.A.) and its subsidiary, the New Economy Development Fund S.A. (TANEO SA). HDB's scope is to improve SMEs' access to finance, to foster innovation, to facilitate investments in infrastructure, to encourage equity investments and other alternative financing sources and to provide business support to SMEs, mainly through shared-risk loans and guarantee facilities, as well as financial expertise to the public sector. The first phase of transformation was completed in April 2019, with the adoption of the new legal framework (Law 4608/2019). The second phase is estimated to be completed by the end of 2019. HDB will deploy a list of new products by using both public and private funds for the support of SMEs within the next five years. HDB will target projects that will have an impact on sustainable growth, regional development, job creation and investments, while at the same time being financially autonomous and sustainable.

Table 18.1. Scoreboard for Greece

Indicator	Unit	2007	2008	2009	2010	2011	2012	2013	2014	2015	2016	2017	2018
					Debt								
Outstanding business loans, SMEs	EUR billion	..	..	..	44.9	41.6	39.1	48.1	48.1	46.9	48.4	44.7	41.1
Outstanding business loans, total	EUR billion	102	124	124	117	113	101	97	95	89	88	82	76.4
Share of SME outstanding loans	% of total outstanding business loans	..	..	..	38.5	36.8	38.8	49.7	50.6	52.6	55.3	54.4	53.8
New business lending, total	EUR billion	..	36.5	36.3	20.7	29.4	21.8	24.3	14.9	6.9	5.8	7.3	11.4
New business lending, SMEs	EUR billion	..	12.5	13.0	4.4	5.2	4.1	3.7	2.3	1.2	1.1	1.1	1.2
Share of new SME lending	% of total new lending	..	34.2	35.6	21.4	17.8	18.9	15.0	15.6	17.0	18.4	15.5	10.18
Outstanding short-term loans, SMEs	EUR billion	..	..	..	..	..	..	..	18.1	17.6	18.8	17.0	15.1
Outstanding long-term loans, SMEs	EUR billion	..	..	..	..	..	..	..	30.1	29.3	29.6	27.7	25.9
Share of short-term SME lending	% of total SME lending	..	..	..	..	..	..	..	37.6	37.6	38.9	38.0	58.4
Government loan guarantees, SMEs	EUR billion	..	..	..	..	..	..	0.37	0.31	0.24	0.56	1.08	1.2
Non-performing loans, total	% of all business loans	4.60	4.30	6.70	8.70	14.2	23.4	31.8	29.4	31.0	30.3	30.5	32.5
Non-performing loans, SMEs	% of all SME loans	..	..	..	..	..	..	..	41.2	44.1	43.2	..	..
Interest rate, SMEs	%	6.57	6.82	4.62	5.53	6.77	6.87	6.51	5.80	5.38	5.32	4.91	4.64
Interest rate, large firms	%	5.32	5.71	3.52	4.27	5.74	5.92	5.77	5.55	4.82	4.61	4.20	3.81
Interest rate spread	% points	1.25	1.11	1.10	1.26	1.03	0.95	0.74	0.25	0.56	0.71	0.71	0.83
Collateral, SMEs	% of SMEs needing collateral to obtain bank lending	..	..	51.4	40.5	49.4	46.7	45.9	46.2	49.2	39.8	25.7	20.7
Percentage of SME loan applications	SME loan applications/ total number of SMEs	..	..	37.9	39.6	30.8	29.9	21.4	25.5	18.8	21.5	17.5	23.0
Rejection rate	1-(SME loans authorised/	..	..	25.8	24.5	33.8	28.3	26.0	21.5	19.9	18.2	16.2	20.5

Indicator	Unit	2007	2008	2009	2010	2011	2012	2013	2014	2015	2016	2017	2018
	requested)												
Utilisation rate	SME loans used/ authorised	..	..	..	..	..	..	..	..	..	..	..	..
Non-bank finance													
Venture and growth capital	EUR million	19.0	32.7	16.7	25.0	10.1	..	4.8	12.6	36.8	38.0	44.5	83.2
Venture and growth capital (growth rate)	%, Year-on-year growth rate	..	72	-49	50	-60	..	..	160	193	3	17	86.9
Leasing and hire purchases	EUR billion	7.28	7.87	7.50	7.28	6.85	6.22	3.36	4.08	4.72	4.40	4.25	3.96
Factoring and invoice discounting	EUR billion	1.28	1.73	1.77	1.73	1.49	1.53	1.41	1.69	1.69	1.72	1.74	1.93
Other indicators													
Payment delays, B2B	Number of days	..	25	34	30	35	40	43	41	36	47	47.	33
Bankruptcies, SMEs	Number	513	359	355	355	445	415	392	330	189	108	123	114
Bankruptcies, SMEs (growth rate)	%, Year-on-year growth rate	..	-30	-1	0	25	-7	-6	-16	-43	-43	14	-7

The full country profile is available at

https://doi.org/10.1787/061fe03d-en

19. Hungary

According to the preliminary data of the Hungarian Central Statistical Office, at the end of 2017, 724 000 enterprises operated in Hungary, 99.86% of which — i.e. 723 000 enterprises — qualified as SMEs.

In 2018, the Hungarian economy expanded at an exceptional rate, exceeding analysts' expectations. The swift rise of Hungarian GDP was substantially influenced by corporate investment growth. In parallel with output and investments, the loans taken out by companies increased more than predicted during the year.

Corporate credit increased by 13.5 per cent annual growth rate in 2018. Half of the expansion was linked to the SME sector. Loans to SMEs rose by 10 percent year-on-year, within which the micro-firm segment expanded the most, with a 14% year-on-year increase.

Banking competition intensified according to Hungarian National Bank's (MNB) report. This trend was accompanied by an improvement in economic prospects and an easing of credit terms. Based on the banks' responses to the Lending Survey, credit conditions were eased for all corporate size categories in the fourth quarter, which mainly affected non-price conditions.

The Funding for Growth Scheme and the Market-based Lending Scheme both contributed to incentivising the SME lending market, however they did not have any significant impact on the lending structure in 2018. Based on the experience gained from these, at the beginning of 2019 the MNB will launch the Funding for Growth Scheme Fix (FGS fix) with more targeted features: a total amount of HUF 1 000 billion to finance new investments by SMEs.

The interest rate on small-amount HUF loans has remained unchanged. There was no major change in the average interest rate of forint loans below EUR 1 million, as they came in at 2.44 per cent, respectively.

2018 was one of the most active years in the history of the Hungarian venture capital and private equity market. Not only the number of transactions but also the total amount invested increased significantly. The majority of transactions were made at the seed stage.

The proportion of guaranteed loans and the ratio of government-backed loan guarantees to GDP is at an exceptionally high level in Hungary, in comparison to other European countries.

Table 19.1. Scoreboard for Hungary

Indicator	Unit	2007	2008	2009	2010	2011	2012	2013	2014	2015	2016	2017	2018
Debt													
Outstanding business loans, SMEs	HUF Billion	5 280	5 823	5 379	4 783	4 797	5 014	5 064	4 831	4 942	4 889	4 802	5 296
Outstanding business loans, total	HUF Billion	8 466	9 613	8 959	8 770	8 825	7 892	7 648	7 761	7 355	7 073	7 545	8 562
Share of SME outstanding loans	% of total outstanding business loans	62.36	60.58	60.05	54.54	54.36	63.53	66.21	62.25	67.20	69.13	63.65	61.86
New business lending, SMEs	HUF Billion	3 851	4 384	3 660	3 531	3 585	3 870	4 662	4 302	3 665	4 187	4 443	3 743
Short-term loans, SMEs	HUF Billion	2 473	2 966	2 832	2 775	2 767	3 052	2 654	2 570	2 424	2 708	2 727	2 002

Indicator	Unit	2007	2008	2009	2010	2011	2012	2013	2014	2015	2016	2017	2018
Long-term loans, SMEs	HUF Billion	1 377	1 418	828	756	818	818	2 008	1 732	1 241	1 478	1 274	1 741
Share of short-term SME lending	% of total SME lending	64.23	67.66	77.37	78.59	77.18	78.86	56.93	59.75	66.14	64.69	68.16	53.48
Government loan guarantees, SMEs	HUF Billion	308.8	352.1	409.2	377.1	343.4	251.9	350.0	346.2	348.7	469.3	525.7	725.5
Government guaranteed loans, SMEs	HUF Billion	381.4	436.4	600.3	472.0	437.2	314.8	458.0	433.8	429.4	568.6	731.0	894.2
Non-performing loans, total (amount)	HUF Billion	..	..	..	832	1 155	1 272	1 124	961	697	577	526	472
Non-performing loans, total	% of all business loans	3.10	4.70	10.10	12.8	17.4	17.7	16.1	13.7	9.6	5.4	3.3	5.5
Non-performing loans, SMEs	% of all SME loans		5.40	8.90	12.8	15.9	20.5	18.6	20.7	13.7	6.3	4.4	3.8
Interest rate, SMEs	%	10.19	11.25	12.31	8.99	9.38	9.7	7.4	5.1	4.7	4.2	3.3	2.44
Interest rate, large firms	%	8.97	10.28	11.07	..	..	8.9	5.9	4.1	2.4	2.8	1.8	2.0
Interest rate spread	% points	1.22	0.97	1.24	..	..	0.80	1.50	1.00	2.30	1.40	1.50	0.44
Collateral, SMEs	% of SMEs needing collateral to obtain bank lending	..	..	..	..	..	..	..	71	64.5	60.1	53.4	..
Rejection rate	1-(SME loans authorised/ requested)	..	..	..	..	..	..	68.8	67	84.4	71.6	49.2	..
Utilisation rate	SME loans used/ authorised	..	..	..	..	..	..	81.5	..	..	..	..	..
Non-bank finance													
Venture and growth capital	HUF Million	3 949	13 782	720	6 982	11 308	19 361	15 880	18 759	27 742	12 070	11 470	28.6
Venture and growth capital (growth rate)	%, Year-on-year growth rate	..	249.00	-94.78	869.72	61.96	71.22	-17.98	18.13	47.89	-56.49	-4.97	149.88
Leasing and hire purchases	HUF Million	..	..	..	..	..	..	..	..	..	274 766	243 743	
Factoring and invoicing	HUF Million	..	..	..	..	..	..	..	..	..	126 038	25 951	
Other indicators													
Payment delays, B2B	Number of days	16.30	19.00	19.00	15.00	22.00	20.00	..	17.40	17.40	..	..	
Bankruptcies, total	Number	153	168	212	232	279	301	376	644	488	377	322	401
Bankruptcies, total (growth rate)	%, Year-on-year growth rate	..	10.35	25.65	9.5	20.4	7.9	24.7	71.3	-24.2	-22.9	-14.4	24.34

The full country profile is available at

https://doi.org/10.1787/061fe03d-en

20. Indonesia

Based on data published by Ministry of Cooperatives and SMEs of Republic of Indonesia, there were 64 194 057 SMEs in 2018, which made up 99.99% of the total business population and employed more than 116 million people. In this report, SMEs consist of micro, small and medium-sized enterprises.

Outstanding loans to all businesses stood at IDR 5 931.61 trillion in 2018, with 19.68% of that amount (IDR 1 167.45 trillion) allocated to SMEs. Outstanding loans continued to grow in double digits in the past eight years (2011-18), with an average yearly growth rate of 16.42%. Outstanding loans to SMEs also rose by 14.82% in this period.

Despite total outstanding loans increasing significantly, non-performing loans (NPLs) remained under 5%. In fact, in the last three years (2016-18), NPLs have been declining both for SMEs (from 4.05% to 3.35%) and for total business (from 2.96% to 2.40%).

The share of short-term loans fell by 16.29% in the 2011-18 period, from IDR 120.80 trillion in 2011 to IDR 101.11 trillion in 2018. Meanwhile long-term loans in the same period grew by 192.49% from IDR 235.9 trillion in 2011 to IDR 1 038.05 trillion in 2018, with a yearly average of around 17.58%. The increasing trend in long-term loans illustrates lenders' higher trust in Indonesian SMEs.

In the period of 2011-2018, interest rates on loans declined for all business, from 14.53% to 12.69% for SMEs and 1.27 percentage points for large company from 12.28% to 11.01%. Interest rates are declining in Indonesia but are still very high compared to the average in other countries.

Financing distributed by the Venture Capital Company shows a significant increase, reaching out IDR 8.46 trillion in 2018, a 94.59% increase compared to 2012. Every year in the 2012-2018 period, the amount of financing grew constantly, with an average growth rate of 13.02%.

Other non-bank finance indicators also gained momentum. Leasing and hire purchases increased by 7.01% in 2018. This indicator shows around 207.54% growth in total during the 2007-2018 periods. Factoring activities exhibit similar trends. During 2007-2018, factoring experienced strong growth (603.80%). Factoring increased by around 16.28% in 2018.

Most SMEs in Indonesia are experiencing problems in accessing financing. Based on this observation, Indonesian Government launched a financing scheme called People Business Credit Programme or Kredit Usaha Rakyat (KUR) in 2007. KUR's objective is to increase SMEs access to finance and works as a bridge for SMEs to obtain a financing scheme from a financial institution. A total of IDR 499.32 trillion have been allocated as part of this programme during 2007-18 and distributed to all provinces in Indonesia. KUR has managed to maintain high-quality credit, with a very low NPL rate. In 2018, the NPL rate for KUR stood at just 0.24%.

Table 20.1. Scoreboard for Indonesia

Indicator	Unit	2007	2008	2009	2010	2011	2012	2013	2014	2015	2016	2017	2018
Debt													
Outstanding business loans, SMEs	IDR trillion	110.1	127.0	127.4	389.0	476.8	551.5	637.3	733.0	792.1	952.2	1 059.2	1 167.5
Outstanding business loans, total	IDR trillion	1 001.9	1 307.7	1 307.8	1 777.8	2 217.5	2 726.8	3 321.2	3 707.7	4 093.9	4 908.4	5 320.1	5 931.6
Share of SME outstanding loans	% of total outstanding business loans	10.99	9.71	10.20	21.86	21.46	20.19	19.15	19.74	19.32	19.38	19.90	19.68
Outstanding short-term loans, SMEs	IDR trillion	..	..	..	102.6	120.8	141.7	195.0	215.4	100.1	115.0	94.3	101.11
Outstanding long-term loans, SMEs	IDR trillion	..	..	..	286.1	354.9	408.7	440.9	516.5	623.8	729.0	901.0	1 038.1
Share of short-term SME lending	% of total SME lending	..	..	..	26.40	25.39	25.74	30.67	29.43	13.83	13.63	9.47	8.88
Government guaranteed loans, SMEs	IDR trillion			17.2*			34.2	40.9	40.3	22.8	94.4	96.7	120.33
Direct government loans, SMEs	IDR trillion	..	0.04	0.41	1.07	1.15	1.25	1.43	1.15	1.56	1.25	0.41	0.04
Non-performing loans, total	% of all business loans	4.08	3.20	3.35	2.55	2.16	1.87	1.77	2.16	2.49	2.40	2.63	2.40
Non-performing loans, SMEs	% of all SME loans	4.80	3.87	4.22	3.97	3.43	3.23	3.19	4.00	4.20	3.35	3.89	3.35
Interest rate, SMEs	%	16.30	16.79	16.60	14.89	14.53	13.99	14.14	14.54	13.99	12.69	13.06	12.69
Interest rate, large firms	%	12	13	13	12.73	12.28	11.60	11.88	12.48	12.51	11.01	11.39	11.01
Interest rate spread	% points	4.14	3.30	3.79	2.16	2.25	2.39	2.26	2.06	1.48	1.68	1.67	1.68
Non-bank finance													
Venture and growth capital	IDR trillion	..	..	..	..	..	4.3	6.0	6.9	7.2	8.5	7.1	8.46
Venture and growth capital (growth rate)	%, Year-on-year growth rate	..	..	..	..	..	..	38.70	14.68	4.38	17.69	-16.26	18.93
Leasing and hire purchases	IDR trillion	36.5	50.7	46.5	53.7	76.6	105.1	117.4	111.0	105.4	97.7	104.8	112.20
Factoring and invoice discounting	IDR trillion	2.2	2.2	2.0	2.3	3.9	5.1	7.7	9.4	10.7	11.5	13.3	15.48

Note: This table contains data from both bank and non-bank sources. Due to availability, post-2016 data includes non-bank data. Another table that includes only non-bank data is to be found in the "Non-bank sources of SME financing" part of the full profile. Data for venture and growth capital, leasing and hire purchases, factoring and invoice discounting are for all businesses, including large enterprises. *Data for 2007-2009.

The full country profile is available at

https://doi.org/10.1787/061fe03d-en

21. Ireland

Irish SMEs account for 99.8 percent of all active enterprises and to just over 68% of those employed.

Debt levels of Irish businesses are declining steadily, and have reduced 43% since 2010, from EUR 27.1 billion to EUR 15.5 billion in 2018.

Gross new lending to core SMEs was EUR 3.5 billion in 2018, representing a 3.2% annual decrease.

Loan approval rates continue to be stable, with 86% of all applications for the period April – September 2018 (excluding "still pending") either being fully or partially approved.

The interest rate spread of 2.15, between large (2.15%) and small loans (4.3%), remains in line with 2017, when it had fallen for the first time since 2007.

The amount of venture capital raised by Irish SMEs declined in 2018, to EUR 738 million, marking a 26% decrease on 2017 figures. Figures for Q1 2019 show that while there was again a decline in funding raised, in underlying terms there has been an increase in activity, with 75 companies receiving funding in Q1 2019 compared to 43 in the same quarter last year.

Bankruptcies decreased again in 2018 after an increase was recorded in 2017, this continues the trend of overall decline since their peak in 2011. Figures for 2018 show a 25% decline compared to 2017 figures, bringing bankruptcies down to their lowest level since 2007.

Significant progress has been made towards resolving SME NPLs in recent years and NPL trends continue to move in a downward trajectory.

In order to mitigate the impact on credit conditions in Ireland due to uncertainties surrounding Brexit, the government has sought to introduce various mitigation measures for SMEs, including the Brexit Loan Scheme. While not targeted specifically at those impacted by Brexit, the Future Growth Loan Scheme and the Business Finance Advisory Hub also aim to aid viable SMEs access appropriate credit.

Some of the main policies introduced to encourage access to credit for small and medium businesses include:

- The Supporting SMEs Online Tool, a cross-government initiative, where small businesses receive a list of available government supports based on their responses to a short questionnaire.
- The Strategic Banking Corporation of Ireland, an initiative designed to increase the availability of funding to SMEs at a lower cost and on more flexible terms than has recently been available on the Irish Market.
- The Credit Guarantee Scheme which encourages additional lending to small businesses by offering a partial government guarantee to banks against losses on qualifying loans to eligible SMEs.
- The Microenterprise Loan Fund which provides support in the form of loans for up to EUR 25 000, available to start-up, newly established, or growing micro enterprises with viable business propositions employing less than 10 people.
- The Credit Review Office which helps SME or Farm borrowers who have had an application for credit of up to EUR 3 million declined or reduced. The Credit Review Office also examines cases where borrowers feel that the terms and conditions of their existing loan, or new loan offer, are unfairly onerous or have been unreasonably changed to their detriment.

Table 21.1. Scoreboard for Ireland

Indicator	Unit	2007	2008	2009	2010	2011	2012	2013	2014	2015	2016	2017	2018
Debt													
Outstanding business loans, SMEs	EUR Billion	..	..	..	27.1	27.34	25.7	24.52	21.4	19.31	16.11	15.82	15.06
Outstanding business loans, total	EUR Billion	56.08	59.57	52.5	42.42	40.31	38.06	36.65	31.79	29.82	28	27.74	29.55
Share of SME outstanding loans	% of total outstanding	..	..	..	63.89	67.82	67.51	66.89	67.32	64.78	57.54	57.04	50.96
New business lending, SMEs	EUR Million	..	..	..	2 284	2 211	1 990	1 905	2 401	2 646	3 235	3 682	3 468
Outstanding short-term loans, SMEs	EUR Billion	17.26	15.02	10.93	6.05	3.81	3.06	3.02	2.39	1.79	2.03	2.52	2.45
Outstanding long-term loans, SMEs	EUR Billion	2.12	1.93	1.34	0.93	0.58	0.54	0.6	0.78	1.09	1	0.73	0.81
Share of short-term SME lending	% of total SME lending	88%	87%	88%	85%	85%	82%	80%	67%	39%	51%	71%	67%
Non-performing loans, total	% of all business loans	..	..	..	..	17.69	23.66	26.14	23.88	17.16	13.92	10	7.7
Non-performing loans, SMEs	% of all SME loans	..	..	..	..	..	41	41	27	26	18.7	22.6	11.1
Interest rate, SMEs	%	6.23	6.67	3.98	3.88	4.68	4.34	4.3	4.78	4.77	4.65	4.28	4.3
Interest rate, large firms	%	5.95	6.19	3.22	2.86	3.33	2.81	2.76	2.98	2.43	2.18	2.13	2.15
Interest rate spread	% points	0.28	0.48	0.76	1.02	1.35	1.53	1.54	1.8	2.34	2.47	2.15	2.15
Collateral, SMEs	% of SMEs needing collateral	..	..	..	..	..	..	..	41	40	46	41	39
Percentage of SME loan applications	SME loan applications/ total SMEs	..	..	..	..	36	39	36	31	30	23	21	20
Rejection rate	1-(SME loans authorised/ requested)	..	..	..	..	30	24	20	14	15	16	15	14
Utilisation rate	SME loans used/ authorised	..	..	..	..	..	..	81	82	84	75	75	83
Non-bank finance													
Venture and growth capital	EUR Million	226	243	288	310	274	269	285	401	522	888	994	738
Venture and growth capital (growth rate)	%, Year-on-year growth rate	..	7.53	18.61	7.67	-11.54	-2	5.95	40.65	30.3	70.1	11.92	-25.75
Other indicators													
Bankruptcies, SMEs	Number	344	613	1 245	1 386	1 410	1 317	1 119	1 007	816	642	720	543
Bankruptcies, SMEs (growth rate)	%, Year-on-year growth rate	..	78.2	103.1	11.33	1.73	-6.6	-15.03	-10.01	-18.97	-21.32	12.15	-24.58

The full country profile is available at

https://doi.org/10.1787/061fe03d-en

22. Israel

Small and medium enterprises (SMEs) constitute the overwhelming majority of companies in Israel. As of 2017, there were 559 567 businesses in Israel and 99.5% of them were SMEs which employed up to 100 workers each.

SME and entrepreneurship policies in Israel are primarily designed by the Ministry of Economy and Industry and implemented by the Israel Innovation Authority (IIA) and the Small and Medium Business Agency (SMBA). While the IIA (formerly known as the Chief Science Office) is focusing on leading technology-based start-ups and SMEs, the SMBA is catering to all SMEs in Israel's main economic sectors through business management training and coaching, subsidised access to finance (for example, through the national loans guarantee programme) and provision of business development centres (MAOF centres).

A central credit database for household and SME was launched in April 2019. The database is expected to improve competition and data accessibility in the Israeli credit market. In January 2017, a law that separates credit card companies and banks was passed as part of a series of moves to enhance competition in the banking industry, and lower financing costs for SMEs. In February 2019 Bank Leumi completed the sale of Leumi Card (the bank's credit card company) to Warburg-Pincus, an American private equity firm. In April 2019 Bank Hapoalim issued 65% of Isracard (the bank's credit card company) in an IPO, after failing to find a buyer. The bank has to sell the rest of its holdings not later than January 2021.

In 2017, the Knesset (Israel's legislature) passed the Ethics of Payments to Suppliers Law (known in the EU as Late Payments Directive). This law determines the maximum period within which payments can be made to suppliers for the sale of goods, provision of services or performance of work. The purpose of the law is to reduce the payment period for the business sector, thereby diminishing the need for working capital credit among SMEs, and to increase transparency in payments.

Table 22.1. Scoreboard for Israel

Indicator	Unit	2007	2008	2009	2010	2011	2012	2013	2014	2015	2016	2017	2018
Debt													
Outstanding business loans, SMEs	ILS billion	169.3	171.2	161.6	173.8	177.7	187.0	186.7	211.9	244.6	259.6	266.1	281.8
Outstanding business loans, total	ILS billion	413.9	460.9	425.2	438.9	458.6	450.4	445.7	447.9	415.6	435.5	444.4	476.9
Share of SME outstanding loans	% of total outstanding business loans	40.9	37.14	38.01	39.6	38.75	41.52	41.89	47.31	58.86	59.61	59.88	59.09
Government loan guarantees, SMEs	ILS million	27	17	121	164	116	116	215	232	257	184	144	144
Government guaranteed loans, SMEs	ILS million	170	109	757	1 028	890	1 057	1 951	2 112	2 340	1 838	1 600	1 604
Non-performing loans, total	% of all business loans	..	..	..	..	..	..	..	..	2.77	2.18	1.57	1.25
Non-performing loans, SMEs	% of all SME loans	..	..	..	..	..	..	..	..	2.13	1.77	1.5	1.31
Interest rate, SMEs	%	..	..	..	..	..	..	..	..	3.96	3.84	4.02	4.06
Interest rate, large firms	%	..	..	..	..	..	..	..	..	2.95	2.89	3.05	2.98
Interest rate spread	% points	..	..	..	..	..	..	..	..	1.02	0.95	0.97	1.08
Non-bank finance													
Venture and growth capital	USD billion	1.76	2.08	1.12	1.22	2.08	1.88	2.95	3.77	4.75	5.10	5.52	6.47
Venture and growth capital (growth rate)	%, year-on-year growth rate	..	18.2	-46.2	8.9	70.5	-9.6	57.3	27.6	26.1	7.2	8.3	17.3
Other indicators													
Payment delays, B2B	Number of days	..	..	..	..	..	..	..	..	..	57.2	53	28
Bankruptcies, SMEs	Number	..	..	2 061	2 834	3 737	5 000	5 610	5 322	5 175	7 900	..	..
Bankruptcies, SMEs (growth rate)	%, year-on-year growth rate	..	..	..	37.51	31.86	33.8	12.2	-5.13	-2.76	52.66	..	..

The full country profile is available at

https://doi.org/10.1787/061fe03d-en

23. Italy

Small and medium-sized enterprises dominate the business landscape in Italy, accounting for nearly 80% of the industrial and service labour force, and generating about two-thirds of turnover and value added.

Weak cyclical conditions in the second half of the year swiftly affected lending markets: after increasing at a sustained pace throughout 2018, business loans resumed their decline in the first half to 2019. Credit weakened slightly for large firms, but contracted markedly for smaller ones, exacerbating an already sluggish loan dynamics.

Credit standards remained loose overall, but gradually tightened from the second half of 2018, owing to higher funding costs for banks and a gloomier economic outlook. Business borrowing rates stood at historically low levels, but collateral requirements remained stable at a high level compared with the past.

Credit quality continued to improve, partly reflecting the cyclical upswing observed in recent years: the ratio of SME new non-performing loans to outstanding loans fell below the levels observed before the global financial crisis. The stock of non-performing loans dropped further, mainly as a result of large sales.

Equity financing for SMEs rose sharply in 2018 compared to the previous year, driven by an unprecedented growth in the early stage segment; resources devoted to firms of all sizes almost tripled, after plummeting by more than 40% in 2017.

Business-to-business payment delays stabilised overall, but the economic slowdown gradually led to a worsening in payment patterns: both agreed timeframes and average delays in the settlement of invoices increased somewhat for smaller firms.

Bankruptcies fell for the fourth year in a row, down by nearly 7% compared to the previous year and well below the peak observed in 2014.

The wide range of policies enacted or ramped up in response to the financial crisis gradually shifted in recent years from a broad-based countercyclical support to more targeted initiatives aimed at pursuing specific goals.

Credit guarantee schemes traditionally played a crucial role in easing SME access to finance. The Central Guarantee Fund continued to expand its activity, reaching a new high in 2018: it provided EUR 13.7 billion in guarantees for EUR 19.3 billion worth of loans. Its recent reform, aimed at better fitting the need of the potential beneficiaries through the introduction of a new evaluation system of firms' creditworthiness, came into effect in early 2019.

Long-term individual savings plans (piani individuali di risparmio or PIR) were introduced in early 2017 to channel private savings towards investments in financial instruments issued by Italian companies. In order to foster the development of small and medium-sized enterprises, the 2019 Budget Law amended the rules on PIR funds by requiring them to invest part of the portfolio in financial instruments issued by Italian SMEs and in venture capital funds. However, these investments were relatively risky and characterised by low liquidity, partly owing to the limited size of the markets for securities issued by smaller firms. Since January 2019, net subscriptions virtually dried up following legislative changes.

Initiatives have been recently undertaken to support the development of a more mature innovation ecosystem. The National Innovation Fund, established by the 2019 Budget Law, is slated to become one of the leading European venture capital operators, acquiring qualified minority stakes in start-ups, scale-ups and innovative SMEs, while acting as a catalyst for private and international capital.

Table 23.1. Scoreboard for Italy, 2007-18

Indicator	Unit	2007	2008	2009	2010	2011	2012	2013	2014	2015	2016	2017	2018
Debt													
Outstanding business loans, SMEs	EUR billion	187	191	193	210	206	204	196	192	188	175	170	165
Outstanding business loans, total	EUR billion	998	1067	1057	1122	1134	1118	1061	1025	1016	985	960	959
Share of SME outstanding loans	% of total business loans	18.7	17.9	18.3	18.7	18.2	18.2	18.5	18.7	18.5	17.8	17.7	7.2
Short-term loans, SMEs	EUR billion	59	56	52	50	48	47	42	39	35	31	28	27
Long-term loans, SMEs	EUR billion	115	120	125	136	133	128	122	115	112	103	101	100
Total short and long-term loans, SMEs	EUR billion	174	177	177	186	181	175	164	155	147	134	130	127
Share of short-term loans, SMEs	% of total short and long-term SME loans	34.0	31.9	29.3	26.9	26.4	26.6	25.7	25.3	23.8	22.9	22.0	21.3
Direct government loans, SMEs	EUR million	337	373	255	276	272	252	390	597	392	418	431	684
Government guaranteed loans, SMEs (CGF)	EUR million, flows	2 300	2 353	4 914	9 119	8 378	8 190	10 811	12 935	15 065	16 703	17 462	19 314
Government loan guarantees, SMEs (CGF)	EUR million, flows	1 146	1 160	2 756	5 225	4 435	4 036	6 414	8 392	10 216	11 570	12 260	13 731
Non-performing loans, SMEs	EUR million	..	22 865	27 953	35 243	38 033	43 812	48 387	53 715	56 189	54 947	50 604	46 928
Non-performing loans, SMEs	% of total SME loans	..	12.0	14.5	16.8	18.4	21.5	24.6	28.0	30.0	31.3	29.8	28.4
Interest rate, SMEs	%	6.3	6.3	3.6	3.7	5.0	5.6	5.4	4.4	3.8	3.2	3.1	3.1
Interest rate, large firms	%	5.7	4.9	2.2	2.2	3.3	3.8	3.4	2.6	2.1	1.8	1.8	1.8
Interest rate spread	%	0.6	1.4	1.4	1.5	1.7	1.8	2.0	1.8	1.7	1.4	1.3	1.3
Collateral, SMEs	%	54	54	52	53	55	54	55	55	56	57	57	57
Rejection rate	% of firms reporting that they had not obtained some or all of the credit requested	3.1	8.2	6.9	5.7	11.3	12.0	8.9	8.4	6.0	4.0	4.3	4.6
Utilisation rate	SME loans used / authorised	79.7	80.7	80.7	82.8	83.6	85.7	86.7	87.2	86.9	84.7	84.4	84.8
Non-bank finance													
Venture capital investments	EUR million	66	115	98	89	82	135	82	43	74	103	133	324

Indicator	Unit	2007	2008	2009	2010	2011	2012	2013	2014	2015	2016	2017	2018
(early stage), SMEs													
Growth capital investments (expansion), SMEs	EUR million	295	440	260	263	500	504	438	230	170	155	161	125
Growth capital investments (expansion), total	EUR million	641	796	371	583	674	926	914	1179	333	710	337	816
Other indicators													
Payment delays, B2B (all firms)	Average number of days	..	20.4	21.3	17.3	16.2	17.5	17.3	16.1	15.0	13.4	12.3	12.2
Bankruptcies, total	Number	6 163	7 509	9 379	11 238	12 160	12 544	14 133	15 694	14 743	13 536	12 073	11 254
Bankruptcies, total	%, Year-on-year growth rate	..	21.8	24.9	19.8	8.2	3.2	12.7	11.0	-6.1	-8.2	-10.8	-6.8
Incidence of insolvency, total	per 10 000 enterprises	11.5	13.7	17.0	20.3	21.6	22.0	25.0	27.9	26.4	24.1	21.5	20.0

The full country profile is available at

https://doi.org/10.1787/061fe03d-en

24. Japan

Japanese SMEs accounted for 99.7% of all businesses and employed 34 million individuals, or approximately 70.1% of the private sector labour force in 2014.

Lending to SMEs decreased every year between 2007 and 2012, reaching a total decrease of 6.6% over that period. In 2013, outstanding SME loans rose by 1.5%, and have continued to increase since then, reaching JPY 271.5 trillion in 2016 and JPY 282.1 trillion in 2017 (+3.9%).

Average interest rates on new short-term loans in Japan were very low and declined continuously between 2007 and in 2017, more than halving from 1.64% to 0.61%. Long-term interest rates on new loans followed a broadly similar pattern, declining from 1.7% in 2007 to 0.8% in 2017, and were thus only slightly higher than short-term interest rates.

Japanese venture capital investments peaked in FY 2007 at JPY 193 billion, and decreased by 29.5% and 36% in FY 2008 and 2009 respectively. Since 2009, VC investments have been inconsistent. In 2017, VC investments totalled JPY 197 billion, a 29.6% increase from 2016.

Leasing volumes to SMEs plummeted in the aftermath of the financial crisis, dropping by almost 40% between 2007 and 2009. Between 2010 and 2013, leasing volumes recovered. In 2016, leasing volumes were JPY 2.56 trillion and they increased slightly to JPY 2.57 trillion in 2017, but still remain well below 2007 levels.

SME bankruptcies, which account for more than 99% of all bankruptcies in Japan, decreased by more than 40% between 2007 and 2017, reaching a 27-year low of 8 397 (-0.5% from 2016).

Total non-performing business loans have continuously declined since 2013, after having experienced erratic movement over the 2007-12 period. In 2016, total NPLs declined by 2.91% to JPY 11 787 billion in 2016 and by 2.52% to JPY 10 483 billion in 2017.

The Japanese Government offers financial support for SMEs, in the form of a credit guarantee programme and direct loans for SMEs. In March 2018, the total amount of outstanding SME loans was approximately JPY 267 trillion (provided by domestically licensed banks and credit associations). The outstanding amount of the credit guarantee programme was JPY 22.2 trillion (covering 1.3 million SMEs), and the outstanding amount of the direct loan programme was JPY 21.2 trillion, (covering 1 million of Japan's 3.81 million SMEs).

Table 24.1. Scoreboard for Japan

Indicator	Unit	2007	2008	2009	2010	2011	2012	2013	2014	2015	2016	2017
Debt												
Outstanding business loans, SMEs	JPY trillion	260.8	259.1	253.1	248.3	245.6	243.6	247.2	251.7	258.4	265.6	275.4
Outstanding business loans, total	JPY trillion	374.5	385.0	379.3	366.1	366.9	370.4	369.7	387.2	395.2	405.1	415.5
Share of SME outstanding loans	% of total outstanding business loans	69.64	67.31	66.72	67.82	66.94	65.76	66.87	65.00	65.38	65.57	66.29
Value of CGCs loan guarantees (Government loan guarantees, SMEs)	JPY trillion	29.4	33.9	35.9	35.1	34.4	32.1	29.8	27.7	25.8	23.9	22.2
Non-performing loans, total (amount)	JPY trillion	17.1	17.1	16.8	16.6	17.2	17.3	15.3	13.9	12.8	11.8	10.5
Non-performing loans, total	% of all business loans	4.56	4.45	4.42	4.54	4.68	4.66	4.14	3.60	3.23	2.91	2.52
Prime lending rate for short-term loans	%	1.88	1.68	1.48	1.48	1.48	1.48	1.48	1.48	1.48	1.48	1.48
Prime lending rate for long-term loans	%	2.30	2.40	1.65	1.60	1.40	1.20	1.20	1.10	1.10	0.95	1.00
New short-term interest rate (Not only for businesses)	%	1.64	1.53	1.23	1.10	1.04	1.02	0.91	0.88	0.80	0.67	0.61
New long-term interest rate (Not only for businesses)	%	1.73	1.67	1.46	1.29	1.21	1.16	1.10	1.00	0.94	0.80	0.80
Outstanding short-term interest rate (Not only for businesses)	%	1.67	1.49	1.26	1.19	1.10	1.03	0.88	0.85	0.78	0.62	0.58
Outstanding long-term interest rate (Not only for businesses)	%	2.05	1.99	1.76	1.65	1.54	1.42	1.30	1.19	1.10	0.97	0.90
Non-bank finance												
Venture capital investments (all stages total)	JPY billion	193	136	87	113	124	102	181	117	130	152	197
Venture capital investments (all stages total)	%, year-on-year growth rate	..	-29.53	-36.03	29.89	9.73	-17.74	77.45	-35.36	11.11	16.92	29.60
Venture capital (seed and early stage)	% (share of all stages)	..	..	36.80	32.50	44.30	57.80	64.50	57.20	62.80	68.30	62.90
Venture capital (expansion and later stage)	% (share of all stages)	..	..	63.20	67.50	55.70	42.20	35.50	42.80	37.20	31.70	37.1
Leasing, SMEs	JPY billion	3 471	2 822	2 100	2 139	2 231	2 284	2 645	2 363	2 604	2 566	2 570
Other indicators												
Bankruptcies, SMEs	Thousands	14.0	15.5	15.4	13.2	12.7	12.1	10.8	9.7	8.8	8.4	8.4
Bankruptcies, SMEs	%, year-on-year growth rate	..	10.76	-0.82	-13.96	-4.22	-4.81	-10.18	-10.37	-9.43	-4.17	-0.50
Bankruptcies, total	Thousands	14.1	15.6	15.5	13.3	12.7	12.1	10.9	9.7	8.8	8.4	8.4
Bankruptcies, total	%, year-on-year growth rate	..	11.04	-1.06	-13.95	-4.41	-4.79	-10.47	-10.35	-9.44	-4.15	-0.49

The full country profile is available at

https://doi.org/10.1787/061fe03d-en

25. Kazakhstan

In 2018, SMEs made up 96.7% of all businesses in Kazakhstan. The share of people employed by SMEs was 37.5% of the total employed population. SMEs contributed 28.9% to the country's GDP that same year (according to preliminary data for 9 months of 2018).

SME lending was on the rise in Kazakhstan since 2014 up to 2017. In 2017-2018 the SME loan portfolio has decreased. In 2018 the SME loan portfolio has decreased by 15.2%, at the same time, new lending to SMEs (over the period) increased by 14.0% over the last year. Due to the fact that the portfolio of loans to SMEs decreased, the share of loans to SMEs in the total portfolio of business loans also decreased to 28.3%. Despite the growth of new lending to SMEs (for the period), their share in the total amount of new business lending decreased to 18.5%. This indicates the growth of new lending (for the period) to large enterprises.

Interest rates for SMEs have fluctuated over the reference period, growing steadily from a record low of 11.5% in 2014 to 14.0% in 2016. In 2018, the rate was 12.7%, while that of large enterprises was 11.2%.

Among non-bank sources of finance, leasing has the largest market and is steadily growing. In 2018, leasing and hire purchases were almost 4.6 times their 2010 level.

Non-performing loans with arrears of more than 90 days (NPL) in banks' portfolio among both total business loans and SME loans decreased in 2018 to 7.4% and 9.3% respectively. Commercial banks fulfil requirements of the National Bank of Kazakhstan concerning maximum appropriate NPL level of no more than 10% of the total loan portfolio.

An important role in maintaining SMEs' access to lending is played by the state, which places funds in commercial banks to provide concessional lending to SMEs during shortages of liquidity in the market. The largest placement of state funds for SME lending took place in 2018. The main part of loans was allocated in 2014-2016 to support SMEs in the manufacturing industry at a rate of 6% per annum, which are issued by banks on a revolving basis. Despite the fact that the largest part of the funds was allocated in 2014-2016, these funds are still used for lending to SMEs on a revolving basis. In addition, the State allocates new funds annually.

Since 2010, the government, through "Damu" Entrepreneurship Development Fund, has provided subsidised interest rate expense and loan guarantees for SMEs under the "Business Roadmap 2020" Programme. A new financial instrument in Kazakhstan, loan guarantees are becoming popular very quickly, escalating from just three guarantees in 2010 to 4 853 at the beginning of 2019.

Table 25.1. Scoreboard for Kazakhstan

Indicator	Unit	2007	2008	2009	2010	2011	2012	2013	2014	2015	2016	2017	2018
Debt													
Outstanding business loans, SMEs	KZT billion	1 508	1 571	1 708	1 389	1 341	1 412	1 283	1 788	2 060	3 105	2 789	2 364
Outstanding business loans, total	KZT billion	5 220	5 605	5 879	5 892	6 849	7 534	8 110	8 532	9 027	9 234	8 568	8 348
Share of SME outstanding loans	% of total outstanding business loans	28.89	28.02	29.06	23.58	19.58	18.74	15.83	20.95	22.83	33.62	32.55	28.32
New business lending, total	KZT billion	7 764	5 373	3 742	3 291	4 795	5 774	6 109	8 044	7 345	7 724	7 615	9 412
New business lending, SMEs	KZT billion	1 870	1 273	753.10	690 15	794 48	1 050	889 71	1 198	1 279	1 984	1 524	1 737
Share of new SME lending	% of total new lending	24.08	23.70	20.13	20.97	16.57	18.18	14.56	14.90	17.41	25.68	20.02	18.46
Short-term loans, SMEs	KZT billion	296	298	236	206	219	277	199	392	390	826	411	366
Long-term loans, SMEs	KZT billion	1 211.2	1 273	1 472	1 183	1 122	1 135	1 084	1 395	1 670	2 279	2 377	1 820
Share of short-term SME lending	% of total SME lending	19.66	18.96	13.82	14.83	16.34	19.64	15.51	21.95	18.93	26.60	14.75	16.75
Government loan guarantees, SMEs	KZT million	..	..	..	339	2 060	3 854	3 336	7 284	11 021	11 952	17 016	21 728
Government guaranteed loans, SMEs	KZT million	..	..	..	677	4 238	10 991	7 090	15 423	26 964	26 903	42 783	51 216
Direct government loans, SMEs	KZT billion	5.5	125.2	257.4	132.9	82.7	78.2	85.8	188.4	236.9	247.3	230.5	272.9
Non-performing loans, total	% of all business loans	..	..	..	..	..	29.80	31.15	23.55	7.95	6.72	9.31	7.38
Non-performing loans, SMEs	% of all SME loans	..	..	..	..	..	22.33	22.40	11.74	12.69	8.79	9.58	9.33
Interest rate, SMEs	%	14.28	15.67	14.01	13.34	12.49	12.10	12.46	11.48	12.95	14.01	13.66	12.71
Interest rate, large firms	%	12.77	14.88	14.04	12.72	11.08	10.58	10.07	10.01	13.47	14.49	12.39	11.22
Interest rate spread	% points	1.51	0.79	-0.03	0.62	1.41	1.52	2.39	1.47	-0.52	-0.48	1.27	1.49
Non-bank finance													
Leasing and hire purchases	KZT billion	..	..	..	60.4	80.1	84.5	106.8	129.0	126.6	167.0	176.5	277.6
Factoring and invoicing	KZT million	..	..	..	..	..	7 889	15 125	33 160	37 655	..	..	..
Other indicators													
Bankruptcies, total	Number	0	2	3	8	36	77	125	143	257	516	1 978	3 493
Bankruptcies, total (growth rate)	%, year-on-year growth rate	..	..	50.00	166.67	350.00	113.89	62.34	14.40	79.72	100.78	283.33	76.59

The full country profile is available at

https://doi.org/10.1787/061fe03d-en

26. Korea

The share of outstanding SME loans has increased continuously from 2014, with a KRW 41 trillion increase in 2018. Meanwhile, the stock of outstanding loans for large firms decreased during the same period, by approximately KRW 0.5 trillion, resulting in an increase in the share of outstanding SME loans.

Outstanding short-term loans as a share of total loans have declined continuously between 2007 (75%) and 2018 (50%). Both the level of outstanding short-term loans and the level of outstanding long-term loans have increased continuously from 2007. However, the growth rate of outstanding short-term loans has been higher than that of outstanding long-term loans.

While the level of government guaranteed loans has been on the rise since 2011, government guaranteed loans to SMEs as a share outstanding business loans to these firms has decreased continuously from 2012. Between 2017 and 2018, the volume of government-guaranteed loans rose by 2.8%. The amount of direct lending to SMEs in 2018 was KRW 4.4 trillion, which is about 0.6% of all outstanding business loans to SMEs.

Since 2013, the rate of non-performing loans has decreased continuously. 1.1% of all SME loans were non-performing in 2018, below the 2017 figure (1.17%). On the other hand, 1.88% of all business loans were non-performing in 2018, indicating that large business loans are more liable to be non-performing than SME loans.

Interest rates for SMEs increased by about 0.2 percentage points from 3.62% to 3.82% in 2018. On the other hand, interest rates for large firms increased by about 0.14 percentage point from 3.31% to 3.45% in 2018, resulting in higher interest rate spread between loans to SMEs and to large firms. However, SME interest rates are still quite low on average.

Venture and growth capital investments increased rapidly in 2018. The growth rate of venture and growth capital was 43.89%, with investments going from KRW 2.38 trillion to KRW 3.42 trillion.

Leasing and hire purchases volumes rose by 0.05% in 2018, which implies that these instruments were stable in 2018.

Since the global financial crisis, the number of bankruptcies has steadily decreased. Payment delays decreased by 1.5 days, on average, in 2018.

Table 26.1. Scoreboard for Korea

Indicators	Units	2007	2008	2009	2010	2011	2012	2013	2014	2015	2016	2017	2018
Debt													
Outstanding business loans, SMEs	KRW trillion	369	422	443	441	455	462	489	522	561	610	655	696
Outstanding business loans, total	KRW trillion	425	511	531	541	586	618	654	706	756	776	817	857
Share of SME outstanding loans	% of total business loans	86.8	82.6	83.5	81.5	77.7	74.7	74.7	74.0	74.2	78.6	80.2	81.2
Outstanding Short-term loans, total; loans for operation	KRW trillion	319	375	373	372	388	395	405	419	426	414	419	429
Outstanding Long-term loans, total; loans for equipment	KRW trillion	106	136	158	169	197	223	249	287	330	362	398	428
Share of short-term loans; loans for operation	KRW trillion	75.0	73.4	70.3	68.7	66.3	63.9	61.9	59.3	56.3	53.4	51.3	50.1
Government loan guarantees, SMEs	KRW trillion	40	43	56	56	55	57	60	60	61	63	66	68
Government guaranteed loans, SMEs	% of SME business loans	10.8	10.0	12.7	12.7	12.2	12.3	12.2	11.5	10.9	10.3	10.0	9.7
Direct government loans, SMEs	KRW billion	2 480	2 635	4 812	3 098	2 957	3 149	3 715	3 270	3 902	4 551	4 666	4 415
Non-performing loans, total	% of all business loans	0.81	1.41	1.6	2.6	1.73	1.66	2.39	2.09	2.56	2.06	1.76	1.88
Non-performing loans, SMEs	% of all SME loans	0.99	1.93	1.8	3.11	2.17	1.96	2.11	1.94	1.64	1.3	1.11	1.10
Interest rate, SMEs	%	7.04	7.61	6.18	6.52	6.36	5.93	5.11	4.69	3.95	3.63	3.62	3.82
Interest rate, large firms	%	6.27	6.81	5.62	5.98	5.81	5.50	4.87	4.51	3.79	3.40	3.31	3.45
Interest rate spread	%	0.76	0.79	0.56	0.54	0.55	0.43	0.24	0.18	0.16	0.24	0.31	0.37
Rejection rate	%, 1-(SME loans authorised/ requested)	..	..	..	..	..	..	..	6.90	3.70	12.20	12.90	15.50
Non-bank finance													
Venture and growth capital	KRW billions	992	725	867	1 091	1 261	1 233	1 385	1 639	2 086	2 150	2 380	3 425
Venture and growth capital (growth rate)	%	..	-26.9	19.7	25.8	15.6	-2.2	12.3	18.4	27.2	3.1	10.7	43.9
Leasing and hire purchases	KRW trillions	10.3	11.7	7.1	10.6	11.1	10.5	11.9	13.2	15.0	17.4	20.2	21.2
Other indicators													
Payment delays, SMEs	Number of days past due date	11.0	12.1	9.9	12.1	11.7	9.1	9.7	10.0	9.2	13.3	8.9	7.4
Bankruptcies, total	Number	2 294	2 735	1 998	1 570	1 359	1 228	1 001	841	720	555	494	469
Bankruptcies, growth rate	Year-on-year growth rate, %	..	19.2	-26.9	-21.4	-13.4	-9.6	-18.5	-16.0	-14.4	-22.9	-11.0	-5.1

The full country profile is available at

https://doi.org/10.1787/061fe03d-en

27. Latvia

Growth of the Latvian economy was considerably faster in 2017 and 2018 than in the previous years. Export, investments, private and public consumption are growing steadily. Export volumes have reached their highest-ever level. An increase is observed in almost all sectors of the national economy. Overall, in the three first quarters of 2018, the gross domestic product (GDP) increased by 4.7% achieving a higher increase than in 2017, when GDP increased by 4.6%. Taking into account economic growth in countries of the European Union (EU), as well as investments available from EU funds, economic growth is expected to remain stable also in 2019, even though at a slower rate.

In Latvia, 99.8% of economically active merchants and commercial companies are SMEs, and 92.1% of these SMEs are micro-enterprises.

Loans to SMEs dominate in the banking sector's lending to non-financial corporations (NFCs), as SMEs play an important role in the domestic economy of Latvia – loans to SMEs comprised 74% (at the end 2018) of total loans to domestic NFCs. The outstanding amount of banking sector loans to SMEs decreased in 2018 by 8.3%. However, to a large extent this is attributed to structural changes in the Latvian banking sector (for instance, the withdrawal of the credit institution's licence). Excluding one-off effects, the SMEs loan stock did not change significantly (-1.0% year-on-year). In 2018, the new lending (flow) to SMEs was slightly higher than in 2017 (by 3.9%). Overall, the economic environment remains favourable, driven by investment growth and domestic demand. The balanced economic growth is expected to continue (the Bank of Latvia forecasts 2.9% real GDP growth in 2019) and will support credit demand.

Venture and growth capital increased in 2017 from EUR 79.4 million to EUR 120 million. In 2018, 3 new acceleration funds in addition to several seed, start-up and growth capital funds were introduced to the market to facilitate the development of venture capital investments.

The state promotes access to funding (through its micro-lending, start-up, and loans programme) for firms lacking the financial credibility (collateral, net worth, cash flow and credit history) that is necessary to access funding from commercial banks or private investors.

Currently, state support programmes are introduced via the JSC Development Finance Institution Altum (ALTUM), a state-owned development finance institution offering aid and financial tools to various target groups. ALTUM develops and implements state aid programmes to compensate for market shortcomings that cannot be resolved by private financial institutions.

Table 27.1. Scoreboard for Latvia

Indicator	Unit	2007	2008	2009	2010	2011	2012	2013	2014	2015	2016	2017	2018
Debt													
Outstanding business loans, SMEs	EUR million	7 727	8 672	8 376	7 764	7 035	6 154	5 404	4 939	4 771	4 942	4 482	4 110
Outstanding business loans, total	EUR million	8 865	10 359	9 681	8 888	8 212	7 474	7 058	6 379	6 274	6 373	5 887	5 591
Share of SME outstanding loans	% of total outstanding business loans	87.16	83.71	86.52	87.34	85.67	82.34	76.57	77.43	76.05	77.55	76.1	73.52
New business lending, total	EUR million	..	..	..	..	1 708	1 914	1 965	1 268	1 346	1 795	1 347	1 312
New business lending, SMEs	EUR million	..	..	..	..	1 506	1 625	1 613	1 020	947	1 399	974	1 012
Share of new SME lending	% of total new lending	..	..	..	..	88.20	84.90	82.08	80.47	70.39	77.95	72.3	77.19
Outstanding short-term loans, SMEs	EUR million	2 653	3 203	3 262	3 009	2 682	2 349	1 852	1 570	1 672	1 371	1 287	1 229
Outstanding long-term loans, SMEs	EUR million	5 048	5 409	4 912	4 701	4 353	3 805	3 552	3 369	3 099	3 571	3 195	2 894
Share of short-term SME lending	% of total SME lending	34.4	37.2	39.9	39	38.1	38.2	34.3	31.8	35.1	27.7	28.7	29.8
Non-performing loans, total	% of all business loans	0.7	3.2	20.2	20.8	16.4	9.7	6.9	5.9	4.4	2.7	3.1	2.5
Non-performing loans, SMEs	% of all SME loans	0.8	3.7	22.4	23.4	18.8	11.7	8.4	7.2	5.7	3.3	3.8	3.3
Interest rate, SMEs	%	8.3	8.9	7.9	7.1	5.8	4.5	4.5	4.7	4.5	4.4	3.8	3.8
Interest rate, large firms	%	6.6	7.1	5.2	4.3	4	3.6	3.8	3.3	3.1	2.5	2.6	2.7
Interest rate spread	% points	1.7	1.8	2.7	2.8	1.8	0.9	0.7	1.4	1.4	1.9	1.2	1.1
Non-bank finance													
Venture and growth capital	EUR million	..	..	..	..	..	..	..	37.95	51.98	79.37	101	118
Venture and growth capital (growth rate)	%, Year-on-year growth rate	..	..	..	..	..	..	..	..	36.97	52.69	27.76	16.45
Leasing and hire purchases	EUR million	1 576	1 594	1 145	841	810	867	875	864	932	939	1 034	..
Factoring and invoice discounting	EUR million	227.24	301.90	149.13	60.68	90.96	96.15	108.01	114.47	151.81	165.99	152.64	..
Other indicators													
Bankruptcies, SMEs	Number	..	1 620	2 581	2 549	822	880	820	959	803	730	588	..
Bankruptcies, SMEs (growth rate)	%, Year-on-year growth rate	..	..	59.32	-1.24	-67.75	7.06	-6.82	16.95	-16.27	-9.09	-19.45	..

The full country profile is available at

https://doi.org/10.1787/061fe03d-en

28. Lithuania

SMEs account for 99.6% of all enterprises operating in Lithuania, the majority of them (81.9%) being micro-enterprises. Most SMEs (80.4%) have chosen the legal form of private limited liability company and are primarily engaged in wholesale or retail trade activities (almost a third of all SMEs).

Equity capital and credits issued by non-banks (e.g. trade payables) are the main sources of funding for SMEs. As of 2017, equity capital financed almost half of SMEs' assets, while slightly more than a third of assets were acquired through non-bank credits. Nevertheless, banks play an important role in financing SMEs. As of 2017, almost 13% of all SME assets were financed via bank loans.

Although SMEs account for the vast majority of enterprises and create almost 70% of gross value added, their share of total business loans remains considerably smaller. By the end of 2018, this share amounted to 40% of the total portfolio of loans to non-financial enterprises. Furthermore, even though outstanding SME loans have been growing (+ 23% and + 5 % over 2014-18 and 2018 respectively), their share in the total portfolio of loans to non-financial enterprises has barely changed over the years.

Previously, SMEs rarely used alternative sources of financing in Lithuania. However, when banks started to tighten funding conditions in 2018 and 2019, the need for such sources significantly increased. The survey of non-financial enterprises conducted by the Bank of Lithuania in H1 2019 indicates that 35% of micro-enterprises need alternative sources of financing (e.g. crowd funding, business angels, equity funds), i.e. 10 percentage points more than six month ago. Regardless of this figure, a very small share of these enterprises are using such sources. For example, while there are clear legal regulations for crowdfunding in Lithuania and a significant number of enterprises providing such services, surveys show crowdfunding was actively used by only 1.2% of the surveyed micro-enterprises. Nevertheless, the popularity of alternative financing sources is increasing. For example, in 2018 new loans issued by crowd funding platforms contained EUR 8.54 million (EUR 1.29 million in 2017) while new loans issued by MFIs declined (see Table 28.1).

The government supports SMEs by ensuring that they benefit from favourable conditions to obtain the necessary financing to start a business. Loans with preferential rates are granted under the EU Entrepreneurship Promotion Fund over the 2014-20 period. SMEs may also get loans with preferential rates from the Venture Capital Fund II. Moreover, when a company does not have sufficient collateral, it may apply to the state-controlled enterprise *UAB Investicijų ir verslo garantijos* (Investment and business guarantees, INVEGA), which provides a guarantee of loan repayment. In addition, municipalities provide significant support to SMEs: when starting business, small enterprises may expect their set-up costs, part of interest payments and other expenses to be compensated.

Table 28.1. Scoreboard for Lithuania

Indicator	Unit	2007	2008	2009	2010	2011	2012	2013	2014	2015	2016	2017	2018
Debt													
Outstanding business loans, SMEs	EUR million	..	..	..	..	..	..	..	3 143	3 231	3 404	3 723	3 920
Outstanding business loans, total	EUR million	8 409	9 864	7 978	6 816	6 906	7 047	6 828	7 404	7 740	8 611	9 252	9 700
Share of SME outstanding loans	% of total outstanding business loans	..	..	..	..	..	..	..	42.45	41.74	39.53	40.24	40.41
New business lending, total	EUR million	7 759	9 452	7 252	4 868	3 792	3 220	3 236	3 128	4 275	4 248	4 639	4 028
Government guaranteed loans, SMEs	EUR million									148.4	218.8	241.6	
Non-performing loans, total (NFCs)	% of all business loans	..	..	..	..	..	..	..	10.31	8.39	6.25	5.04	4.05
Non-performing loans, SMEs	% of all SME loans	..	..	..	..	..	..	..	17.54	14.11	11.18	8.59	6.60
Interest rate, SMEs	%	6.61	6.33	4.70	4.55	4.97	3.35	3.47	3.19	2.97	2.96	2.79	3.52
Interest rate, large firms	%	6.04	5.76	4.26	4.35	4.44	3.27	2.86	1.65	2.03	2.27	2.07	3.07
Interest rate spread	% points	0.57	0.57	0.44	0.20	0.53	0.08	0.61	1.54	0.94	0.69	0.72	0.45
Collateral, SMEs	% of SMEs needing collateral to obtain bank lending							76.20	70.40	67.10	71.70	79.10	73.10
Rejection rate	1-(SME loans authorised/ requested)	..	..	..	19.1	15.6	19.0	10.2	22.8	8.6	10.5	15.6	27.0
Non-bank finance													
Leasing and hire purchases	EUR million	..	..	..	1 756	1 547	1 452	1 527	1 521	1 660	2 111	2 463	2 880
Factoring and invoice discounting	EUR million	..	..	..	151	200	231	348	359	407	434	517	464
Other indicators													
Payment delays, B2B	Number of days	..	..	..	..	..	..	..	..	..	26	27	30
Bankruptcies, SMEs	Number	606	954	1 842	1 637	1 272	1 401	1 552	1 685	1 983	2 732	2 970	2 090
Bankruptcies, SMEs (growth rate)	%, Year-on-year growth rate	..	57.43	93.08	-11.13	-22.30	10.14	10,78	8.57	17.69	37.77	8.71	–29.63

The full country profile is available at

https://doi.org/10.1787/061fe03d-en

29. Luxembourg

SMEs account for 99.5% of all non-financial firms in Luxembourg. In 2016, SMEs employed approximately 67% of the labour force and generated 65% of economy's total value added.

New business lending to all firms increased in 2018 compared to 2017 but remained well below the peak of 2008. New loans to SMEs (defined as loans below EUR 1 million) continued to increase in 2018 but at lower pace than loans to all enterprises. Therefore, the share of new SMEs lending decreased to 10.89%, which is lower than the 12.8% of 2017.

In 2018, the interest rate for SMEs amounted to 1.73%, down from 5.72% in 2008. The interest rates for SMEs remained systematically higher than the interest rate for large firms over the period 2007-18, with a gap of 46 basis points in 2018. In relative terms, interests payed by SMEs are 36.8% higher than interest payed by large firms.

Alternative forms of financing such as venture capital and factoring may hold high potential for SMEs seeking finance. In 2018, nearly EUR 112 million of venture capital were invested in Luxembourgish firms.

Bankruptcies in Luxembourg increased from 904 in 2017 to 1191 in 2018, marking the peak of the 2007-2018 period.

The simplified limited liability company (SARL-S), also dubbed "1-1-1 companies" (one person, one euro, in one day), is gaining popularity. In the period January-July 2018, 10.3%, of all registrations had the legal form of SARL-S compared to the 7.7% in 2018 and 6% in 2017. The SARL-S is intended to facilitate the development of new business activities and it can be created more quickly than a regular SARL-S.

Table 29.1.Scoreboard for Luxembourg

Indicator	Unit	2007	2008	2009	2010	2011	2012	2013	2014	2015	2016	2017	2018
Debt													
New business lending, total	EUR million	113 817	181 792	166 287	111 898	111 568	105 854	100 444	92 349	83 076	87809	80 264	95 853
New business lending, SMEs	EUR million	12 800	14 555	14 754	15 441	17 979	15 593	13 713	10 765	10 142	9 395	9 698	10 440
Share of new SME lending	% of total new lending	11.25	8.01	8.87	13.80	16.11	14.73	13.65	11.66	12.21	10.70	12.08	10.89
Non-performing loans, total	% of all business loans	0.12	0.18	0.44	0.48	0.64	0.59	0.52	0.41	0.40	0.27	0.38	0.40
Interest rate, SMEs	%	5.51	5.72	2.81	2.71	2.68	2.22	2.05	2.08	1.88	1.75	1.76	1.73
Interest rate, large firms	%	4.96	4.97	2.59	2.30	2.62	1.86	1.64	1.47	1.42	1.20	1.21	1.26
Interest rate spread	% points	0.54	0.75	0.21	0.41	0.06	0.35	0.41	0.62	0.46	0.55	0.55	0.47
Percentage of SME loan applications	SME loan applications/ total number of SMEs	..	..	..	..	18.20	..	25.80	16.40	23.00	26.15	18.93	32.28
Non-bank finance													
Venture and growth capital	EUR thousand	103 343	298 650	49 021	132 917	281 484	86 212	31 090	128 472	144 368	196 346	59 145	112 046
Venture and growth capital (growth rate)	%, Year-on-year growth rate	..	188.99	-83.59	171.14	111.77	-69.37	-55.23	230.97	13.00	34.10	-69.85	89.44
Factoring and invoice discounting	EUR million	..	..	349	321	180	299	407	339	..	..	..	..
Other indicators													
Bankruptcies, SMEs	Number	659	574	693	918	978	1 050	1 049	850	873	961	904	1 191
Bankruptcies, SMEs (growth rate)	%, Year-on-year growth rate	..	-12.90	20.73	32.47	6.54	7.36	-0.10	-18.97	2.71	10.08	-5.93	31.75

The full country profile is available at

https://doi.org/10.1787/061fe03d-en

30. Malaysia

SMEs represent the vast majority of firms in the Malaysian economy, outnumbering large enterprises, both in terms of number and employment. According to the released Economic Census 2016, SMEs accounted for 98.5% of total business establishments in Malaysia in 2015.

Finance is becoming increasingly important for Malaysian companies, as reflected by the 9.3% growth in outstanding SME loans in 2016 (MYR 299.8 billion, from MYR 274.4 billion in 2015). Outstanding SME loans continued to grow in 2017, albeit at a slightly slower pace, increasing by 5.3% to MYR 315.7 billion. As total outstanding loans did not grow as rapidly, the share of SME lending in total business lending increased to 50.6% in 2017, from 48.7% in 2016 and 46.7% in 2015.

The annual average interest rate on SME loans by banking institutions (BIs) decreased from 7.8% in 2015 to 6.6% in 2016, but again increased slightly to 7.0% in 2017.

As of the end of December 2017, there were a total of 110 registered corporations within the Venture Capital and Private Equity sector (101 venture capital corporations (VCC) or venture capital management corporations (VCMC) and 9 private equity managing corporations (PEMC) or private equity corporations (PEC)). A total of MYR 7.0 billion are under management within these funds, which represents an increase of 7.7% year-on-year. Investments made in 2017 decreased significantly by 26.6%, to MYR 417.8 million, from MYR 569.5 million in 2016.

In 2017, the Credit Guarantee Corporation Malaysia Berhad (CGC) recorded a lower approval value of MYS 3.4 billion, as compared to MYS 4.2 billion in 2016, mainly due to the increased penetration to the microenterprise market segment, with lower average financing size. This is evidenced by the double-digit growth of 14.0% in the number of SME accounts approved, from 7 568 in 2016 to 8 637 in 2017.

Impaired financing, a proxy for non-performing loans, of the overall financial sector stood at 3.3% of total business loans, stable from 2016 and 2015 (3.3% and 3.2% respectively). Despite the rapid expansion of bank credit to SMEs, SME impaired financing substantively decreased from a peak of 7.5% in 2010, to 3.2% in 2017, and was thus almost on par with the share of large firms.

Since its inception in 2004, the National SME Development Council (NSDC) has continued to steer SME development in Malaysia by setting the strategic direction, and by formulating policies to promote the growth of SMEs across all sectors. The success of the NSDC can be measured through a number of outcomes, such as the adoption of a national definition for SMEs, the development of an SME database and statistics, the monitoring and analyse of SME performances to facilitate policy formulation, the streamlining dissemination of information on SMEs, the development of SME financial infrastructures and the endorsement of the formulation of an SME Masterplan.

More recently, the policy focus of the authorities has been to further expand the non-bank possibilities for risk capital, particularly to enhance access to finance for SMEs that are innovative, high-growth and active in new growth areas. The advent of Financial Technologies (FinTech) is transforming the financial landscape and these are expected to offer more financing alternatives to SMEs, including equity crowdfunding, investment account platforms (IAP) and peer-to-peer (P2P) lending.

Table 30.1. Scoreboard for Malaysia

Indicator	Unit	2007	2008	2009	2010	2011	2012	2013	2014	2015	2016	2017
Debt												
Outstanding business loans, SMEs	MYR billion	128.0	138.9	141.6	141.2	165.3	187.6	211.0	243.7	274.4	299.8	315.7
Outstanding business loans, total	MYR billion	290.7	328.3	343.1	375.3	422.0	465.1	499.8	545.9	588.1	616.0	623.8
Share of SME outstanding loans	% of total outstanding business loans	44.00	42.30	41.30	37.60	39.17	40.34	42.22	44.64	46.66	48.66	50.60
New business lending, total	MYR billion	163.1	129.0	104.9	141.1	171.4	169.5	178.8	196.4	179.3	178.7	200.0
New business lending, SMEs	MYR billion	63.2	58.9	50.9	62.2	75.2	84.7	78.3	77.7	72.0	74.6	70.7
Share of new SME lending	% of total new lending	38.77	45.70	48.50	44.06	43.90	49.94	43.78	39.57	40.12	41.77	35.33
Share of short-term SME loans outstanding	% of total SME lending	..	..	..	..	..	..	28.73	26.52	24.18	23.61	24.10
Share of long-term SME loans outstanding	% of total SME loans	..	..	..	..	..	..	71.27	73.48	75.82	76.39	75.90
Guarantee and Financing Schemes	No. of accounts (in thousands)	13.00	10.37	14.07	7.67	7.50	2.15	2.37	6.84	8.23	7.57	8.64
Guarantee and Financing Schemes	MYR million	4 567	3 014	3 112	2 495	2 861	1 066	1 546	3 175	3 356	4 224	3 380
Impaired financing, total (amount)	MYR billion	..	20.2	18.1	23.6	21.3	18.4	17.7	17.9	18.9	20.5	20.8
Impaired financing, total	% of all business loans	..	6.16	5.29	6.28	5.05	3.97	3.55	3.27	3.21	3.32	3.33
Impaired financing, SMEs (amount)	MYR billion	..	9.9	8.9	10.6	9.6	8.5	8.2	8.6	8.9	8.9	10.1
Impaired financing, SMEs	% of all SME loans	..	7.12	6.28	7.50	5.78	4.53	3.89	3.51	3.24	2.96	3.19
Interest rate, SMEs	%	..	6.39	5.50	5.69	5.74	5.72	6.06	7.18	7.81	6.60	7.00
Interest rate, large firms	%	..	6.08	5.08	5.00	4.92	4.79	3.79	5.41	5.11	5.06	4.82
Interest rate spread	% points	..	0.31	0.42	0.69	0.82	0.94	2.28	1.77	2.69	1.54	2.17
Collateral, SMEs	% of SMEs needing collateral to obtain bank lending	..	..	..	..	..	..	49.11	51.85	46.08	41.56	43.58
Non-bank finance												
Total investment as at end of the period	MYR billion	1.78	1.93	2.59	3.39	3.59	2.76	3.43	3.25	2.22	2.92	2.45
Total investment as at end of the period	%, Year-on-year growth rate	53.90	8.13	34.06	31.05	5.81	23.12	24.52	5.45	31.58	31.61	16.05
Leasing and Factoring	MYR million	..	..	..	..	721	918	1 099	1 170	1 086	834	1 280

Note: Malaysia uses the term "Impaired financing" instead of "non-performing loans" and "Total investment as at end of the period" instead of "Venture and growth capital".

The full country profile is available at

https://doi.org/10.1787/061fe03d-en

31. Mexico

In Mexico there are 4 million SMEs, of which 97.4% are microenterprises that represent 12.4% of total gross production (TGP) and employ 47.2% of the workforce.

In 2018, the average interest rates varied according to the amounts of the loans and the size of the borrowing company. For large companies, the average interest rate was approximately 11.78%; For SMEs, the average was 17.70%.

In recent years, the Mexican government has developed a series of initiatives to support entrepreneurs and strengthen the access of SMEs to finance. These initiatives have included programs to promote the entrepreneurship of young people and women and programs to strengthen alternative financial instruments, in particular the use of venture capital by SMEs.

Guarantee funds have also been used to develop more specific programmes. For example, government initiatives were developed to support the provision of credit to previously ignored companies, such as construction companies, travel agencies, real estate development, rural tourism, small taxpayers and government SME providers.

Finally, the increase in competition among financial intermediaries has generated a significant improvement in credit conditions, which has resulted in longer loan maturities and lower interest rates.

Table 31.1. Scoreboard for Mexico

Indicator	Unit	2007	2008	2009	2010	2011	2012	2013	2014	2015	2016	2017	2018
Debt													
Outstanding business loans, SMEs	MXN billion	...	...	199.0	220.9	256.8	310.9	423.6	481.7	548.1	738.1	821.3	..
Outstanding business loans, total	MXN billion	...	...	975.1	1054.3	1218.7	1299.5	1424.7	1518.7	1758.3	2059.6	2357.5	..
Share of SME outstanding loans	% of total outstanding business loans			20.4	21.0	21.1	23.9	29.7	31.7	31.2	35.8	34.8	..
New business lending, total	MXN billion	...	...	...	79.3	164.4	80.8	125.3	93.9	239.6	301.3	297.9	..
New business lending, SMEs	MXN billion	...	...	...	21.9	35.9	54.1	112.6	58.2	66.4	190.0	83.2	..
Share of new SME lending	% of total new lending				27.7	21.8	67.0	89.9	61.9	27.7	63.1	27.9	..
Outstanding short-term loans, SMEs	MXN billion	11.1	41.3	39.1	30.8	30.0	36.9	34.3	12.5	17.7	21.7	32.1	23.8
Outstanding long-term loans, SMEs	MXN billion	10.8	22.4	38.5	36.6	44.2	60.1	80.9	89.0	90.1	107.1	99.1	115.3
Share of short-term SME lending	% of total SME lending	50.6	64.8	50.4	45.7	40.4	38.0	29.8	12.3	16.4	16.8	24.5	17.1
Government loan guarantees, SMEs	MXN billion	0.8	1.1	1.9	2.3	3.0	3.0	3.7	4.3	3.2	2.7	1.9	4.0
Government guaranteed loans, SMEs	MXN billion	21.9	63.8	77.7	67.4	74.3	96.9	115.1	101.6	107.8	128.8	84.3	84.3
Direct government loans, SMEs	MXN billion	...	...	29.5	30.8	53.3	63.0	88.1	135.4	183.8	111.1	131.2	139.1
Non-performing loans, total	% of all business loans			1.9	1.9	2.2	2.1	3.6	3.2	3.1	2.3	2.2	1.6
Interest rate, SMEs	%	19.9	16.2	12.1	11.9	11.4	11.2	9.9	9.2	9.1	11.0	17.0	17.7
Interest rate, large firms	%	7.4	8.0	8.1	7.9	7.7	7.6	6.6	6.0	6.0	8.1	10.6	11.8
Interest rate spread	% points	12.4	8.3	3.9	4.0	3.8	3.6	3.4	3.2	3.1	2.9	6.4	5.9
Non-bank finance													
Venture and growth capital	USD billion	4.1	1.7	1.8	4.3	2.5	4.0	1.8	6.9	11.9	4.5	4.0	1.6
Venture and growth capital (growth rate)	%, Year-on-year growth rate	...	-57.2	2.4	139.9	-41.2	60.9	-54.8	278.3	71.9	-61.8	-12.1	-60.9

Note: Venture capital data were updated for previous years by the by AMEXCAP (association for the private equity industry in Mexico).

The full country profile is available at

https://doi.org/10.1787/061fe03d-en

32. The Netherlands

The recovery of the Dutch economy continued in 2018, with GDP showing a year-on-year growth rate of 1.8%, and unemployment decreasing a further 1.3 percentage point to 3.6%, close to the lowest percentage since 2009.

New lending to SMEs stood at EUR 18 billion in 2018. This represents a slight decrease compared to 2017, when it stood at EUR 21 billion. Total outstanding business loans also decreased slightly, from EUR 328 billion in 2017 to EUR 325 billion in 2018.

Bank loans continue to be the main source of external financing for SMEs in the Netherlands. However, according to CPB's 2019 policy brief, Dutch SMEs had recourse to bank finance less often than their European counterparts did. On the other hand, the percentage of requested loans that were fully authorised rose from 74% in 2015 to 84% in 2018. The interest rate for SME firms (2-250 employees) is higher than for large firms by 2.0 percentage points (respectively 4.1% and 2.1%). The interest rate for large firms decreased by 40 basis points in 2018.

The sum of venture and growth capital investments in the Netherlands has fluctuated over the last decade with peaks in 2008 (EUR 691 million), 2015 (EUR 788 million), 2017 (the highest point so far with EUR 930 million) and 2018 (EUR 868 million). Since 2014, total private equity investments have not dipped below the EUR 700 million mark.

The average number of days before receiving a B2B payment was 28 days in 2018, with the average contractual term being 27 days, as was the case in 2017. The average number of days of delay to receive a B2B payment therefore remains 5 days, a decrease from 2015 by one day, and a considerable decrease compared to preceding years. The number of bankruptcies continued to decrease in 2018, with a year-on-year decrease of 4.4%. The number of bankruptcies is at a lower level than in 2007.

Several programmes are in place to support SMEs' access to finance. These include different guarantee schemes, like the Guarantee Scheme for SMEs (BMKB). Another is Qredits, a microcredit institution, introduced SME loans of various sizes in 2013. Furthermore, the Netherlands is creating a National Promotional Institution named Invest-NL. This institution is due to be established by the end of 2019. The aim of Invest-NL is, among other things, to help SMEs through financing or the development of viable business cases.

Table 32.1. Scoreboard for the Netherlands

Indicator	Unit	2007	2008	2009	2010	2011	2012	2013	2014	2015	2016	2017	2018
Debt													
Outstanding business loans, SMEs	EUR billion	..	..	..	..	..	..	143.3	136.0	130.4	124.1	125.9	127.1
Outstanding business loans, total	EUR billion	258.0	304.8	313.5	313.9	342.1	349.1	346.5	330.5	370.2	349.1	328.3	325.3
Share of SME outstanding loans	% of total outstanding business loans	..	..	..	..	..	..	41.4	41.1	35.2	35.6	38.3	39.1
New business lending, total	EUR billion	..	..	..	123.0	124.9	110.0	97.3	83.7	146.7	122.7	129.8	130.6
New business lending, SMEs	EUR billion	..	..	..	10.2	19.5	18.7	18.8	18.0	18.2	16.0	20.9	18.2
Share of new SME lending	% of total new lending	..	..	..	8.3	15.6	17.0	19.3	21.5	12.4	13.0	16.1	13.9
Outstanding short-term loans, SMEs	EUR billion	..	..	..	..	..	..	30.1	26.8	23.1	19.8	17.9	16.6
Outstanding long-term loans, SMEs	EUR billion	..	..	..	..	..	..	113.3	108.2	107.3	104.3	107.9	110.0
Share of short-term SME lending	% of total SME lending	..	..	..	..	..	..	21.0	19.8	17.7	15.9	14.3	13.1
Government loan guarantees, SMEs	EUR million	..	400.0	370.0	945.0	1040.0	590.0	415.0	473.0	523.0	710.0	646.0	643.0
Non-performing loans, SMEs	% of all SME loans	..	..	..	..	..	..	10.0	10.8	9.5	8.1	8.8	9.2
Interest rate, SMEs	%	5.4	5.7	4.5	6.0	6.4	5.1	4.3	4.1	4.4	3.7	2.9	4.1
Interest rate, large firms	%	..	..	..	..	3.5	3.6	3.4	2.8	2.4	3.2	2.5	2.1
Interest rate spread	% points	..	..	..	..	2.9	1.5	0.9	1.3	2.0	0.5	0.4	2.0
Collateral, SMEs	% of SMEs needing collateral to obtain bank lending	..	..	47.0	45.0	44.0	47.0	50.0	43.0	29.0	34.0	40.0	59.0
Percentage of SME loan applications	SME loan applications/ total number of SMEs	..	..	29.0	22.0	18.0	22.0	21.0	21.0	16.0	14.0	18.0	12.8
Rejection rate	1-(SME loans authorised/ requested)	..	..	31.0	10.0	13.0	28.0	28.0	27.0	7.0	18.0	17.0	16.0
Utilisation rate	SME loans used/ authorised	..	..	72.0	75.0	70.0	50.0	54.0	44.0	89.0	73.0	83.0	84.0
Non-bank finance													
Venture and growth capital	EUR million	498.0	575.0	506.1	323.3	660.0	419.4	389.3	589.9	714.2	704.3	731.2	868.0

Indicator	Unit	2007	2008	2009	2010	2011	2012	2013	2014	2015	2016	2017	2018
Venture and growth capital (growth rate)	%, Year-on-year growth rate	..	15.5	-12.0	-36.1	104.1	-36.5	-7.2	51.5	21.1	-1.4	3.8	18.7
Leasing and hire purchases	% of SMEs	..	..	..	..	..	..	..	..	9.0	16.0	12.0	21.0
Factoring and invoice discounting	% of SMEs	..	..	..	..	..	..	..	..	..	..	..	2.0
Other indicators													
Payment delays, B2B	Number of days	13.2	13.9	16.0	17.0	18.0	18.0	17.0	16.0	6.0	5.0	5.0	5.0
Bankruptcies, SMEs	Number	3 589	3 842	6 942	6 162	6 117	7 349	8 376	6 645	5 271	4 399	3 291	3 144
Bankruptcies, SMEs (growth rate)	%, Year-on-year growth rate	..	7.0	80.7	-11.2	-0.7	20.1	14.0	-20.7	-20.7	-16.5	-25.2	-4.5

The full country profile is available at

https://doi.org/10.1787/061fe03d-en

33. New Zealand

New Zealand has been recognised as the number one country in the world for ease of doing business with the shortest time to start a business; and the first in the world for corruption transparency.

SMEs, when defined as businesses with 0-49 employees, make up 99% of New Zealand businesses.

The upward trend of bank lending to businesses has continued in 2018 with an increase of 4.92% from 2017 to NZD 113.0 million. This was also true for SME bank lending, which reached NZD 68.2 million up from NZD 64.6 million in 2017. This did not significantly affect the share of SME lending of total business lending as it only increased by 0.4% to 60.4%.

Overall the New Zealand financial system is resilient to economic risks. However, it is vulnerable to severe risks, particularly the highly indebted New Zealand households and dairy farms. It is also vulnerable to international risks that could cause a major global economic recession.

Lending conditions for other sectors were also favourable in the second half of 2018. This was particularly true for commercial property loans.

Non-performing loans for all businesses have remained at the same low levels to the past three years at 0.5%. Non-performing loans for SMEs have decreased since 2017 from 0.9% to 0.6% in 2018, now being only slightly above the percentage of total non-performing business loans.

Interest rates for SMEs increased by 0.1% from 2017 to 2018, returning to 2015 levels of 9.4% after a brief decrease in 2016 and 2017. Data on interest rate spread and large business interest rates is no longer available since the Reserve Bank of New Zealand stopped the survey gathering this data.

After a rapid increase from 2016 to 2017, debt finance rejection rates for SMEs have decreased to 9.03% in 2018. This was significantly lower than the 11.7% rejection rate in 2017. The decrease in rejection rates could be caused by the increase in SME outstanding loans as banks were lending more money to SMEs in 2018. The data for rejection rates in New Zealand only includes businesses with 6-49 employees. This could affect the statistics as smaller and micro-businesses are likely to be rejected, which will not be included in the data available.

Growth in the New Zealand venture capital markets has been strong. In 2018, NZD 111.3 million were invested in seed and early stage ventures. This is an increase of 28% from the previous year.

New Zealand has eight licensed peer-to-peer lenders and eight licensed crowdfunding providers. These have been an increasingly popular source of funding for both individuals and businesses over the past few years.

Bankruptcies have continued their downward trend over the last three years to a new low of 1 486 in 2018. This figure only includes personal insolvencies but not corporate liquidations. However, many SME owners rely on their personal assets to finance their business.

Payment delays for business-to-business transactions have stayed almost the same at 5.8 days in 2017 to 5.9 days in 2018. SME payment delays decreased significantly from 6.3 days in 2017 to 5.8 days in 2018. The government has continued promoting e-Invoicing, which will be introduced in late 2019 with the aim to address payment delays. The government is also looking into other ways to address unfair payment terms and delays.

Table 33.1. Scoreboard for New Zealand

Indicator	Unit	2007	2008	2009	2010	2011	2012	2013	2014	2015	2016	2017	2018
Debt													
Outstanding business loans, SMEs	NZD billion	..	..	31.6	32.4	32.1	30.9	32.4	34.2	36.5	60.4	64.6	68.2
Outstanding business loans, total	NZD billion	80.0	87.6	80.4	78.9	79.9	83.0	85.4	89.0	95.0	101.6	107.7	113.0
Share of SME outstanding loans	% of total outstanding business loans	..	..	39.3	41.1	40.2	37.2	37.9	38.4	38.4	59.4	60.0	60.4
Non-performing loans, total	% of all business loans	..	..	1.7	2.1	1.8	1.5	1.1	0.8	0.6	0.5	0.5	0.5
Non-performing loans, SMEs	% of all SME loans	..	..	2.7	2.9	2.8	2.7	2.4	1.6	0.7	1.1	0.9	0.6
Interest rate, SMEs	%	12.2	11.2	9.8	10.1	10.0	9.6	9.5	10.3	9.4	9.2	9.3	9.4
Interest rate, large firms	%	9.0	8.2	5.7	6.3	6.1	6.0	5.4	6.0	5.4	4.6	..	..
Interest rate spread	% points	3.2	3.0	4.1	3.8	4.0	3.5	4.2	4.3	4.0	4.6	..	..
Rejection rate	% (SME loans rejected/ requested)	6.9	11.6	18.4	20.9	11.4	14.6	9.4	8.4	10.6	4.8	11.7	9.0
Non-bank finance													
Venture and growth capital (seed and early stage)	NZD million	29.5	32.6	43.2	53.1	34.8	29.9	53.1	56.4	61.2	69.0	87.0	111.3
Venture and growth capital (seed and early stage) (growth rate)	%, year-on-year growth rate	..	10.3	32.8	22.8	34.5	14.1	77.6	6.3	8.5	12.6	26.2	28.0
Other indicators													
Payment delays, B2B	number of days	..	..	..	..	15.7	13.5	12.7	10.4	7.1	5.9	5.8	5.9
Bankruptcies, total	number	3 585	2 504	2 564	3 054	2 714	2 417	2 188	1 921	1 979	1 996	1 863	1 486
Bankruptcies, total (growth rate)	%, year-on-year growth rate	..	-30.2	2.4	19.1	-11.1	-10.9	-9.5	-12.2	3.0	0.9	-6.7	-20.2

The full country profile is available at

https://doi.org/10.1787/061fe03d-en

34. People's Republic of China

In China, more than 98.64% of all firms are small businesses with 300 or fewer employees, contributing to over 60% of total GDP, 50% of tax income, 75% of job creation and 68% of exports. In 2018, new business creation reached record highs with a total 67.0 million new companies being created, up by 10.4% compared to 2017.

The stock of SME loans increased to CNY 46 477.3 billion in 2017, up 14.7% from 2016. The SME loan share increased from 54.60% to 64.96% over 2014-17. The ratio of short-term loans to total loans for SMEs decreased from 56.10% to 41.62 % over the same period. The ratio of SME loans backed by collateral dropped to 50.28% in 2017, down 1.77 percentage points.

In 2018, interest rates for SMEs and large firms were 5.17% and 5.07%, down 0.61 and 0.33 percentage points, respectively, compared to 2017. The interest rate spread between SMEs and large enterprises has narrowed to 0.1, which means lower financing costs for SMEs. In addition, SMEs were on average charged extra loan fees amounting to about 1.3% of the total bank loan volume. In 2018, the 1-year interest rate in the shadow banking sector ranged from 13%-15%, with a spread of about 9% from formal bank loans.

In 2018, the rejection rate of loan applications for SMEs was 3.69%, down 0.38 percentage points compared to 2017. On average, only 58.36% of loan amounts requested were finally granted. The utilisation rate of SME bank loans was 86.26%.

In 2018, SMEs obtained CNY 167.5 billion from the Shenzhen SME Board, and CNY 98.6 billion from Shenzhen Venture Board, and CNY 60.4 billion from National Equities Exchange and Quotations (NEEQ). Venture capital, leasing and factoring, online lending and crowdfunding continue to remain important sources of SME financing.

In 2018, payment delays for B2B slightly decrease to 38 days, 6 days down compared to the previous year. The ratio of SME non-performing loans to total SME loans was 2.58%, 0.53 percentage points higher than the ratio of non-performing loans for all businesses. The bankruptcy rate for SMEs was 2.85% in 2018 according to survey data, down 22.97% from the previous year.

National Financing Guarantee Fund was established with a registered capital of CNY 66.1 billion in 2018. This fund focuses on assisting small business, and its business covers re-guarantees for SME credit loans or direct PE investments. The National SME development fund had completed 208 investment projects totalling CNY 6.05 billion. National Guide Fund for Venture Investment in Emerging Industries account for an aggregate investment of over CNY 22.5 billion in 2018. Finally, Special Funds for SME Development continued to support SMEs by intensively investing in supporting innovative cities, promoting innovation and entrepreneurship and supporting financing guarantee.

The Chinese Government implemented a national strategy to support financing SMEs and entrepreneurship. During 2009-18, China put forward a series of policy adjustments, such as a differentiated deposit-reserve ratio policy and a sole credit allocation plan for SMEs, to encourage financial institutions to expand SME credit. Broader policy adjustments and reforms were carried out, targeted at easing SME access to diversified financing sources.

Table 34.1. Scoreboard for the People's Republic of China

Indicator	Unit	2007	2008	2009	2010	2011	2012	2013	2014	2015	2016	2017	2018
Debt													
Outstanding business loans, SMEs	RMB billion	..	..	13 616	17 139	21 168	25 356	28 585	33 302	35 300	40 517	46 477	..
Outstanding business loans, total	RMB billion	..	..	24 940	30 292	35 017	39 283	44 019	52 162	53 895	62 578	71 545	..
Share of SME outstanding loans	% of total outstanding business loans	..	..	54.60	56.58	60.45	64.55	64.94	63.84	65.50	64.75	64.96	..
Share of short-term SME lending	% of total SME lending	..	..	..	..	..	..	56.10	49.24	47.56	54.69	40.97	41.62
Direct government loans, SMEs	RMB billion	..	..	..	..	1 550	1 813	2 082	2 470	2 820	..	..	..
Non-performing loans, total	% of all business loans	..	..	..	..	1.26	1.21	1.25	1.49	2.04	2.07	2.05	..
Non-performing loans, SMEs	% of all SME loans	..	..	..	..	1.75	1.65	1.66	1.97	2.59	2.60	2.58	..
Interest rate, SMEs	%	..	..	..	..	..	..	8.39	7.51	5.23	4.77	5.78	5.17
Interest rate, large firms	%	..	..	..	..	..	..	7.72	7.47	5.26	4.89	5.40	5.07
Interest rate spread	% points	..	...	..	..	..	..	0.67	0.04	-0.03	-0.12	0.38	0.10
Collateral, SMEs	% of SMEs needing collateral to obtain bank lending	..	..	..	..	51.59	52.98	54.52	54.76	55.67	52.05	50.28	..
Percentage of SME loan applications	SME loan applications/ total number of SMEs	..	..	..	..	..	..	..	..	69.88	63.06	53.09	58.36
Rejection rate	1-(SME loans authorised/ requested)	..	..	..	..	..	..	6.19	11.97	11.72	6.13	4.07	3.69
Utilisation rate	SME loans used/ authorised	..	..	..	..	..	..	93.51	94.75	94.48	94.03	89.91	86.26
Non-bank finance													
Venture and growth capital (stock)	RMB billion	111	146	161	241	320	331	264	293	336	377	411	..
Venture and growth capital (stock, growth rate)	%, Year-on-year growth rate	..	30.80	10.26	49.93	32.88	3.59	-20.34	11.15	14.59	12.02	9.16	..
Venture and growth capital (incremental)	RMB billion	..	..	..	..	..	25.11	27.90	37.44	46.56	50.55	84.53	..
Venture and growth capital (incremental, growth rate)	%, Year-on-year growth rate	..	..	..	..	..	..	11.11	34.19	24.36	8.57	67.22	..
Leasing and hire purchases	RMB billion	24	155	370	700	930	1 550	2 100	3 200	4 440	5 330	6 060	6 650
Factoring and invoice discounting	EUR billion	..	55.0	67.3	154.6	274.9	343.8	378.1	406.1	352.9	301.6	405.5	411.5
Other indicators													
Payment delays, B2B	Number of days	..	..	..	..	..	..	95.91	72.31	64.44	65.21	44.00	38.00
Bankruptcies, SMEs	Percentage of all SMEs	..	..	..	..	..	..	8	7	5	5	4	3
Bankruptcies, SMEs (growth rate)	%, Year-on-year growth rate	..	..	..	..	..	..	..	-4.36	-24.59	-13.37	-21.78	-22.97

The full country profile is available at

https://doi.org/10.1787/061fe03d-en

35. Peru

Peru's Central Reserve Bank (CRB) forecasts an annual growth of 4.0% in 2019, following similar growth in 2018 and thanks to a better performance of internal private consumption. It is also expected that the terms of trade will experience a slight improvement from -2.9% to -0.7%, due to a reduction on import prices. In addition, the Central Reserve Bank expects to maintain its interest rate to stimulate the economy (2.75%), given that the inflation rate is stable at around 2.0% and that the output gap is negative.

Outstanding business loans grew by 4.9% in 2018. Based on preliminary data, SME outstanding business loans amounted to 20.8% of all outstanding business loans in 2018, which is slightly lower than the share observed in 2017 (21.5%).

It is also important to point out that 2.83% of all outstanding business loans were non-performing loans, a slight increase from 2017 (2.75%). Non-performing loans in the SME sector experienced a insignificant deterioration from 9.05% in 2017 to 10.13% in 2018. On the other hand, the interest rate spread between SME loans and large firm loans fell slightly from 14.6 to 13.7 percentage points by the end of year 2018, according to the Central Reserve Bank.

In 2018, 99.6% of Peruvian enterprises were SMEs (including micro-enterprises, which employ less than ten persons), and they employed 89.1% of the private sector's workforce. Compared to 2017, the SME sector grew by 16.0% in 2018 (in terms of the number of SMEs), a significant recovery compared to recent years, according to the National Tax Administration Bureau. Among these formal enterprises, only 5.5% acceded to the formal financial system in 2018, decreasing from 5.9% in 2017. The reason behind this decrease is that the amount of formal enterprises created on 2018 was much higher than in previous years. Importantly, direct government loans from public banks decreased by 12.3%.

As many as 90.8% of the outstanding loans to SME were provided by private banks, with other types of financial institutions granting the remaining 9.2%. It is important to note that it is not necessary for an enterprise to be formal to obtain a formal credit, because entrepreneurs can access credit as individuals.

Table 35.1. Scoreboard for Peru

Indicator	Unit	2010	2011	2012	2013	2014	2015	2016	2017	2018
					Debt					
Outstanding business loans, SMEs. As of June 30	PEN Billion	16.20	18.65	21.88	24.77	28.21	30.37	32.57	32.54	33.04
Outstanding business loans, total. As of June 30	PEN Billion	71.41	81.29	87.57	104.22	120.35	139.38	146.39	151.13	158.46
Share of SME outstanding loans	% of total outstanding business loans	22.69	22.95	24.98	23.77	23.44	21.79	22.25	21.53	20.85
New business lending, total	PEN Billion	3.99	2.64	2.12	2.78	3.70	1.13	3.03	7.37	12.65
New business lending, SMEs	PEN Billion	3.41	2.29	1.88	2.26	3.30	0.82	2.77	6.59	8.03
Share of new SME lending	% of total new lending	85.42	86.77	88.61	81.27	89.39	72.85	91.68	89.32	63.46
Government loan guarantees, SMEs	PEN Billion	..	..	..	..	..	..	400	..	..
Direct government loans, SMEs	PEN Billion	26	20	26	143	224	234	268	237	208
Non-performing loans, total	% of all business loans	1.93	1.55	1.41	1.56	1.79	1.98	2.29	2.75	2.83
Non-performing loans, SMEs	% of all SME loans	7.82	6.31	5.21	6.27	6.99	8.42	9.07	9.05	10.13
Interest rate, SMEs	%	27.81	25.08	24.41	22.91	22.36	22.83	23.48	23.05	21.55
Interest rate, large firms	%	7.15	8.29	9.06	8.46	8.32	7.90	8.26	8.41	7.83
Interest rate spread	% points	20.66	16.79	15.35	14.45	14.05	14.93	15.22	14.64	13.72
Percentage of SME loan applications	SME loan applications/ total number of SMEs	..	..	..	..	37.82	47.13	58.98	..	..
Rejection rate	1-(SME loans authorised/ requested)	..	..	..	..	5.07	5.25	0.00	..	..
Utilisation rate	SME loans used/ authorised	..	..	..	..	2948.07	94.75	0.00	..	..
					Non-bank finance					
Leasing and hire purchases	PEN Billion	3 267	3 723	4 182	3 807	3 955	3 691	3 540	3 923	2 948
Factoring and invoice discounting	PEN Billion	675	679	657	697	717	740	786	925	916
					Other indicators					
Bankruptcies, all businesses	Number	..	..	..	69 427	89 982	85 190	83 079	87 586	..

Note: *Preliminary data.

The full country profile is available at

https://doi.org/10.1787/061fe03d-en

36. Poland

Since the financial crisis of 2009, Poland's GDP has grown constantly. It reached 5.1% in 2018. SMEs contribution to GDP is steadily increasing. The banking sector is overall sound.

SMEs are the backbone of the Polish economy. In 2017, Polish SMEs employed over 6.7 million employees – 68.3% of all enterprise employees – and accounted for 55.6% of value added by all enterprises and 46.3% of all investment outlays.

The stock of SME outstanding loans in 2018 decreased year-on-year and currently accounts for 53.7% of total business lending. The vast majority of SME loans are long-term loans. The share of SME non-performing loans decreased for the sixth year in a row in 2018.

Venture capital and growth investments have increased significantly since 2014. In 2018, they grew by 78.2% year-on-year.

SME interest rates increased compared to 2017, from 2.95% to 3.4%. The figure in 2018 is lower by 1.9 percentage points than the value at its peak, in 2008. Interest rates for large enterprises stood at 2.9%. The interest rate spread reached 0.5 percentage points in 2018.

Poland offers multiple instruments to support SMEs' access to finance, both at the national and at the regional level. Under the De Minimis Guarantee Scheme, SMEs can obtain loan guarantee covering up to 60% of the loan amount, up to a maximum of PLN 3.5 million. Since its launch in 2013, over 141 000 thousands SMEs have been granted a guarantee under this scheme.

Guarantees and other forms of financial support for SMEs are also offered as part of European Union (EU) cohesion funds as well as other EU programmes (e.g. Programme for the Competitiveness of Enterprises and small and medium-sized enterprises – COSME, Programme for Employment and Social Innovation – EaSI).

Table 36.1. Scoreboard for Poland

Indicator	Unit	2007	2008	2009	2010	2011	2012	2013	2014	2015	2016	2017	2018
						Debt							
Outstanding business loans, SMEs	PLN Billion	..	125.31	127.22	127.00	159.02	164.81	163.93	175.63	185.78	193.63	206.57	208.48
Outstanding business loans, total	PLN Billion	..	233.28	222.08	219.69	264.51	272.25	277.96	300.92	327.27	344.93	366.02	388.25
Share of SME outstanding loans	% of total outstanding business loans	..	53.72	57.29	57.81	60.12	60.54	58.97	58.36	56.77	56.14	56.44	53.70
Outstanding short-term loans, SMEs	PLN Billion	..	31.93	31.25	31.52	38.45	39.88	37.37	40.46	41.60	42.81	43.93	39.30
Outstanding long-term loans, SMEs	PLN Billion	..	90.18	93.24	93.73	116.22	122.23	123.43	130.25	138.33	145.05	156.36	161.89

Indicator	Unit	2007	2008	2009	2010	2011	2012	2013	2014	2015	2016	2017	2018
Share of short-term SME lending	% of total SME lending	..	26.15	25.10	25.17	24.86	24.60	23.24	23.70	23.12	22.79	28.09	24.27
Government loan guarantees, SMEs	PLN Billion	..	..	..	..	..	..	7.00	9.65	8.90	9.36	9.91	10.17
Government guaranteed loans, SMEs	PLN Billion	..	..	..	..	..	..	12.24	17.43	15.86	16.43	17.80	18.17
Non-performing loans, total	% of all business loans	..	6.50	11.58	12.40	10.37	11.78	11.61	11.33	10.31	9.11	8.28	11.32
Non-performing loans, SMEs	% of all SME loans	..	7.46	13.35	14.59	12.33	13.06	12.99	12.75	12.29	10.97	10.04	8.70
Interest rate, SMEs	%	..	5.37	3.82	4.31	4.57	4.86	3.85	3.52	3.00	2.86	2.95	3.43
Interest rate, large firms	%	..	5.62	4.28	4.00	4.45	4.74	3.83	3.40	2.90	2.77	2.76	2.92
Interest rate spread	% points	..	-0.25	-0.46	0.31	0.12	0.12	0.02	0.12	0.10	0.09	0.19	0.51
Collateral, SMEs	% of SMEs needing collateral to obtain bank lending	..	..	..	..	..	..	..	..	..	38.92	30.33	..
Percentage of SME loan applications	SME loan applications/ total number of SMEs	..	..	..	..	..	..	..	..	..	78.55	80.12	..
Rejection rate	1-(SME loans authorised/ requested)	..	..	..	..	..	..	..	..	..	37.20	31.78	..
Utilisation rate	SME loans used/ authorised	..	..	..	..	..	..	..	..	..	66.44	61.83	..
Non-bank finance													
Venture and growth capital	EUR Million	147.5	96.4	70.7	112.7	197.5	127.1	198.2	89.3	140.3	190.7	195.8	349.0
Venture and growth capital (growth rate)	%, Year-on-year growth rate	..	-34.65	-26.70	59.44	75.28	-35.62	55.93	-54.96	57.07	35.97	2.69	78.23
Leasing and hire purchases	PLN Billion	27.11	24.09	21.43	23.92	27.79	26.91	30.42	34.29	37.83	51.01	58.19	66.44
Factoring and invoice discounting	PLN Billion	30.34	45.51	53.16	88.61	95.33	113.06	129.59	152.68	171.64	192.74	222.49	269.63

The full country profile is available at

https://doi.org/10.1787/061fe03d-en

37. Portugal

In 2017, SMEs comprised 99.7% of enterprises in Portugal, employed 72.4% of the labour force and were responsible for 58.1% of the turnover of the non-financial business economy.

In 2018, the global stock of business loans further decreased by 4.8% year-on-year, below the decrease in SME lending which stood at 6.2%. The share of SME loans in total business loans remained slightly above 85% since 2015. It should be noted that the share of SME loans is above 80% for more than a decade.

The decline in SME lending was more pronounced in short-term SME loans, having dropped by 62% over the 2010-18 period. Despite this long term trend, since 2016, the share of short-term in total SME loans is rising. In 2018, such loans registered an increase of 1.8% compared to the previous year, whereas long-term SME loans decreased by 1.6% year-on-year.

The share of government guaranteed loans in total SME loans grew significantly, from 5.4% in 2009 to 10.5% in 2018, demonstrating the sustained public efforts to support SMEs' access to finance.

The average interest rate for SME loans decreased to 3.13% in 2018, marking the sixth year in a row of decline, after the 2012 peak of 7.6%. The interest rate spread between SMEs and large firms increased from 1.9 to 2.2 percentage points between 2009 and 2012, and decreased since then, to 1.2 percentage point in 2018, indicating an improvement in SME financing conditions.

After a continuous decline in venture capital investments since 2007, there were signs of recovery since 2012. Total venture capital investments in 2015 increased again to EUR 59 million, +354% compared to their 2011 value. Nevertheless, the amount of venture capital invested dropped again to EUR 21 million in 2016, a 64.4% decrease from 2015, but recovered in the last two years, and in 2018, total venture capital investments reached EUR 32 million, with an increase of 23.1% year-on-year.

Payment delays rose from 35 days in 2009 to 41 days in 2011, and then almost halved again from 40 days in 2012 to 12 days in 2018, decreasing steadily in the last five years.

Following four years of continuous increase (2009-12) in the number of bankruptcies, 2018 ended with a new 13.1% reduction from 2017, with 2 694 bankruptcies, at pre-crisis levels.

SMEs' access to finance has been a major priority for the government. In this context, several credit lines were made available to facilitate SMEs' access to credit. The government programmes "SME Invest/Growth and *Capitalizar*" offered credit lines with a total stock of EUR 20.2 billion, and long-term maturities (up to 7 years). They also offer preferential conditions, such as subsidised risk-sharing public guarantees, which cover between 50% and 75% of the loan. These credit lines aim to support fixed investment as well as SME working capital.

On the equity side, several venture capital funds and business angels co-investment vehicles have been implemented, totalling EUR 270 million for venture capital investments in the start-up and expansion phases (2017-2020). To reinforce the entrepreneurial ecosystem, the government created in 2018, a venture capital fund with the European Investment Fund (EIF), totalling EUR 100 million, the "Portugal Tech".

The Portuguese Government approved a strategic program, "Capitalizar", to support the capitalization of Portuguese companies, relaunch investment and facilitate SMEs' access to funding, mainly through:

- Financial instruments of direct or indirect participation in companies;
- Special financing instruments to quasi-equity capital;
- Tax measures to encourage firm capitalisation.

Table 37.1. Scoreboard for Portugal

Indicator	Unit	2007	2008	2009	2010	2011	2012	2013	2014	2015	2016	2017	2018
Debt													
Outstanding business loans, SMEs	EUR billion	83.8	91.7	92.3	90.8	87	79.8	73.6	70.9	68.1	66.8	62.7	58.8
Outstanding business loans, total	EUR billion	102	112.4	114	111.5	107.3	98.8	91.8	86.3	79	77.3	72.6	69.1
Share of SME outstanding loans	% of total outstanding business loans	82.17	81.57	80.96	81.45	81.13	80.75	80.13	82.19	86.2	86.4	86.4	85.2
New business lending, total	EUR billion	64.3	61.8	46.3	45.6	45	45.6	49.1	41.2	33.8	29.8	28.8	31.6
New business lending, SMEs	EUR billion	28.9	26.4	23.1	9	14.2	12.5	11.9	11.9	11.9	11.3	10.9	11.2
Share of new SME lending	% of total new lending	44.9	42.78	49.97	19.72	31.63	27.52	24.16	28.79	35.2	37.88	37.74	35.56
Short-term loans, SMEs	EUR billion	..	..	28.9	26.7	23.8	16.7	14.2	11.4	9.8	10.2	10.1	10.3
Long-term loans, SMEs	EUR billion	..	..	58.8	59.2	56.1	53.2	47.8	47.3	46.1	44.6	43.1	42.4
Share of short-term SME lending	% of total SME lending	..	..	32.94	31.09	29.77	23.91	22.94	19.41	17.48	18.69	18.98	19.5
Government guaranteed loans, SMEs	EUR billion	..	..	5	6.8	6.1	5.7	5.8	5.5	5.6	5.7	6.1	6.2
Non-performing loans, total	% of all business loans	1.83	2.44	4.22	4.59	6.94	10.54	13.46	15.05	15.91	15.85	13.46	9.43
Non-performing loans, SMEs	% of all SME loans	4.14	4.38	4.95	5.41	8.18	12.33	15.77	17.32	17.92	17.88	15.1	10.38
Interest rate, SMEs	%	7.05	7.64	5.71	6.16	7.41	7.59	6.82	5.97	4.6	3.83	3.42	3.13
Interest rate, large firms	%	5.29	5.92	3.84	3.91	5.4	5.43	4.97	4.37	3.25	2.69	2.14	1.93
Interest rate spread	% points	1.76	1.72	1.87	2.25	2.01	2.16	1.85	1.6	1.35	1.14	1.28	1.2
Collateral, SMEs	% of SMEs needing collateral to obtain bank lending	..	..	85.95	86.3	85.16	84.76	83.42	84.88	88.88	88.78	89.71	89.57
Non-bank finance													
Venture and growth capital	EUR million	120.8	65.3	60.8	68.9	110.7	59.6	127.6	175.9	114.9	44.9	70.8	364.5
Venture and growth capital (growth rate)	%, Year-on-year growth rate	..	-45.9	-6.9	13.4	60.6	-46.2	114.1	37.9	-34.7	-60.9	57.5	414.6
Leasing and hire purchases	EUR billion	..	..	5.3	5.2	3.4	3	2.7	2.4	2.3	2.3	2.2	2.2
Factoring and invoice discounting	EUR million	..	..	621	733	402	338	376	476	547	441	421	454
Other indicators													
Payment delays, B2B	Number of days	39.9	33	35	37	41	40	35	33	21	20	20	12
Bankruptcies, SMEs	Number	2 612	3 528	3 815	4 091	4 746	6 688	6 030	4 019	4 714	3 620	3 099	2 694
Bankruptcies, SMEs (growth rate)	%, Year-on-year growth rate	..	35.1	8.1	7.2	16	40.9	-9.8	-33.3	17.3	-23.2	-14.39	-13.1

The full country profile is available at

https://doi.org/10.1787/061fe03d-en

38. Russian Federation

The definition of SMEs in the Russian Federation differs from the EU definition, hindering accurate international comparisons.

There are more than 6.2 million micro, small, and medium-sized enterprises in Russia (as of May 2019), accounting for about 22.3% of GDP and employing around 26.3% of the workforce.

New SME loans doubled between 2008 and 2013, but in 2014 there was slight decline (-6%) which was followed by a sharp 28% drop in 2015. In 2016, the downward trend continued (-3%). This movement reversed in 2017 and 2018, as new SME loans increased respectively by 15% and 11%.

In 2018, the continuous (2014-2017) decline in outstanding SMEs loans turned into weak growth (+1%).

Lending conditions tightened considerably in 2014-2015, with an increase of the central interest rate from 5.5% to 17%, but this trend reversed in 2016-2018, when interest rates sharply decreased as a result of an easing of monetary policy, and the launch of new state programmes of preferential lending for SMEs.

The interest rate spread between loans charged to SMEs and to all non-financial enterprises increased in 2015, shrank more than twofold in 2016, and increased slightly again in 2017. In 2018, the decline continued and the indicator reached its historical minimum.

Venture capital (VC) and Private equity (PE) have grown steadily over the 2008-13 period, doubling from 2008 and reaching USD 26.3 billion by the end of 2013. In 2014, there was a slight decrease of 1%, which in the next 2 years was followed by a strong decline (14% in 2015 and 13% in 2016). In 2017, the decline was replaced by low growth (4 %). In 2018, this trend continued, with 8% growth.

Non-performing SME loans doubled between 2013 and 2017 from 7.08% to 14.93% of all loans. In 2018 this indicator decreased slightly, but remained at high levels (12.38%).

In 2018, government initiatives to legalise self-employment were launched. The pilot project started in four regions. In addition, a large-scale state programme to promote entrepreneurship was launched.

One of the factors that could limit the development of entrepreneurship in 2019 is the increase in the tax burden (growth in VAT rate from 18% to 20%).

Table 38.1. Scoreboard for the Russian Federation

Indicator	Unit	2008	2009	2010	2011	2012	2013	2014	2015	2016	2017	2018
Debt												
Outstanding business loans, SMEs	RUB billion	2 523	2 648	3 228	3 843	4 494	5 161	5 117	4 885	4 469	4 170	4 215
Outstanding business loans, total	RUB billion	12 997	12 412	13 597	17 061	19 580	22 242	27 785	29 885	28 204	29 219	32 229
Share of SME outstanding loans	% of total outstanding business loans	19.41	21.33	23.74	22.53	22.95	23.20	18.42	16.35	15.84	14.27	13.08
New business lending, total	RUB billion	..	18 978	20 662	28 412	30 255	36 225	38 530	34 236	35 580	38 453	45 005
New business lending, SMEs	RUB billion	4 090	3 003	4 705	6 056	6 943	8 065	7 611	5 460	5 303	6 117	6 816
Share of new SME lending	% of total new lending		15.82	22.77	21.31	22.95	22.26	19.75	15.95	14.90	15.91	15.15
Government loan guarantees, SMEs	RUB billion	..	..	..	24	28	30	22	..	102	141	146,4
Government guaranteed loans, SMEs	RUB billion	..	..	..	51	62	65	48	..	172	234	312
Non-performing loans, total	% of all business loans		5.83	5.43	4.30	4.57	4.31	4.59	5.61	6.91	6.66	6.51
Non-performing loans, SMEs	% of all SME loans	2.93	7.56	8.80	8.19	8.39	7.08	7.71	13.64	14.23	14.93	12.38
Interest rate, SMEs	%	..	..	..	..	..	..	16.09	16.44	13.03	10.84	10.08
Interest rate, large firms	%	..	..	..	..	..	..	12.94	12.95	11.70	9.41	9.17
Interest rate spread	% points	..	..	..	..	..	..	3.15	3.49	1.33	1.43	0.91
Non-bank finance												
Venture and growth capital	USD million	14 327	15 192	16 787	20 092	24 126	26 251	25 991	22 386	19 566	20 398	22 065
Venture and growth capital (growth rate)	%, Year-on-year growth rate	...	6.04	10.50	19.69	20.08	8.81	-0,99	-13.87	-12.60	4.25	8.17
Leasing and hire purchases	RUB billion	..	..	..	..	2 530	2 900	3 200	3 100	3 200	3 450	4 300
Factoring and invoice discounting	RUB billion	..	..	361	725	1 230	1 600	1 650	1 400	1 530	1 850	2 630

The full country profile is available at

https://doi.org/10.1787/061fe03d-en

39. Serbia

SMEs dominate the Serbian business economy, accounting for 99% of all enterprises. In 2018, SMEs employed more than 65% of the labour force and accounted for 57.4% of total gross value added and for 37% of total exports. Sector-specific data indicates that most SMEs belonged to the trade sector (26.0%), followed by the manufacturing sector (15.4%), professional, scientific and innovative activities (12.8%), and transportation and storage (10.0%).

Results from the 2018 SME lending conditions survey conducted by the National Bank of Serbia indicate that SME financing conditions continued to improve, prolonging a trend that started in 2014. These improvements are linked to the country's achievement and maintenance of a more macro-economically stable environment, as well as to the Central Bank's relaxation of monetary policy and successful work on resolutions for dealing with NPLs, which have lowered the country's risk premium.

In 2018, new bank lending to SMEs increased by 17.2% year-on-year. The share of new SMEs loans among total corporate loans likewise increased by 1.8 percentage points to 44.5% in 2018. The stock of SMEs loans in 2018 increased by 12% year-on-year to EUR 6.5 billion. As a result, the share of outstanding SME loans in total corporate loans stood at 31.2%. Long-term loans amounted to 77.2% of total SMEs loans.

Lending conditions as captured by interest rate levels continue to improve. Interest rates for SME loans in or indexed to foreign currencies decreased to 4.2% in 2018 (from 4.6% in 2017 and 5.7% in 2016), however the interest rate spread between large companies and SMEs increased slightly to 1.9 percentage points (from 1.8 percentage points in 2017). On the Serbian dinar-denominated loans side, interest rates on loans to large companies decreased faster than interest rates on SME loans, thus the interest rate spread on RSD-denominated loans increased to 2.4 percentage points (from 1.9 percentage points in 2017). More specifically, interest rates on RSD-denominated loans to SMEs declined from 6.9% in 2017 to 6.3% in 2018.

The rejection rate (that is, the percentage of SME loan applications that are rejected) decreased to 17.1% in 2018 (from 28.3% in 2017), while the utilisation rate (the percentage of used SME loans among all SME loans that were approved) increased to 95% in 2018 (from 90.6% in 2017). At the same time, the share of loans requiring collaterals (excluding bills of exchange) decreased to 53.1% in 2018 (from 53.8% in 2017).

The share of NPLs in total SMEs loans continued to improve in 2018 and stood at 6.1% (compared to 9.9% in 2017). This is a strong signal supporting the successful implementation of the NPL Resolution Strategy, which affected not only the SME segment but the whole corporate sector, whose NPL share decreased to 5% in 2018 from 10.4% in 2017.

Table 39.1. Scoreboard for Serbia

Indicator	Unit	2007	2008	2009	2010	2011	2012	2013	2014	2015	2016	2017	2018
Debt													
Outstanding business loans, SMEs	EUR Million	2 858	3 994	3 966	4 202	4 320	4 352	4 061	4 779	5 340	5 552	5 802	6 497
Outstanding business loans, total	EUR Million	13 598	19 044	19 268	19 777	20 028	20 460	19 154	18 724	18 677	18 362	19 150	20 847
Share of SME outstanding loans	% of total outstanding business loans	21.02	20.97	20.58	21.25	21.57	21.27	21.20	25.52	28.59	30.24	30.30	31.16
New business lending, total	EUR Million	..	..	..	..	8 862	9 043	7 093	6 765	8 461	10 130	10 966	12 339
New business lending, SMEs	EUR Million	2 027	3 409	3 015	3 190	3 323	2 771	2 302	2 717	3 332	4 038	4 688	5 495
Share of new SME lending	% of total new lending	..	..	..	..	37.49	30.64	32.45	40.16	39.38	39.86	42.75	44.53
Outstanding short-term loans, SMEs	EUR Million	1 000	1 265	1 356	1 436	1 308	1 257	1 386	1 405	1 348	1 380	1 451	1 483
Outstanding long-term loans, SMEs	EUR Million	1 858	2 729	2 610	2 766	3 012	3 096	2 675	3 374	3 993	4 172	4 350	5 013
Share of short-term SME lending	% of total SME lending	34.98	31.67	34.20	34.17	30.28	28.87	34.13	29.40	25.24	24.86	25.01	22.83
Government guaranteed loans, SMEs	EUR Million	0	0	298	523	390	569	342	750	126	13	14	15
Non-performing loans, total	% of all business loans	..	14.56	19.84	20.70	22.33	19.19	24.52	24.64	21.71	17.22	10.41	5.05
Non-performing loans, SMEs	% of all SME loans	6.72	10.56	18.86	21.00	22.64	26.15	28.05	27.08	26.69	20.16	9.91	6.15
Interest rate, SMEs	%	10.69	10.90	10.57	10.06	9.72	8.15	8.03	7.25	6.31	5.69	4.58	4.23
Interest rate, large firms	%	6.32	8.04	7.23	7.36	7.88	6.60	6.34	5.18	3.87	3.13	2.78	2.30
Interest rate spread	% points	4.37	2.85	3.35	2.70	1.85	1.55	1.70	2.07	2.44	2.56	1.79	1.93
Collateral, SMEs	% of SMEs needing collateral to obtain bank lending	31.62	38.78	43.14	44.51	45.59	53.00	55.06	53.13	53.79	42.70	53.85	53.09
Percentage of SME loan applications	SME loan applications/ total number of SMEs	..	..	..	..	..	..	..	..	14.94	16.46	16.89	15.46
Rejection rate	1-(SME loans authorised/ requested)	18.66	17.25	28.42	27.13	15.77	32.02	32.18	25.15	24.52	28.18	28.32	17.09
Utilisation rate	SME loans used/ authorised	71.75	81.66	88.20	67.76	83.83	86.11	87.92	86.47	87.86	88.05	90.58	94.99

The full country profile is available at

https://doi.org/10.1787/061fe03d-en

40. Slovak Republic

SMEs dominate the Slovak economy, accounting for 99.5% of the business population (excluding self-employed individuals). The number of SMEs increased by 1.7% in 2018, and micro-enterprises accounted for a considerable portion of this growth, growing by 1.8% year-on-year.

Credit conditions and access to finance for SMEs improved in 2018, which was reflected not only in an increase in the volume of existing and new bank loans but also in a decline in non-performing loans. The amount of outstanding business loans has been growing since 2013, increasing by 5.2% in 2018 from 2017, to EUR 15 281 million. More than half of SMEs' outstanding business loans (61.8%) were long-term, while short-term loans accounted for 38.2% (EUR 5 842 million) of SMEs' outstanding business loans.

Favorable credit conditions increased interest in bank financing for all size categories of enterprises. Despite a decrease in the share of SMEs in the total volume of new lending, the volume of SMEs' new business lending increased year-on-year by 8.4%.

The share of non-performing SME loans among all SME loans was higher (5.7%) than the share of non-performing loans among all business loans (4.1%) in 2018. Both shares, however, decreased in 2018.

Interest rates on SME loans fell from 3.8% in 2012 to 3.0% in 2017 and remained unchanged in 2018. The drop in SME interest rates over these years has been making finance available to more SMEs. Interest rates for self-employed entrepreneurs reached 5.2% in 2018, 0.1 percentage points lower than in the previous year. This improvement in SMEs' access to credit financing indicates that credit conditions have been gradually improving over the reference period.

After last year's significant decline in the volume of venture and growth capital caused by the closure of funding support under the JEREMIE initiative for the 2007-2013 programming period, there was a recovery in 2018. The amount of venture capital investments increased year-on-year by 85.6% to EUR 5.4 million in 2018. The majority of investments were focused on established SMEs – to expand production capacities, to develop market potential or further development of product or service. Compared to SME bank financing, the amount of venture capital invested in 2018 is still negligible.

The payment discipline of SMEs has not changed over the past 3 years - average business-to-business (B2B) payment delays remained stable at 19 days.

SME bankruptcies, which totalled 252 over the year, accounted for 98.4% of all bankruptcies in 2018. Despite the decreasing trend, the number of SME bankruptcies for 2018 is still higher than in the pre-crisis period.

The government has continued to implement several policies that seek to improve SMEs' access to finance. Primarily, these consist of loan and guarantee provisions to SMEs by specialised state banks (The Slovak Guarantee and Development Bank and Eximbank) and the Slovak Business Agency.

Table 40.1. Scoreboard for the Slovak Republic

Indicator	Unit	2007	2008	2009	2010	2011	2012	2013	2014	2015	2016	2017	2018
Debt													
Outstanding business loans, SMEs (1)	EUR billion	9.1	12.1	12	12	10.6	11	10.7	11.9	13.2	13.5	14.6	15.3
Outstanding business loans, SMEs (2)	EUR billion	..	..	..	..	..	5.9	6.7	6.9	7.4	8.7	8.9	9.2
Outstanding business loans, total	EUR billion	13.9	15.7	15.2	15.2	16.1	15.5	15.1	14.8	16.1	16.9	18.1	18.9
Share of SME outstanding loans (1)	% of total outstanding business loans	65.7	77.12	79.39	79.39	65.77	71.11	71.07	80.22	81.7	79.81	80.46	80.66
New business lending, total	EUR billion	8.49	9.44	7.56	9.12	10.69	11.69	11.88	12.5	11.78	8.67	9.5	10.72
New business lending, SMEs (2)	EUR billion	..	..	..	..	..	2.36	2.63	2.6	3.09	3.13	3.17	3.46
Share of new SME lending	% of total new lending	..	..	..	..	..	20.2	22.16	20.83	26.2	36.14	33.37	32.29
Outstanding short-term loans, SMEs	EUR million	4 609	4 797	4 981	4 987	4 188	4 481	4 532	5 385	5 766	5 394	5 695	5 842
Outstanding long-term loans, SMEs	EUR million	4 527	7 295	7 051	7 059	6 412	6 557	6 202	6 517	7 404	8 129	8 832	9 439
Share of short-term SME lending	% of total SME lending	50.45	39.67	41.4	41.4	39.51	40.6	42.22	45.24	43.78	39.89	39.21	38.23
Government loan guarantees, SMEs	EUR million	82	99	81	70	84	87	38	26	60	46	32	39
Government guaranteed loans, SMEs	EUR million	115	157	143	139	167	136	157	186	244	184	88	116
Direct government loans, SMEs	EUR million	117	160	139	146	168	209	152	159	172	177	120	132
Non-performing loans, total	% of all business loans	..	..	6.8	8.4	8.3	7.9	8.3	8.6	7.4	6.5	5	4.12
Non-performing loans, SMEs(2)	% of all SME loans	..	..	..	..	..	10.4	9.9	10.3	9	8.1	6.65	5.68
Interest rate, SMEs	%	5.5	4.6	3	3.2	3.2	3.8	3.6	3.8	3.4	3.1	3	3
Collateral, SMEs	% of SMEs needing collateral to obtain bank lending	100	100	100	100	100	100	100	100	100	100	100	100
Percentage of SME loan applications	SME loan applications/ total number of SMEs	..	..	..	..	17	..	16	..	23	18	22	17
Rejection rate	1-(SME loans authorised/ requested)	..	..	..	..	20	..	15	..	13	5	13	10
Non-bank finance													
Venture and growth capital	EUR million	7	8	14.4	11.4	11.5	7	9	9	12.7	17.1	2.9	5.4
Venture and growth capital (growth rate)	%, year-on-year growth rate	..	14.3	80	-20.8	0.9	-39.1	28.6	-0.3	41.7	34.4	-83	85.57
Other indicators													
Payment delays, B2B	Number of days	20	8	13	17	20	21	19	17	24	19	19	19
Bankruptcies, SMEs	Number	169	251	276	344	363	339	377	409	350	273	285	252
Bankruptcies, SMEs (growth rate)	%, year-on-year growth rate	..	48.5	10	24.6	5.5	-6.6	11.2	8.5	-14.4	-22	4.4	-11.6

Note: (1) SME loans classified according to the national/ EU definition of SMEs; (2) No EU definition used - SME loans classified based on banking standards.

The full country profile is available at

https://doi.org/10.1787/061fe03d-en

41. Slovenia

Slovenian SMEs employ 72% of the workforce in the business economy (436 000 persons employed), and produce 64% of the value added (EUR 13 billion). Micro firms account for more than one third of all employment in the business economy, while the share of large firms in both employment and value added are below the OECD average, in line with the small size of the economy.

Firms manufacturing coke and petroleum are comprised only of SMEs. Otherwise, SMEs dominate mostly the service sector in terms of employment. Relative to the OECD average, the share of SMEs is significantly higher in the ICT sector and in manufacture of machinery. On the other hand, employment in textiles and apparel and in electrical equipment manufacturing activities is relatively more concentrated in large companies. (OECD, forthcoming publication).

Table 41.1. Scoreboard for Slovenia

Indicator	Unit	2007	2008	2009	2010	2011	2012	2013	2014	2015	2016	2017	2018
Outstanding business loans, SMEs	EUR billion	7.30	8.12	7.86	9.67	9.79	9.53	5.70	4.31	4.12	4.35	4.61	4.71
Outstanding business loans, total	EUR billion	16.80	19.94	19.86	20.83	20.09	18.64	14.14	11.21	10.04	9.31	9.31	9.18
Share of SME outstanding loans	% of total outstanding business loans	43.45	40.71	39.59	46.43	48.75	51.14	40.29	38.47	41.01	46.79	49.52	51.33
New business lending, total	EUR billion	..	..	..	10.25	12.38	9.21	6.71	5.99	4.95	3.92	3.48	3.64
New business lending, SMEs	EUR billion	..	..	..	6.09	7.17	5.81	3.78	3.30	2.88	2.23	2.21	2.13
Share of new SME lending	% of total new lending	..	..	..	59.36	57.93	63.06	56.34	54.99	58.07	56.90	63.55	58.54
Outstanding long-term loans, SMEs	EUR billion	2.09	2.53	2.15	2.76	3.09	3.19	1.74	0.79	0.61	0.78	0.80	0.83
Share of short-term SME lending	% of total SME lending	5.21	5.59	5.71	6.91	6.70	6.34	3.96	3.53	3.51	3.58	3.82	3.88
Government loan guarantees, SMEs	EUR million	28.62	31.19	27.33	28.54	31.55	33.47	30.51	18.22	14.70	17.87	17.26	17.72
Non-performing loans, total	% of all business loans	3.00	4.00	8.00	13.00	20.00	27.00	25.00	23.00	21.00	10.00	8.00	5.00
Non-performing loans, SMEs	% of SME loans	4.00	7.00	11.00	15.00	23.00	29.00	36.00	39.00	35.00	17.00	11.00	7.00
Interest rate, SMEs	%	7.11	7.51	7.09	5.80	6.00	5.89	5.84	5.14	3.66	2.93	2.73	2.98
Interest rate, large firms	%	5.69	6.25	5.06	5.07	5.17	4.84	4.48	4.16	2.84	2.15	2.24	2.01
Interest rate spread	% points	1.42	1.26	2.03	0.72	0.83	1.05	1.36	0.97	0.82	0.78	0.49	0.97

The full country profile is available at

https://doi.org/10.1787/061fe03d-en

42. South Africa

Although estimates vary, the number of micro, small and medium enterprises (SMEs) in South Africa rose by 3%, from 2.18 million in the first quarter of 2008 to 2.25 million in the second quarter of 2015 (Bureau for Economic Research (BER), 2016). Of the 2.25 million SMEs, 1.5 million were informal, concentrated in the trade (wholesale and retail) and accommodation sector.

The evidence regarding firm dynamics in South Africa suggests that scaling up is a significant challenge for most SMEs. For instance, average annual growth rates are positively related with firm size, such that larger firms exhibit higher average growth. Lack of access to markets, technology, business infrastructure, information etc., are some of the constraints for SMEs scaling up.

According to the South African Reserve Bank data on bank statistics, total SME credit exposure to banks was ZAR 617 billion at the end of 2017, which accounts for 28% of total business loans. As indicated below, the low level of SME financing appears to be emanating from the demand side as the vast majority of SMEs indicates that they do not borrow from financial institutions, particularly banks.

Owner-funded capital represents, by far, the most widely used source of finance, followed by investments by family and business partners.

SME non-performing loans in the banking sector have declined since 2010, falling from 5.2% to 2.5% in 2017. The economic recovery following the 2009 recession and prudent lending criteria have likely contributed to the improvement. At 2.53% in 2017, the ratio of non-performing loans of SMEs was higher than that of total corporates (1.3%) by more than one percentage point.

Government funding for SMEs is provided through grants and financing by development finance institutions (DFIs). The outstanding direct government loans to SMEs at the end of 2017 amount to ZAR 11.48 billion, which accounted for 1.8% of all SME loans.

Credit guarantees are also in use in South Africa. ZAR 297 million were provided in 2017 by the IDC and SEFA up from ZAR 243 million in 2016, after having declined significantly in 2013 and in 2014.

The South African Government is also working on the establishment of a registry for movable assets and of a database with credit information. Both initiatives aim to make lending less risky and should therefore make bank financing more widely available.

Table 42.1. Scoreboard for South Africa

Indicator	Unit	2007	2008	2009	2010	2011	2012	2013	2014	2015	2016	2017
Debt												
Outstanding business loans, SMEs	ZAR million	..	423 691	411 212	388 090	411 280	454 012	512 504	545 271	579 823	638 525	617 846
Outstanding business loans, total	ZAR billion	..	1 441	1 276	1 373	1 481	1 648	1 791	1 965	2 323	2 377	2 239
Share of SME outstanding loans	% of total outstanding business loans	..	29.39	32.23	28.26	27.76	27.55	28.61	27.75	24.96	26.87	27.59
Government loan guarantees, SMEs	ZAR million	8	99	226	201	439	227	105	105	223	243	298
Direct government loans, SMEs	ZAR million	..	4 829	4 909	5 915	6 900	7 383	7 269	8 748	10 565	10 898	11 481
Non-performing loans, total	% of all business loans	..	1.40	2.96	2.91	2.11	1.97	1.84	1.54	1.64	1.48	1.29
Non-performing loans, SMEs	% of all SME loans	..	2.89	5.23	5.20	4.07	3.36	2.92	2.94	2.51	2.55	2.53
Non-bank finance												
Venture and growth capital	ZAR million	468	551	242	194	211	288	183	273	372	872	..
Venture and growth capital (growth rate)	%, Year-on-year growth rate	..	17.74	-56.08	-19.83	8.76	36.49	-36.46	49.18	36.26	134.41	..
Other indicators												
Bankruptcies, SMEs	Number	3 151	3 300	4 133	3 992	3 559	2 716	2 374	2 064	1 962	1 934	1 868
Bankruptcies, SMEs (growth rate)	%, Year-on-year growth rate	..	4.73	25.24	-3.41	-10.85	-23.69	-12.59	-13.06	-4.94	-1.43	-3.41

The full country profile is available at

https://doi.org/10.1787/061fe03d-en

43. Spain

99.7% of all non-financial corporations (NFCs) in Spain in December 2017 were SMEs, employing 63.8% of the business labour force. Of these, micro-enterprises dominated with a share of 89.8% of all enterprises.

The expansion of the Spanish economy continued in 2018. GDP growth was 2.6%, somewhat down on 2017. Growth remained very intensive in employment creation. The slight slowdown observed was in line with expectations, but the composition of GDP was very different: domestic demand continued to be very robust, set against the significant slowdown in exports. Activity and world trade were affected by the tightening of global financial conditions and heightening uncertainty over trade conflicts and the Chinese authorities' difficulties in redressing this economy's debt.

After an intense contraction of the SME lending during the financial crisis, the activity and business performance of NFCs in general recovered, in particular those SMEs in particular, which began to grow in 2014, and continued all along the period 2015-2018, as did the improvement in their financing conditions.

Short-term loans, for the first year in the recent period, recorded a reduction as a percentage of total loans. In the case of SMEs, at end-2018, 89.7% of lending was short term, which is a higher share than for large corporations and implies that SMEs are more dependent on credit institutions in the refinancing process than large enterprises.

As regards SME credit conditions, the trend of declining interest rates and interest rate spreads, along with a stabilisation of credit conditions, initiated in 2012, continued. The interest rate spreads between loans to SMEs and large corporates also continued to narrow over the same period, progressively falling from the peak 230 basis points (bp) in 2012 to 20 bp in 2018.

General government financing to non-financial corporations has stabilized in the last 3 years. In particular, financing to SMEs during 2018, showed a very moderate increase. This was, however, compatible with a greater availability of liquid funds and easier credit conditions from private-sector banks, so that SMEs found it easier to access private credit rather than public financing.

The economic recovery and the higher demand, along with improved credit conditions, were also evidenced in lower company mortality (bankruptcies). This was also favoured by various insolvency legislation reforms that have stimulated agreements between creditors and the business continuity.

The latest available information on venture capital investments which relates to 2017, indicates equity financing and the related investments with respect to the seed, start-up and expansion stages in that year (EUR 1 146 million) decreased by 1.2 vis-a-vis 2016.

Table 43.1. Scoreboard for Spain

Indicator	Unit	2007	2008	2009	2010	2011	2012	2013	2014	2015	2016	2017	2018
Debt													
Outstanding business loans, SMEs	EUR billion	..	..	..	..	..	..	..	293	258	247	263	229
Outstanding business loans, total	EUR Billion)	893	952	915	896	840	708	609	545	518	493	477	446
Share of SME outstanding loans	% of total outstanding business loans	..	..	..	..	..	..	..	53.79	49.85	50.10	55.14	51.35
New business lending, total	EUR Billion)	991	929	868	665	527	485	393	357	393	323	339	347
New business lending, SMEs	EUR Billion	394	357	263	210	174	146	134	147	165	170	184	175
Share of new SME lending	% of total new lending	39.76	38.43	30.30	31.58	33.02	30.10	34.10	41.18	41.98	52.63	54.28	50.43
Outstanding short-term loans, SMEs	EUR	379	346	246	196	166	139	126	135	154	153	163	157
Outstanding long-term loans, SMEs	EUR	15	11	17	14	8	7	9	11	12	17	21	18
Share of short-term SME lending	% of total SME lending	96.19	96.92	93.54	93.33	95.40	95.21	93.33	92.47	92.77	90.00	88.59	89.71
Government loan guarantees, SMEs	EUR Million	5 550	7 700	11 000	10 100	12 000	11 000	13 000	9 100	7 600	6 500	3 110	0
Government guaranteed loans, SMEs	EUR Million	5 210	7 053	5 906	7 236	7 502	4 974	2 064	938	273	109	42	30
Direct government loans, SMEs	EUR Million	10 103	12 384	19 916	23 740	26 221	23 599	23 648	22 588	21 481	20 734	20 525	20 625
Non-performing loans, total	% of all business loans	..	..	..	5.81	7.84	10.43	13.62	12.51	10.12	9.11	7.79	..
Interest rate, SMEs	%	5.96	5.51	3.63	3.78	4.95	4.91	4.79	3.86	3.01	2.44	2.15	1.89
Interest rate, large firms	%	5.33	4.30	2.16	2.57	3.36	2.61	2.69	1.99	1.97	1.56	1.56	1.69
Interest rate spread	% points	0.63	1.21	1.47	1.21	1.59	2.30	2.10	1.87	1.04	0.88	0.59	0.20
Collateral, SMEs	% of SMEs needing collateral to obtain bank lending	..	..	..	35.19	34.36	31.45	30.00	31.22	28.24	25.89	26.04	24.05
Percentage of SME loan applications	SME loan applications/ total number of SMEs	..	..	38.07	36.25	34.67	31.89	31.49	34.36	33.81	32.80	28.14	28.60
Rejection rate	1-(SME loans authorised/ requested)	..	..	22.74	15.87	12.83	18.47	12.85	9.77	7.87	6.95	4.75	5.95
Non-bank finance													
Venture and growth capital	EUR Million	..	3 336	3 596	3 600	2 675	2 145	1 473	1 437	1 112	1 160	1 146	..
Venture and growth capital (growth rate)	%, Year-on-year growth rate	..	..	7.79	0.11	-25.69	-19.81	-31.33	-2.44	-22.62	4.32	-1.21	..
Other indicators													
Payment delays, B2B	Number of days	5.00	5.00	14.00	12.00	6.00	9.00	16.00	11.00	9.00	8.00	8.00	..
Bankruptcies, SMEs	Number	894	2 550	4 463	4 187	4912.00	6627.00	7517.00	5096	3927	3305	3 310	3 250
Bankruptcies, SMEs (growth rate)	%, Year-on-year growth rate	..	185.23	75.02	-6.18	17.32	34.91	13.43	-32.21	-22.94	-15.84	0.15	-1.81

The full country profile is available at

https://doi.org/10.1787/061fe03d-en

44. Sweden

In 2017, around 99% of limited liability companies with employees in Sweden were SMEs. They accounted for about 53% of total employment and 45% of GDP.

The stock of SME debt from banks and other financial institutions was SEK 1 290 billion in 2017, up by 10% in comparison with 2016. SME debt as a share of total outstanding debt was just above 40% in 2017, a slight increase from the previous year.

Surveys of bank managers' views on business loan volumes indicate that loans to SMEs have increased since Q1 2012 and continue to increase; this development is concurrent with decreasing low interest rates on bank loans over the period.

The repo rate – the main policy rate of the Swedish Central bank (*Sw. Riksbanken*) remains negative, but was increased in January 2019 from -0.5% to -0.25%. The repo rate dipped below zero in February 2015, and has remained negative ever since.

Private equity investments in Swedish companies in the venture and growth stages stood at EUR 499 million in 2018, an increase of 1.67% from the previous year. Alternative finance volumes in Sweden totalled EUR 196 million in 2018, of which EUR 126 million was alternative business funding.

Almi's lending decreased by 27% to SEK 1 857 million in 2017. The Swedish National Export Credits Guarantee Board issued guarantees totalling SEK 2.2 billion to SMEs in 2018, a 29% increase from 2017.

The Swedish parliament (*Riksdag*) adopted a proposal to address the structure of public financing for innovation and sustainable growth in June 2016 (the government's bill 2015/16:110). A primary aim of the revised public financing structure is to clarify and simplify the system of state venture capital (VC) financing. Its purpose is also to improve the efficiency of public resources and contribute to the development and renewal of Swedish industry. A key feature of the new structure is the establishment of a new joint stock company, Saminvest AB, a fund of funds that invests in privately managed VC firms focusing on development-stage companies. In 2018, Saminvest AB invested in 6 VC funds, which in turn made 56 investments in growth firms.

Table 44.1. Scoreboard for Sweden

Indicator	Unit	2007	2008	2009	2010	2011	2012	2013	2014	2015	2016	2017	2018
Debt													
Outstanding business loans, SMEs	SEK Billion	..	..	..	..	..	930	964	1 003	1 073	1 173	1 290	..
Outstanding business loans, total	SEK Billion	..	..	..	..	..	2 683	2 722	2 812	2 901	2 962	3 189	..
Share of SME outstanding loans	% of total outstanding business loans	..	..	..	..	..	34.66	35.39	35.67	36.99	39.60	40.46	..
Outstanding short-term loans, SMEs	SEK Billion	..	..	..	..	..	211	217	249	262	316	339	..
Outstanding long-term loans, SMEs	SEK Billion	..	..	..	..	..	719	747	754	811	857	951	..
Share of short-term SME lending	% of total SME lending	..	..	..	..	..	22.71	22.50	24.83	24.44	26.92	26.28	..
Direct government loans, SMEs	SEK Million	1 422	1 716	3 231	2 112	2 023	2 161	2 200	2 354	3 241	3 324	2 559	1 857
Non-performing loans, total	% of all business loans	0.08	0.46	0.83	0.78	0.65	0.70	0.61	1.24	1.17	1.04	1.12	0.49
Interest rate, SMEs	%	4.86	5.66	2.43	2.59	4.17	4.07	3.29	2.71	1.75	1.56	1.50	1.53
Interest rate, large firms	%	3.99	4.84	1.71	1.64	3.01	3.03	2.64	2.15	1.35	1.21	1.14	1.05
Interest rate spread	% points	0.87	0.82	0.72	0.95	1.16	1.04	0.65	0.56	0.40	0.34	0.37	0.48
Non-bank finance													
Venture and growth capital	EUR Million	566.3	504.8	361.7	699.4	422.4	335.5	357.3	375.6	280.8	290.9	491.2	499.4
Venture and growth capital (growth rate)	%, Year-on-year growth rate	..	-10.86	-28.34	93.37	-39.61	-20.58	6.50	5.13	-25.25	3.61	68.83	1.67
Other indicators													
Payment delays, B2B	Number of days	..	..	..	..	..	20.00	24.00	15.00	9.00	9.00	10.00	14
Bankruptcies, SMEs	Number	2 469	3 139	3 913	3 342	3 449	3 808	3 777	3 355	2 998	2822.00	3 019	3 392
Bankruptcies, SMEs (growth rate)	%, Year-on-year growth rate	..	27.14	24.66	-14.59	3.20	10.41	-0.81	-11.17	-10.64	-5.87	6.98	12.24

The full country profile is available at

https://doi.org/10.1787/061fe03d-en

45. Switzerland

Only 0.8% of all Swiss enterprises are large and SMEs continue to dominate the enterprise landscape, constituting 99.2% of all firms.

Switzerland exhibited a real GDP growth of 2.5% in 2018, an increase of 1.4 percentage points from 2017.

Total outstanding SME loans rose by 4.6% in 2018, reaching CHF 441 billion, a higher growth rate compared to the 2017 figure of 2.4%.

Over the 2007-18 period, SME loans expanded by 36.6%, while overall corporate lending rose by 45.4%.

Lending standards remained unchanged in 2018, while demand for credit slightly increased.

The average interest rate charged to SMEs decreased in 2018 to 1.96% after the 2017 increase, while the interest rate spread between large and small companies decreased to 71 basis points.

Venture and growth capital investments experienced in 2018 a 33.8% decrease, following a large increase in 2017.

Crowdfunding activities are increasing rapidly (+38% in 2018), also supported by the lack of specific crowdfunding legislation. Recently, the government has taken steps to make the regulatory framework friendlier to the industry, and particularly to financial technology companies.

Payment delays in the business-to-business sector have significantly decreased over the last few years, from 12 days in 2008 to 6 days in 2018, illustrating that liquidity problems have significantly diminished.

In Switzerland, there are four guarantee cooperatives that help promising SMEs obtain bank loans of up to CHF 500 000. Loan guarantee volumes increased steadily over 2007-2010, declined slightly in 2011, and continued to grow in the following six years. The Parliament amended the Federal Law on Financial Aid for guarantee organisations: since 1 July 2019, the Law allows for guarantees up to CHF 1 million.

Table 45.1. Scoreboard for Switzerland

Indicator	Unit	2007	2008	2009	2010	2011	2012	2013	2014	2015	2016	2017	2018
Debt													
Outstanding business loans, SMEs	CHF million	323 093	344 840	343 866	363 566	377 630	384 438	404 793	402 346	403 681	412 005	422 065	441 332
Outstanding business loans, total	CHF million	401 647	426 489	433 485	458 689	480 922	489 116	513 631	526 532	525 042	538 709	550 365	583 934
Share of SME outstanding loans	% of total outstanding business loans	80.44	80.86	79.33	79.26	78.52	78.60	78.81	76.41	76.89	76.48	76.69	75.58
Government loan guarantees, SMEs	CHF million	104	148	187	215	210	219	227	238	244	254	255	262
Interest rate, SMEs	%	..	..	2.21	2.11	2.08	2.01	1.99	2.05	2.07	2.04	2.09	1.96
Interest rate, large firms	%	..	..	1.35	1.23	1.16	1.11	1.16	1.16	1.30	1.25	1.30	1.25
Interest rate spread	% points	..	..	0.86	0.88	0.92	0.90	0.83	0.89	0.78	0.79	0.79	0.71
Collateral, SMEs	% of SMEs needing collateral to obtain bank lending	..	..	76.00	75.01	76.56	76.75	74.86	78.78	79.64	79.88	81.86	81.70
Utilisation rate	SME loans used/ authorised	71.00	70.00	71.00	70.00	69.00	71.00	72.00	72.00	71.76	71.68	70.59	70.30
Non-bank finance													
Venture and growth capital	EUR million	319.8	300.9	308.5	330.1	227.6	245.8	216.8	237.2	394.3	452.4	1195.9	790.7
Venture and growth capital (growth rate)	%, Year-on-year growth rate	..	-5.91	2.53	7.00	-31.05	8.00	-11.80	9.41	66.23	14.73	164.35	-33.88
Other indicators													
Payment delays, B2B	Number of days	12	13	13	11	10	9	9	7	7	7	7	6
Bankruptcies, SMEs	Number	4 314	4 221	5 215	6 255	6 661	6 841	6 495	5 867	6 098	6 684	6 710	6 878
Bankruptcies, SMEs (growth rate)	%, Year-on-year growth rate	..	-2.16	23.55	19.94	6.49	2.70	-5.06	-9.67	3.94	9.61	0.39	2.50

The full country profile is available at

https://doi.org/10.1787/061fe03d-en

46. Thailand

In 2016, there were approximately 3.01 million SMEs in Thailand, which constituted 99.7% of all enterprises. They altogether contributed to 42.2% of the country's GDP and accounted for 78.5% of total private sector employment.

According to the criteria defined by the Ministry of Industry, SMEs are categorized by the number of employees and the value of total fixed assets (excluding land).

SMEs are able to access financing through commercial bank loans. In 2017, outstanding SME loans totaled THB 4 220 624 billion, representing 50.47% of all outstanding business loans. Furthermore, SMEs are able to source funds from other financial institutions, the capital market, crowdfunding and venture capital.

Some SMEs still face problems including collateral constraints and a lack of credit history, which limit their access to bank loans. Government policies have been put into place to address these constraints.

For example, the Thai Credit Guarantee Corporation (TCG) provides credit guarantees for viable SMEs to ensure that SMEs with insufficient collateral have access to bank loans.

Moreover, The Business Collateral Act B.E. 2558 (2015) simplified the process of security interest creation and expanded the types of collateral which SMEs can register and use to secure loans.

In addition, to boost SMEs' financial access in a sustainable manner, the government has also launched capacity-building programmes to enhance SMEs' competitiveness.

Table 46.1. Scoreboard for Thailand

Indicator	Unit	2007	2008	2009	2010	2011	2012	2013	2014	2015	2016	2017
Outstanding business loans, SMEs	THB billion	2 365	2 410	2 222	2 376	2 743	3 084	3 513	3 710	3 918	3 989	4 220
Outstanding business loans, total	THB billion	4 629	5 117	4 863	5 298	6 080	6 723	7 473	7 774	8 017	8 066	8 362
Share of SME outstanding loans	% of total outstanding business loans	51.06	47.09	45.70	44.85	45.11	45.87	47.00	47.73	48.87	49.45	50.47
Government loan guarantee, SMEs	THB billion	..	..	..	73	113	180	244	270	309	331	353
Non-performing loans, total	% of all business loans	8.23	5.77	5.32	3.96	2.97	2.36	2.13	2.07	2.55	2.88	3.01
Non-performing loans, SMEs	% of all SME loans	..	..	7.11	5.38	3.97	3.46	3.29	3.11	3.5	4.35	4.37

Source: Bank of Thailand and Thai Credit Guarantee Corporation (Outstanding loans and non-performing loans include only Thai commercial banks, excluding specialized financial institutions).

The full country profile is available at

https://doi.org/10.1787/061fe03d-en

47. Turkey

SME lending grew steadily over the whole 2007-2018 period, with the exception of a minor decline of 1.6% in 2009. SME loans grew by 19% in 2018. The share of SME loans in total business loans remained broadly stable, at 32.3%, slightly below the Scoreboard median (38%).

Venture and private equity investments show an erratic pattern. After reaching a peak in 2011, investments remained subdued in the years after, until 2017, when new investments surpassed 2011 levels for the first time. In 2018, a 108% increase from 2017 was observed. Non-performing loans (NPLs) ratio for both business loans and SME loans rose significantly in 2018, to 4.01% and 6.69%, respectively. Nevertheless, these levels remains lower than the previous peak levels in 2009.

The number of bankruptcies decreased from 131 firms in 2017 to 105 in 2018. Company closures, including sole proprietorships, totalled 38 698 enterprises in 2018, decreased from 42898 enterprises in 2017, highlighting that bankruptcies (upon court verdict) constitute a relatively uncommon phenomenon in Turkey.

In 2012, the Turkish Government enacted a law to stimulate the development of the business angel industry. A secondary legislation came into force in 2013. The purpose of the law and the secondary legislation was the establishment of a legal framework and the provision of generous tax incentives for licensed angel investors.

The government also introduced regulation regarding fund of funds, which enables the Ministry of Treasury and Finance to transfer capital to a fund of funds under certain conditions in 2014. In 2017, the fund of funds law, which regulated capital contribution of the Ministry of Treasury and Finance (Turkish Treasury) to funds of funds was changed. With this change Ministry of Treasury and Finance has the authority to invest not only fund of funds but also venture capital funds. Secondary legislation of Direct Investment to Venture Capital Funds came into force on 5 June 2018.

KOSGEB constitutes the main body for executing SME policies in Turkey. It provides 11 different support programmes and supports collateral costs for SMEs with considerable outreach throughout Turkey.

In 2018, KOSGEB made some changes in its support programmes with a vision to give priority to SMEs that produce innovative, technological and high value-added products, who want to carry these products to international markets and who are export-oriented. In this direction, KOSGEB made innovations in its support models in order to extend the technology to the base through SMEs, strengthen the manufacturing industry, support domestic and national production for the production of imported products domestically, increase internationalization and enable large and small business cooperation. Additionally, in the field of entrepreneurship, KOSGEB has established a new entrepreneurship model with a focus on medium-high and high-tech fields.

At the end of 2018 KOSGEB has introduced a new loan interest support programme. The new model provides resource efficiency, facilitates access to finance for enterprises in high value added sectors and is easily accessible throughout the year. SMEs can be classified as Entrepreneurial Enterprises, Project Oriented Enterprises, Technology Based Enterprises and Enterprises in Strategic Priority Sectors. Classified SMEs can benefit from investment, working capital, export and emergency support loan types with subsidised loan rates. In 2016, Turkey passed a bill on movable collateral in commercial transactions.

The goal of the reform is to increase access to finance against valuable tangible and intangibles assets such as receivables, machinery, inventory and stock, which comprise 78% of SMEs' total assets. This reform led to the creation of 22 361 security rights in 2017, 2018 and the first six months of 2019, amounting for security right to TRY 526.3 billion, USD 41.6 billion US Dollars and EUR 30.2 billion Euros and actual financial amount is TRY 51.1 billion Turkish Liras, USD 8.2 billion, and EUR 1.03 billion. The most used assets are receivables, machines and inventories respectively.

Table 47.1. Scoreboard for Turkey

Indicator	Unit	2007	2008	2009	2010	2011	2012	2013	2014	2015	2016	2017	2018
Debt													
Outstanding business loans, SMEs	TRY billion	76.5	84.6	83.3	125.5	162.8	199.7	271.4	333.3	388.7	420.5	513.2	611.3
Outstanding business loans, total	TRY billion	190.6	250.3	262.7	353.2	459.0	528.8	715.5	884.6	1 100.1	1 314.4	1 609.8	1 890.2
Share of SME outstanding loans	% of total outstanding business loans	40.14	33.80	31.70	35.52	35.47	37.77	37.94	37.67	35.34	32.00	31.88	32.34
Government loan guarantees, SMEs	TRY billion	0.1	0.3	0.6	0.9	1.1	1.1	1.1	1.4	1.6	5.3	236.7	94.5
Government guaranteed loans, SMEs	TRY billion	0.1	0.4	0.8	1.3	1.6	1.6	1.5	1.9	2.3	7.2	262.6	107.9
Direct government loans, SMEs	USD million	552	842	997	855	1 174	928	2 632	1 709	1 764	1 749	284.5.	457
Non-performing loans, total	% of all business loans	3.8	3.7	4.91	3.43	2.61	2.82	2.69	2.64	2.68	2.9	2.81	4.01
Non-performing loans, SMEs	% of all SME loans	3.62	4.79	7.64	4.49	3.1	3.17	3.12	3.27	3.92	4.9	4.71	6.69
Non-bank finance													
Venture and growth capital*	TRY million	13.7	0.9	6.3	47.6	373.2	110.1	335.5	124.4	135.3	343.2	435.1	904
Venture and growth capital (growth rate)*	%, year-on-year growth rate	..	-93.76	639.58	652.9	684.82	-70.5	204.78	-62.93	8.77	153.64	26.79	108
Leasing and hire purchases	TRY billion	11.7	14.4	11.1	10.7	15.1	17.2	25.0	29.5	36.7	44.0	52.0	60.7
Factoring and invoice discounting	TRY billion	6.2	5.6	8.4	12.4	14.2	16.3	20.1	24.7	25.0	31.0	41.6	31.4
Other indicators													
Bankruptcies, total	Number	52	47	50	68	72	141	69	99	108	222	131	105
Bankruptcies, Total (growth rate)	%, year-on-year growth rate	..	-9.6	6.4	36.0	5.9	95.8	-51.1	43.5	9.1	105.6	-41.0	-19.8

Note: (*) The data presented in this section do not refer to outstanding values but show the new investments each year.

The full country profile is available at

https://doi.org/10.1787/061fe03d-en

48. Ukraine

SMEs prevail in the Ukrainian economy, accounting for 99.98% of the total business population (both legal enterprises and individual entrepreneurs). SMEs employ almost 81% of the labour force and generate 65% of total sales. Most SMEs belong to the trade sector (26.16%), agriculture (14.19%) and industry (11.82%)

In the wake of the economic crisis of 2014, employment and value added among SMEs have shown growth since 2016. Over all sectors and regions, employment in SMEs increased by 1%. The recovery continued in 2017 and 2018.

Today, the state policy is focussing specifically on SMEs, particularly on the financing of SMEs. This is evidenced by the approval of the Strategy for Small and Medium-sized Enterprise Development in Ukraine (hereafter - SME Development Strategy) in 2017 and of the Action Plan for Implementing the Strategy of SME Development in Ukraine (hereafter - Action Plan) in 2018. The access of SMEs to finance is one of the key priorities of these two programmes, which will run until 2020.

In Ukraine, banks play an important role in financing SMEs. There are fourteen banks operating on the market that actively provide services to SMEs at the national level and eight at the regional level. However, indicators on the size of the banking system only became available recently (the National Bank of Ukraine started to publish data on credit and credit rates by borrower size on 23 November 2017). That is, it is possible to analyse the dynamics only in a short-term perspective for now.

Results from the survey on SME lending conditions conducted by the National Bank of Ukraine show that businesses' demand for credit is growing. In particular, an increase is predicted for SME lending, as well as for short-term and national currency loans for businesses.

At the same time, according to another survey conducted by the European Business Association in 2018, 52% of respondents indicated that credits are "expensive" and difficult to obtain. Only 19% of respondents considered that credits are accessible.

The main driver for demand is businesses' need for working capital, which they are mostly unable to cover with their own funds. Additionally, banks indicate an increase in the approval of SMEs' credit applications and a gradual easing of lending standards for SMEs. Financial institutions expect further growth in the demand for all types of business loans. The most optimistic predictions concern SME loans.

In 2018, new SMEs loans accounted for 33% of total new business lending.

State banks as well as commercial banks in Ukraine have a range of financial and consulting services which target SMEs specifically. These include bank guarantees, blank credits for SMEs of all sizes, bill avalization, receipt of new and used transport vehicles, machinery and equipment, etc.

The following trends in Ukrainian SMEs financing can be outlined: financing of firms in the agricultural sector, financing of innovative enterprises, regional financial support programmes, state financial support programmes and international support programmes through Ukrainian banks. In particular, measures include the compensation of agricultural equipment costs, credit secured with future harvests, investment financing, energy efficiency loans, lines of credit without collateral, structured trade financing, etc.

Emphasis is being placed on the financing of innovative enterprises and start-ups. Thus, different ministries have established funds that aim at encouraging inventions and scientific approaches in business ventures.

The funds introduce grants and financing mechanisms after the company has gone through competitive selection. Furthermore, regional programmes play an important role in SMEs' financing.

Most state programmes focus on themes such as financial support at the start of the business, support for agricultural companies, tax and duty privileges, and "green tariffs".

International support programmes, which are implemented through Ukrainian banks, provide credit funds to Ukrainian SMEs that meet the programme's requirements. Usually, the programmes targets entrepreneurs in rural areas and SMEs that operate in strategic sectors (agriculture, forestry and fisheries, manufacturing, hospitality, provision of electricity, gas and steam). The international support programmes involves the provision of a grant and targeted programmes by donor organisations.

While international financing is usually less costly than bank financing, most international donor programmes take the availability of transparent information and reporting into account, which the majority of SMEs lack.

Table 48.1. Scoreboard for Ukraine

Indicator	Unit	2007	2008	2009	2010	2011	2012	2013	2014	2015	2016	2017	2018
Debt													
Outstanding business loans, SMEs	UAH billion	..	..	..	..	..	..	..	..	..	..	443	445
Outstanding business loans, total	UAH billion	271	460	482	520	597	626	716	809	807	837	845	874
Share of SME outstanding loans	% of total outstanding business loans	..	..	..	..	..	..	..	..	..	..	52.42	50.86
New business lending, total	UAH billion	627	724	685	958	1 079	1 121	1 330	1 231	1 213	1 446	1 407	2 011
New business lending, SMEs	UAH billion	..	..	..	..	..	..	..	..	..	..	..	678
Share of new SME lending	% of total new lending	..	..	..	..	..	..	..	..	..	..	..	33.74
Outstanding short-term loans, SMEs	UAH billion	..	..	..	..	..	..	..	..	..	..	200	215
Outstanding long-term loans, SMEs	UAH billion	..	..	..	..	..	..	..	..	..	..	243	230
Share of short-term SME lending	% of total SME lending	..	..	..	..	..	..	..	..	..	..	45.12	48.34
Interest rate, SMEs	%	..	..	..	..	..	..	..	..	..	..	..	17.35
Interest rate, large firms	%	..	..	..	..	..	..	..	..	..	..	..	17.70
Interest rate spread	%	..	..	..	..	..	..	..	..	..	..	..	-0.35
Non-bank finance													
Venture and growth capital	UAH billion	..	..	..	0.020	0.024	0.059	0.089	0.039	0.132	0.088	0.259	0.337
Venture and growth capital (growth rate)	%	..	..	..	..	20.00	145.83	50.85	-56.18	238.46	-33.33	194.32	30.08
Leasing and hire purchases	UAH billion	12	8	2	3	9	9	25	6	5	10	13	22
Factoring and invoice discounting	UAH billion	0	1	2	6	7	12	10	24	17	17	31	48
Other indicators													
Bankruptcies, all businesses	Number of subjects of entrepreneurial activity	..	..	..	..	..	9 540	7 168	6 098	6 292	6 007	4 920	4 075
Bankruptcies, all businesses (growth rate)	%	..	..	..	..	..	..	-24.86	-14.93	3.18	-4.53	-18.10	-17.17

The full country profile is available at

https://doi.org/10.1787/061fe03d-en

49. United Kingdom

Developments in 2018 showed a marked divide between continued growth in alternative sources of finance and little change in bank lending. The main measures of bank lending to SMEs remained flat in nominal terms: driven, in no small part, by continued economic uncertainty and increasing SME reluctance to use external finance to invest and grow.

The outstanding stock of bank lending to SMEs, the principal component of SME finance markets, continued to decline in real terms. Total stock at GBP 166 billion at year end 2018 was significantly below historic levels against a backdrop of benign credit conditions, increasing credit availability and persistently low interest rates. Gross flows of bank lending in 2018 were little changed on 2017, closely matched by repayments, resulting in a slightly reduced net lending figure of GBP 0.5 billion in 2018.

More positively, outside of bank lending, there was an increase in usage of other types of finance signalling a more diverse funding environment for SMEs. The most commonly used forms of alternative finance, invoice finance (2%) and asset finance (3%), showed continued if slower growth in 2018, whilst the value of equity finance received by SMEs also increased (5%). Moreover, P2P business lending and P2P invoice finance grew apace in 2018, by 18% and 105% respectively, albeit from much smaller 2017 baselines.

On the demand side a range of indicators signalled generally low or declining SME demand for external finance despite conditions remaining broadly accommodative. UK Finance data show deposits held by SMEs rose to a record high in Q4 2018 to almost GBP 195 billion, a 15% increase on the previous year. At the same time there has been a continued reduction in SME usage of overdrafts.

More broadly, just 36% of SMEs reported using any type of external finance in 2018, compared to 44% in 2012. A majority (8 in 10) of SMEs who reported retaining good credit balances said this reduced their need for external finance. A similar percentage of SMEs have growth plans based on what they can afford to self-fund, and almost three quarters report they would accept a slower rate of growth rather than borrow. Overall, a much smaller proportion of SMEs (3%) applied for new and renewed bank facilities in 2018.

Reluctance to use external finance could reflect recent increases in economic uncertainty. Almost 1 in 4 SMEs report political uncertainty and the current economic climate as major obstacles to growth. Despite these concerns, one in two SMEs still aspire to grow over the next 12 months and fewer SMEs are citing access to finance as a major obstacle.

The UK Government, the Department for Business, Energy and Industrial Strategy and the British Business Bank will continue to work with a wide range of partners to promote and encourage SME access to, and take up of, external finance throughout the devolved nations and regions of the United Kingdom. For example, in June 2018 the British Business Bank launched a new website that offers independent and impartial information on different finance options for scale-up, high growth and potential high growth businesses.

On the supply side the British Business Bank has introduced the British Patient Capital programme, to enable long term investment into high growth potential companies across the UK, and further extended the ENABLE Guarantee programme to provide funding to banks supporting smaller housebuilders to access external finance.

Table 49.1. Scoreboard for the United Kingdom

Indicator	Unit	2008	2009	2010	2011	2012	2013	2014	2015	2016	2017	2018
						Debt						
Outstanding business loans, SMEs	GBP billion	..	..	..	189	176	166	167	164	166	165	166
Outstanding business loans, total	GBP billion	..	..	..	504	472	448	435	430	449	466	467
Share of SME outstanding loans	% of total outstanding business loans	..	..	..	37.5	37.3	37.1	38.4	38.3	36.9	35.5	34.8
New business lending, total	GBP billion	..	..	..	..	146	163	190	205	234	259	273
New business lending, SMEs	GBP billion	..	..	..		38	43	53	58	59	57	58
Share of new SME lending	% of total new lending	..	..	..		26.1	26.4	28.2	28.2	25.3	22.2	21.1
Government loan guarantees, SMEs	GBP million	..	61	52	32	43	51	45	34	31	32	30
Government guaranteed loans, SMEs	GBP million	..	626	529	326	288	337	298	226	207	216	199
Direct government loans, SMEs	GBP million	..	..	..	..	0.8	60.6	70.7	62.0	82.6	106.8	85.5
Interest rate, SMEs	%	4.54	3.47	3.49	3.52	3.71	3.60	3.43	3.33	3.22	3.16	3.44
Interest rate, large firms / PNFCs *	%	3.49	2.35	2.10	2.25	2.41	2.20	2.45	2.11	2.60	2.43	2.70
Interest rate spread	% points	1.05	1.12	1.39	1.27	1.30	1.40	0.98	1.22	0.62	0.73	0.74
Collateral, SMEs	% of SMEs needing collateral to obtain bank lending	..	..	..	25	31	31	34	40	45	56	41
Percentage of SME loan applications	SME loan applications/ total number of SMEs	..	..	..	7	6	4	5	4	3	2	2
Rejection rate	1-(SME loans authorised/ requested)	..	..	..	..	31	32	23	18	19	20	17
						Non-bank finance						
Venture and growth capital	GBP billion	..	..	..	1.9	1.6	1.6	2.2	2.4	2.7	4.2	4.2
Venture and growth capital (growth rate)	%, Year-on-year growth rate	..	..	..		-16.8	-0.6	40.5	9.9	8.6	57.0	0.5
Leasing and hire purchases	GBP billion	..	..	..	11.4	12.2	12.9	14.4	15.8	16.7	18.3	18.8
Factoring and invoice discounting	GBP billion	..	..	..	9.4	9.5	9.9	11.1	10.6	10.8	11.8	12.0
						Other indicators						
Bankruptcies, SMEs	Thousands	..	..	..	22.3	21.4	20.0	17.6	15.9	17.9	18.5	18.7
Bankruptcies, SMEs (growth rate)	%, Year-on-year growth rate	..	..	..	..	-3.9	-11.6	-6.9	-9.8	12.1	3.6	1.4

Note: * Break in data series and definition from 2016.

The full country profile is available at

https://doi.org/10.1787/061fe03d-en

50. United States

During the 2010-18 recovery period, U.S. real GDP posted an average annual growth rate of 2.3%. While this growth rate was slightly lower than the 2.9% average recorded during the longer post-WWII period, it was sufficient to absorb excess labour supply created during the 2008-09 recession. The employment-to-population ratio rose continuously from 42% during March of 2010 to 45% during July of 2018, not far from the recent peak ratio 47% recorded during March of 2000. During this period, the index of real output per hour posted an average annual growth rate of 0.7%, while the index of real compensation per hour posted an average annual growth rate of 0.6%.

Net formation of employer firms and employer SMEs rebounded modestly since 2012, but as of 2015 they both stood 2.5% lower than their peak 2007 levels. However, the Bureau of Labor Statistics point to a continued growth during 2016 and 2017 with levels surpassing 2007 highs.

SME loan origination (flow data) indicates the new supply of loans to SMEs. It posted solid gains from October 2009 through September 2015, but then declined during the next sixteen months, bottoming during February 2017. 2018 marked a slight uptick in new lending to SMEs. Stock data show the value of small loans going to businesses declined continuously from 2008Q2 to 2013Q3, but then posted a modest recovery thereafter.

Since early 2010, bankers have been loosening lending standards for loans to large firms and SMEs, and SME surveys report that loan availability is near historical highs. However, the same data sources point to soft demand for SME loans. Interest rates for SME loans posted dramatic declines during 2006Q3 to 2009Q3, and then posted a flat to modest downward trend up to 2015Q4, when they started to rise.

At USD 29 trillion, SBA's loan guarantees are remaining at high levels. The number of guarantees have underperformed their dollar value, but nonetheless stood about 24% higher than 2009 lows as of the end of 2017. Like other SBA capital access programmes, SBIC financing rebounded strongly during the 2010-15 period, reaching USD 6.3 billion during 2015, more than tripling the USD 1.9 billion low recorded in 2009. More recently, and partly mirroring the decline in the overall VC market, the SBIC programme experienced a 4.7 and 4.4% decline during 2016 and 2017 respectively. The pattern of venture capital deals mirrors the pattern seen in the SME loan markets, where the number of contracts underperform their dollar value. As of 2017, the number of VC deals has not surpassed the 2014 high of 10 509, all the while their dollar value as of 2018 stood at 132, much higher than the previous 2015 high of USD 82.2 billion.

Total bankruptcy filings have been on a continuous decline since 2011. Business bankruptcies started their continuous decline a year earlier. As a result, business bankruptcies during 2018 were 63% lower than 2009 peak levels. Delinquency rates of SME loans are at or near historical lows, with 31-90 days delinquency rates ranging 1.0-1.5%, and 91-180 delinquency rates remaining below 0.5%.

Table 50.1. Scoreboard for the United States

Indicator	Unit	2007	2008	2009	2010	2011	2012	2013	2014	2015	2016	2017	2018
Debt													
Outstanding business loans, SMEs. As of June 30	USD billion	687	711	695	652	608	588	585	590	599	613	619	633
Outstanding business loans, total. As of June 30	USD trillion	2.28	2.57	2.52	2.30	2.35	2.55	2.67	2.87	3.07	3.32	3.46	3 62
Share of SME outstanding loans	% of total outstanding business loans	30.1	27.7	27.6	28.4	25.9	23.1	21.9	20.6	19.5	18.5	17.9	17.5
New business lending, SMEs	USD: Index	119	94	74	77	97	100	105	120	147	140	140	145
Government loan guarantees, SMEs	USD billion	21	16	15	22	19	23	23	24	28	29	32	29
Government guaranteed loans, SMEs	Number of loans (in thousand)	108	66	57	66	52	54	53	61	70	69	71	63
Non-performing loans, total	% of all business loans	1.22	1.88	3.91	3.46	2.01	1.34	1.00	0.80	0.87	1.57	1.33	1.12
Non-performing loans, SMEs	% of all SME loans	2.14	2.62	3.24	2.62	1.90	1.44	1.21	1.22	1.22	1.28	1.34	1.41
Interest rate, SMEs	%	7.96	5.16	3.82	4.09	3.95	3.76	3.55	3.39	3.33	3.46	4.94	5.16
Interest rate, large firms	%	8.05	5.09	3.25	3.25	3.25	3.25	3.25	3.25	3.26	3.51	4.10	4.90
Interest rate spread	% points	-0.09	0.08	0.57	0.84	0.70	0.51	0.30	0.14	0.07	-0.05	0.84	0.26
Collateral, SMEs	% of SMEs needing collateral to obtain bank lending	..	..	..	..	..	..	..	..	..	..	92.90	94.30
Percentage of SME loan applications	SME loan applications/ total number of SMEs	..	..	..	..	..	..	..	..	..	..	55.20	67.30
Rejection rate	1-(SME loans authorised/ requested)	..	..	..	..	..	..	..	..	..	..	44.80	32.70
Utilisation rate	SME loans used/ authorised	..	..	..	..	..	..	..	..	..	..	47.50	46.60
Non-bank finance													
Venture and growth capital	USD billion	36	37	27	31	44	42	47	72	82	76	82	132
Venture and growth capital (growth rate)	%, Year-on-year growth rate	..	3.1	-27.0	15.6	42.1	-6.1	13.6	51.6	14.3	-8.0	8.4	59.4
Leasing and hire purchases	USD billion	595	613	508	449	361	376	395	401	416	382	388	391
Factoring and invoice discounting	USD billion	..	..	..	..	146	100	111	130	105	99	98	104
Other indicators													
Payment delays, B2B	Percent of Domestic Invoices Overdue	..	..	..	..	..	..	25.9	..	46.6	..	40.3	..
Bankruptcies, all businesses	Number (in thousand)	28.3	43.5	60.8	56.3	47.8	40.1	33.2	27.0	24.7	24.1	23.2	22.2
Bankruptcies, all businesses (growth rate)	%, Year-on-year growth rate	43.8	53.8	39.7	-7.5	-15.1	-16.2	-17.1	-18.8	-8.3	-2.5	-4.0	-4.0

The full country profile is available at

https://doi.org/10.1787/061fe03d-en

Annex A. Methodology for producing the national scoreboards

Financing SMEs and Entrepreneurs: An OECD Scoreboard provides a framework to monitor trends in SMEs' and entrepreneurs' access to finance – at the country level and internationally – and supports the formulation and evaluation of policies in this domain.

The individual country profiles present data for a number of core indicators, which measure trends in SME debt and equity financing, credit conditions, solvency and policy measures. The set of indicators and policy information provide governments and other stakeholders with a consistent framework to evaluate whether SME financing needs are being met, to support the design and evaluation of policy measures, and to monitor the implications of financial reforms on SME access to finance. Consistent time series for country data permit an analysis of national trends in participating countries. It is mainly by comparing trends that insights are drawn from the varying conditions in SME financing across countries. The focus on analysis of changes in variables, rather than on absolute levels, helps overcome existing limitations to cross-country comparability of the core indicators, due to differences in definitions and reporting practices.

This Annex describes the methodology for producing the national country profiles, discusses the use of proxies in case of data limitations or deviation from preferred definitions, and addresses the limits in cross-country comparability. It also provides recommendations for improving the collection of data on SME finance.

Scoreboard indicators and their definitions

Core indicators

Trends in financing SMEs and entrepreneurs are monitored through 17 core indicators, which assess specific questions related to access to finance. These core indicators meet the following criteria:

- Usefulness: the indicators must be an appropriate instrument to measure how easy or difficult it is for SMEs and entrepreneurs to access finance and to help policy makers formulate or adjust their policies and programmes.
- Availability: the data for constructing the indicators should be readily available in order not to impose new burdens on governments or firms.
- Feasibility: if the information for constructing the indicator is not publicly available, it should be feasible to make it available at a modest cost, or to collect it during routine data exercises or surveys.
- Timeliness: the information should be collected in a timely manner so that the evolving conditions of SME access to finance can be monitored. Annual data may be more easily available, but should be complemented by quarterly data, when possible, to better capture variability in financing indicators and describe turning points.
- Comparability: the indicators should be relatively uniform across countries in terms of the population surveyed, content, method of data collection and periodicity or timeliness.

Data sources and preferred definitions

The data in the national Scoreboards are supplied by country experts with access to the information needed from a variety of supply-side and demand-side sources.

Most of the Scoreboard indicators are built on supply-side data, that is, data provided by financial institutions and other government agencies. There are several indicators which are based on demand-side surveys of SMEs. However, not all countries undertake such surveys. Use is made of quantitative demand-side data, as collected by SME surveys, to complement the picture and improve the interpretative power of the OECD Scoreboard. Whereas a plethora of qualitative SME surveys (i.e. opinion surveys) exist, quantitative demand-side surveys are less common. Experience shows that qualitative information based on opinion survey responses must be used cautiously. The broader perception of entrepreneurs about access to finance and credit conditions, emanating from such opinion surveys, has its own value though and complements the hard data provided in the quantitative analysis. Furthermore, the cross-country comparability of national surveys remains limited, as survey methodologies and the target population differs from country to country. Comparable demand-side surveys are undertaken on a regular basis by the European Central Bank and the European Commission, which provide an example of the benefits that can come from standardised definitions and methodology across countries when conducting demand-side surveys.

In order to calculate monitor the core indicators, data are collected for 22 variables. Each variable has a preferred definition (see Table A A.1.), intended to facilitate time consistency and comparability. In a number of cases, however, it is not possible for countries to adhere to the "preferred definition" of an indicator, due to data limitations or differences in reporting practices, and a proxy is used instead. For this reason, in each country profile the data are accompanied by a detailed table of definitions and sources for each indicator.

Table A A.1. Preferred definitions for core indicators

Indicator	Definition/ Description	Sources
Outstanding business loans, SMEs	Bank and financial institution loans to SMEs, amount outstanding (stocks) at the end of period; by firm size using the national definition of SME or, if necessary, loan amounts less than EUR 1 million or an equivalent threshold that is deemed appropriate on a case-by-case basis	Supply-side data from financial institutions
Outstanding business loans, total	Bank and financial institution business loans to all non-financialenterprises, outstanding amounts (stocks)	Supply-side data
New business lending, total	Bank and financial institution business loans to all non-financialenterprises over an accounting period (i.e. one year), flows	Supply-side data
New business lending, SMEs	Bank and financial institution loans to SMEs over an accounting period (i.e. one year), flows; by firm size using the national definition of SME or, if necessary, loan amounts less than EUR 1 million or an equivalent threshold that is deemed appropriate on a case-by-case basis	Supply-side data
Short-term loans, SMEs	Loans equal to or less than one year; outstanding amounts or new loans	Supply-side data
Long-term loans, SMEs	Loans for more than one year; outstanding amounts or new loans	Supply-side data
Government loan guarantees, SMEs	Government guarantees available to banks and other financial institutions, stocks or flows	Supply-side data
Government guaranteed loans, SMEs	Loans guaranteed by government, stocks or flows	Supply-side data
Direct government loans, SMEs	Direct loans from government, stocks or flows	Supply-side data
Interest rate, SMEs	Average annual rates for new loans, base rate plus risk premium; for maturity less than one year; and amounts less than EUR 1 million	Supply-side data
Interest rate, large firms	Average annual rates for new loans, base rate for loans equal to or greater than EUR 1 million; for maturity less than one year	Supply-side data
Collateral, SMEs	Percentage of SMEs that were required to provide collateral on latest bank loan	Demand-side survey
Percentage of SME loan applications	SME loan applications divided by the total number of SMEs in the country, in %	Supply-side data or survey
Rejection rate	1-(SME loans authorised/ requested), in %	Supply-side survey

Utilisation rate	SME loans used/ authorised, in %	Supply-side survey
Venture and growth capital investments	Seed, start-up, early stage and expansion capital (excludes buyouts, turnarounds, replacements)	VC association (supply side)
Leasing and hire purchases	New production of hire purchases and leasing, which covers finance leases and operating leases of all asset types (automotive, equipment and real estate) and also includes the rental of cars, vans and trucks.	Business associations (supply side)
Factoring and invoice discounting	Factoring turnover volumes which includes invoice discounting, recourse factoring, non-recourse factoring, collections (domestic factoring), export factoring, import factoring and export invoice discounting (international factoring)	Business associations (supply side)
Non-performing loans, total	% of total business loans	Supply-side data
Non-performing loans, SMEs	% of total SME loans	Supply-side data
Payment delays, B2B	Average number of days delay beyond the contract period for the Business to Business segment (B2B)	Demand-side survey
Bankruptcies, SMEs	Number of enterprises ruled bankrupt; or number bankrupt per 10 000 or 1 000 SMEs	Administrative data

Share of SME loans in total business loans: This ratio captures the allocation of credit by firm size, that is, the relative importance of SME lending in the national credit market. The business loan data, which are used in the construction of several indicators in the Scoreboard, include overdrafts, lines of credit, short-term and long-term loans, regardless of whether they are performing or non-performing loans. In principle, this data does not include personal credit card debt and residential mortgages.

Share of SME new lending in total new business lending: This ratio equally captures the allocation of credit by firm size, but for new loans (flows). Flows, which are measured over an accounting period (i.e. one year), are expected to reflect short-term events and are therefore more volatile than stocks, which measure the value of an asset at a given point in time, and thus reflect latest flows, as well as values that may have cumulated over time, net of depreciation.

Share of short-term loans in SME loans: This ratio shows the debt structure of SMEs or whether loans are being used to fund current operations or investment and growth needs. However, caution has to be used in interpreting this indicator, because it is affected by the composition of short-term loans versus long-term loans in the SME loan portfolio of banks. Indeed, the share of long-term loans could actually increase during a financial crisis, because it is easier for the banks to shut off short-term credit.

SME government loan guarantees, SME government guaranteed loans, SME direct government loans: These indicators show the extent of public support for the financing of SMEs in the form of direct funding or credit guarantees. By comparing government loan guarantees with guaranteed loans, information can be drawn on the take up of government programmes and on their leverage effect.

SME interest rates and interest rate spreads: These indicators describe the tightness of the market and the (positive or negative) correlation of interest rates with firm size.

Collateral required: This indicator also shows tightness of credit conditions. It is based on demand-side surveys where SMEs report if they have been explicitly required to provide collateral for their last loan. It is not available from supply-side sources, as banks do not generally divulge this information.

SME rejection rate: This indicator shows the degree to which SME credit demand is met. An increase in the ratio indicates a tightening in the credit market as more credit applications have been turned down. A limitation in this indicator is that it omits the impact of "discouraged" borrowers. However, discouragement and rejection seem to be closely correlated, as the number of discouraged borrowers tends to increase when credit conditions become tighter and a higher proportion of credit applications are refused.

SME utilisation rate: This ratio also captures credit conditions, more precisely the willingness of banks to provide credit, and is therefore sometimes used in addition to or instead of the rejection rate. An increase of this ratio indicates that a higher proportion of authorised credit is being used by entrepreneurs and SMEs, which usually occurs when credit conditions are tightening.

Venture capital and growth capital investments: This indicator shows the ability to access external equity in the form of seed, start-up, early stage venture capital as well as expansion capital and is ideally broken down by the investment stage. It excludes buyouts, turnarounds and replacement capital, as these are directed at restructuring and generally concern larger enterprises.

Leasing and hire purchases: This indicator contains information on the use of leasing and hire purchases. New production of leasing includes finance leases and operating leases of all asset types (automotive, equipment and real estate) as well as the rental of cars, vans and trucks.

Factoring and invoice discounting provides information on factoring turnover volumes, including invoice discounting, recourse factoring, non-recourse factoring, collections (domestic factoring), export factoring, import factoring and export invoice discounting (international factoring).

SME non-performing loans/SME loans: This indicator provides information about the relative performance of SME loans in banks' portfolio, that is, the riskiness implied by exposure to SME loans. It can be compared with the overall ratio of non-performing loans to all business loans to determine whether SMEs are more risky.

Payment delays: This indicator contributes to assess SME cash flow problems. Business-to-business (B2B) payment delays show supplier credit delays and how SMEs are coping with cash flow problems by delaying their payments and are more relevant to assess cash flow problems compared with business-to-consumer or business-to-government data.

SME bankruptcies or bankruptcies per 10 000 or per 1 000 SMEs: This indicator is a proxy for SME survival prospects. Abrupt changes in bankruptcy rates demonstrate how severely SMEs are affected by economic crises. However, the indicator likely underestimates the number of SME exits, as some SMEs close their business even when not being in financial difficulties. Bankruptcies per 10 000 or per 1 000 SMEs are the preferred measures, because this indicator is not affected by the increase or decrease in the total number of enterprises in the economy.

Inflation-adjusted data

Differences in inflation levels across countries hamper comparability of trends over time. For the second time in the 2017 edition of this report, indicators in the trends chapter therefore have been adjusted for inflation when appropriate. For this purpose, the GDP deflator from the OECD Economic Outlook publication, deflating nominal values into real values, is used. This deflator is derived by dividing an index of GDP (measured in current prices) by a chain volume index of GDP. It is therefore a weighted average of the price indices of goods and services consumed by households; expenditure by government on goods, services and salaries; fixed capital assets; changes in inventories; and exports of goods and services minus imports of goods and services.1 It is a very broad indicator of inflation and, given its comprehensiveness, it is thus suitable to deflate current price nominal data into a real terms prices basis for measures of national income, public expenditure and other economic variables with a focus beyond consumer items.

Inclusion of median values

In order to facilitate interpretation of the data, median values of core indicators are included when appropriate in Chapter 1 of this publication. This enables a better assessment of how participating countries are positioned in terms of the assessed core indicators on SME financing. Given the limited comparability of some indicators, this relative position needs to be interpreted carefully and within the country-specific

[1] OECD (2009), *OECD Factbook 2009: Economic, Environmental and Social Statistics*, OECD Publishing, Paris. DOI: http://dx.doi.org/10.1787/factbook-2009-en

context, however. Median values rather than average values are displayed because they are less sensitive to outliers in the data.

SME target population

The SME target population of the Scoreboard consists of non-financial "employer" firms, that is, firms with at least one employee besides the owner/ manager, which operate a non-financial business. This is consistent with the methodology adopted by the OECD-Eurostat Entrepreneurship Indicators Programme to collect data about business demography. The target group excludes firms with no employees or self-employed individuals, which considerably reduces the number of firms that can be considered SMEs. For most of the countries in the report, data are available for this target population. However, not all countries collect data at the source and compile them in accordance with these criteria. Therefore, in a few cases data include financial firms and/or self-employed individuals. This is mostly the case in countries reporting financial indicators based on loan size, rather than the target population, or when sole proprietorships/ self-entrepreneurs cannot be distinguished from the SME population at the supply-side level of reporting.

Timeframe for data collection

The data in the present report cover the period 2007 to 2017, which includes three distinct economic stages: pre-crisis (2007), crisis (2008-09) and recovery (2010-17). Specific attention is given to the period 2016-17, in order to identify the most recent trends in SME finance and policies.

Data sources

Deviations from preferred definitions of indicators

Data limitations and country-level specific reporting practices imply that the national Scoreboards may deviate from the preferred definitions of some core indicator. Some of the main deviations in definition of variables and data coverage are discussed below.

SME loans

The OECD Scoreboard aims to collect business loan data that include overdrafts, lines of credit, short-term loans, and long-term loans, regardless of whether they are performing or non-performing loans. Additionally, it aims to exclude personal credit card debt and residential mortgages. However, for some countries, significant deviations exist from this preferred SME loan definition. For instance, in some cases, credit card debt is included in SME loans, and it cannot be determined which part corresponds to consumer credit card debt and which part is business credit card debt. In other cases, lines of credit and overdrafts are excluded, while a number of other products are indeed included in SME loans, such as securitised loans, leasing and factoring.

In some countries, central banks do not require any reporting on SME lending. In these cases the SME loans are estimated from SME financial statements available from tax authorities.

SME loans requested, authorised and used

The indicators on SME loans authorised and SME loans requested, which are used to calculate the rejection rate, are obtained from demand-side surveys. However, not all countries undertake such surveys, or, if they do, the results are not necessarily comparable. This also constitutes an area, where substantial data improvements could be made, such as enriching the analysis by the inclusion of an indicator on the level of discouragement to apply for a bank loan. To capture discouragement, this indicator should ideally be analysed in tandem with the number of loan applications. If both, loan applications and rejection rates decrease over the same period, this would suggest a higher level of discouragement. As presumably the least credit-worthy firms are deterred from applying for a loan, this could also be indicative of the average riskiness of SME lending.

Another potential improvement concerns the granularity and level of detail of the data; it might be possible to distinguish the rejection rate according to the type of loan (e.g. specific rejection rates on overdrafts, term loans, credit card loans and so on), to separate partial rejections from full rejections, including more analysis on the (likely) reason(s).

A similar problem holds true for the utilisation rate; which consists of SME loans used divided by SME loans authorised. A decline in this ratio suggests that the credit market is easing, or that banks have been providing more credit than has been used. Again, not every country has reliable survey data on the SME loans used and caution is warranted when making comparisons across countries.

Government loan guarantees and guaranteed loans

The report includes data on government loan guarantees and on the value of loans backed by government guarantees. Supply-side data are the best source of information on loan guarantees. There are many sources for such guarantees: local, regional or central governments. In some countries, an important volume of guarantees is also provided by mutual guarantee schemes. These are private schemes that typically benefit from public support, in the form of direct funding or counter-guarantees. However, the various loan guarantees schemes, public, private and mixed, are not always consolidated to obtain national figures. Therefore, the OECD Scoreboard reports mostly on government loan guarantees which are readily available at central government level. This is also a way to avoid the double-counting of guarantees that have multiple layers, given the existence of counter-guarantees at other levels (regional or supra-national). Still, cross-country differences exist in the degree to which the reported data include all government guarantee programmes, or only large ones.

In some cases, lack of awareness and reporting make it difficult to collect data on guaranteed SME loans. In fact, SMEs are not always aware that their loan is backed by a government guarantee and banks do not usually report this information. When these guaranteed SME loans are reported, they usually represent the full value of the loan and not the portion of the loan that is actually backed by a public institution guarantee. Nevertheless, this figure has a value of its own when compared to the total amount of SME loans outstanding. Also, it allows the calculation of the leverage effect of government guarantees to SMEs (ratio of guaranteed SME loans to corresponding government guarantees).

SME credit conditions

Significant differences exist across countries in the calculation for SME interest rates. While there is agreement that “fees” should be included in the “cost” of the SME loans, it appears to be particularly difficult to determine which “fees”, among the various charges applied to firms, to include in the interest rates. In most cases, the interest rate charged on SME loans, net of any fee, is reported. The additional fees, however, represent a rather significant cost for SMEs that is not being captured by the current indicators built on supply-side data, particularly in the case of small SME loans. In this regard, demand-side surveys could be used to collect information on the total cost of funding.

Central banks usually do not collect key pieces of information on SME access to finance, such as the collateral required for SME loans. Banks consider this to be confidential information. A rough approximation can be obtained from demand-side information, that is, the percentage of SMEs required to provide collateral on new loans. This measure is currently used in the OECD Scoreboard, and more transparent reporting by banks on the terms of their SME lending is recommended to improve information on SME credit conditions.

Equity financing

The present report monitors external equity, that is, venture and growth capital. Venture capital is usually reported by stage of development: seed, start-up and early expansion capital. Later stage expansion capital, referred to as growth capital, is also reported. Buyouts, turnarounds and replacement capital are excluded from venture and growth capital. Country classification systems do not always break down private equity data into these categories and most do not break it down by firm size. Indeed, at present, the lack of a standard international definition of venture capital limits cross-country comparability. Also, venture capital data are sometimes collected by private venture capital associations, which rely on voluntary reporting and whose membership may be incomplete. There is a need for greater standardisation of venture capital data reporting, in terms of both the definition used for the different stages of investment, and the methodology employed to collect data.[2]

Asset-based finance

Most of the indicators of the Scoreboard relate to bank finance, although in practice SMEs and entrepreneurs also rely on other financing options. Including statistics on the use of asset-based finance allows for a more complete overview of trends of access to finance for SMEs and entrepreneurs. Asset-based financing covers a variety of instruments whereby a firm obtains cash based on the value of a particular asset, rather than on credit standing. These instruments include asset-based lending, factoring, hire purchases and factoring.

Asset-based lending is any sort of lending secured by an asset (such as accounts receivable, inventory, real estate, equipment). As these loans are usually issued by banks, information on asset-based loans is already covered in the indicator on SME loans, and a separate indicator is not required. More detailed information on the composition of bank loans would, however, shed light on the importance of asset-based lending and what assets are most often used as a security.

The indicator on leasing covers either the new production (i.e. a flow indicator) of finance leases and operating leases of all asset types (automotive, equipment and real estate) and also includes the rental of cars, vans and trucks. Leasing is an agreement whereby the owner of an asset provides the right to use the asset for a specified period of time in exchange for a series of payments. Information on hire purchases, which are agreements where the purchaser agrees to pay for the goods in parts or percentages over a number of months and which is very similar to leasing is also covered.. Factoring is a type of supplier financing where firms sell their credit-worthy accounts receivable at a discount and receive immediate cash. Data on factoring turnover volumes includes all turnover that is covered by invoice discounting, recourse factoring, non-recourse factoring, collections (domestic factoring), export factoring, import factoring and export invoice discounting (international factoring).

It is important to note that these data usually do not distinguish between SMEs and large corporations, and a breakdown of data according to the size of the lessees does not exist in most countries, although research indicates that leasing and other forms of asset-based finance are very often used by SMEs. Increasing the number of countries providing data and deriving information on the take-up of asset-based finance by firm size, either directly or through a proxy, constitutes an important avenue for future research.

Non-performing loans

There is also a great deal of latitude in how banks define non-performing loans. The generally accepted threshold of 90-day arrears, i.e. payments of interest and principal past due by 90 days or more, is indeed used by many of the Scoreboard countries, but not all. Even when this same threshold is adopted, there is

---

2 See Annex C in OECD (2013), Entrepreneurship at a Glance 2013, OECD Publishing, Paris, for a detailed discussion on the international comparability of venture capital data.

a great deal of variation across countries in the measurement of SME non-performing loans. In some cases, these are measured as a percentage of the entire SME loan portfolio and in other cases they are not. In addition, it is common practice to classify loans that are unlikely to be repaid in full as non-performing, even when the threshold of 90-day arrears is not met. The circumstances, under which loans are considered unlikely to be repaid, and hence deemed non-performing, vary substantially across countries and financial institutions. Caution is therefore warranted when interpreting this data.

When compared to the non-performing loans ratio of large firms, this indicator provides a good description of the performance of SME loans on a national level, irrespective of the particularity of the national definition. In addition, if the changes in the non-performing ratio are analysed over time, the indicator has value for cross-country comparisons.

Payment delays and bankruptcies

Payment delays and bankruptcy data are usually collected for all enterprises and not broken down by firm size. Since SMEs account for more than 97% of the enterprises in the participating countries, the national figures for payment delays and bankruptcy rates were used in this report. However, bankruptcies are hard to compare across countries because of different bankruptcy costs, legislation and behaviour in the face of bankruptcy. In some cases, bankruptcy procedures take a long time and so bankruptcies only show up in later periods rather than during the crisis period.

Payment delays are reported as delays beyond the contractual date on a B2B or on a broader B2B and B2C basis. Reporting of payment delays is important, given that it captures an additional source of cash flow constraints for SMEs. The reporting of both indicators and the comparison of B2B with B2C delays can also be used to uncover whether and how SMEs make use of such payment delays to resolve short-term cash flow issues in lieu of working capital credit facilities.

Differences in definitions of an SME

One of the biggest challenges to comparability is represented by existing differences in the statistical definition of an SME by banks and national organisations across countries. Greater harmonisation continues to prove difficult due to the different economic, social and political concerns of individual countries. In addition, within-country differences exist: some banks and financial institutions do not use their national statistical definitions for an SME but a different definition to collect data on SME financing.

In many cases, the national authorities collect loan data using the national or EU definition for an SME, based on firm size, u sually the number of employees or the annual turnover (see Box A A.1).

Box A A.1. What is an SME?

While there is no universal definition of an SME and several criteria can be used in the definition, SMEs are generally considered to be non-subsidiary firms which employ less than a given number of employees. This number of employees varies across countries. The most frequent upper limit designation of an SME is 250 employees, as in the European Union. However, some countries set the limit at 200, while the United States considers SMEs to include firms with fewer than 500 employees. Small firms are mostly considered to be firms with fewer than 50 employees while micro-enterprises have less than 10. Medium-sized firms have between 50 and 249 employees. Turnover and financial assets are also used to define SMEs: in the EU, the turnover of an SME cannot exceed EUR 50 million and the annual balance sheet should not exceed EUR 43 million

Source: OECD (2006), The SME Financing Gap (Vol. I): Theory and Evidence, OECD Publishing, Paris

In other cases, the SME loan data are based not on firm size but rather on a proxy, that is, loan size.[3] However, the size of the SME loan can differ among countries and sometimes even among banks within the same country.

Several reasons are advanced for not compiling financial statistics based on firm size including:

- Banks do not collect data by firm size;
- It is too expensive to collect such data;
- Breaking down loan data by firm size would jeopardise confidentiality and are not gathered or communicated as a consequence.

Experience gained from the OECD Scoreboard suggests that loan data broken down by firm size are already in the financial system but are not extracted unless banks are under a regulatory obligation to provide them. Experience also suggests that the challenges mentioned above could be addressed quite easily. For instance, confidentiality requirements in theory could be met through the use of judicious sub-grouping. In this case, resolution of this issue could be found if national regulatory authorities were to make the provision of this information mandatory for banks.

Table A A.2. Difference between national statistical and financial definitions of SMEs

Country	National statistical definition of SMEs	Indicator	Definition of SMEs used
Australia	Size of firm: less than 200 employees	Business loans, SMEs	Loan size: amounts outstanding under AUD 2 million
		Interest rate, SMEs	Loan size: amounts outstanding under AUD 2 million
Austria	Size of firm: 1 – 249 employees	Business loans, SMEs	Loan size: amounts up to EUR 1 million
		Short- and long-term loans, SMEs	Loan size: amounts up to EUR 1 million
		Government loan guarantees and government guaranteed loans, SMEs	Firm size: enterprises with less than 250 employees

3 Recent studies by the World Bank provide evidence that loan size is an adequate proxy for size of the firm accessing the loan. See for instance Ardic O.P., Mylenko N., Saltane V. (2012), “Small and medium enterprises: a cross-country analysis with a new data set”, Pacific Economic Review, Vol. 17, Issues 4, pp. 491-513.

		Direct government loans, SMEs	Firm size: enterprises with less than 250 employees
		Rejection rate	Firm size: enterprises with less than 250 employees
		Interest rate, SMEs	Loan size: amounts up to EUR 1 million
Belgium	Size of firm: less than 250 employees	Business loans, SMEs	Firm size: enterprises with less than 250 employees
		SME loans authorised and used	Firm size: enterprises with less than 250 employees
		Interest rate, SMEs	Loan size: amounts up to EUR 1 million
Brazil	annual turnover of up to BRL 4.8 million	Outstanding business loans, SMEs	Loan size: amounts up to BRL 100 million
			Measured on a client-facility-month basis
Canada	Size of firm: 1-499 employees	Business loans, SMEs	Loan size: amounts up to CAD 1 million
		Short- and long-term loans, small businesses	Firm size: enterprises with 1-99 employees
		Government guaranteed loans, SMEs	Firm size: annual sales (turnover) lower than CAD 5 million
		Direct government loans, SMEs	Firm size: annual sales (turnover) less than CAD 25 million
		Risk premium for small businesses	Firm size: enterprises with 1-99 employees
		Loans authorised and requested, small businesses	Firm size: enterprises with 1-99 employees
		Collateral, small businesses	Firm size: enterprises with 1-99 employees
Chile	Annual sales of firm: up to UF 100 000	Business loans, SMEs	Loan size: amounts up to UF 18 000
		Short- and long-term loans, SMEs	Loan size: amounts up to UF 18 000
		Government guaranteed loans, SMEs	Firm size: annual sales up to UF 100 000 or annual exports up to UF 400 000
		Direct government loans, SMEs	Less than 12 hectares and capital up to UF 3 500
		Loans authorised and requested, SMEs	Firm size: annual sales up to UF 100 000
		Non-performing loans, SMEs	Loan size: amounts up to UF 18 000
		Short-term and long-term interest rate, SMEs	Loan size: amounts up to UF 18 000
		Payment delays, SMEs	Loan size: amounts up to UF 18 000
China	The definition of SMEs differs according to sector.		The definition of SMEs differs according to sector.
		Short- and long-term loans, SMEs	The definition of SMEs differs according to sector.
		Government loan guarantees, SMEs	The definition of SMEs differs according to sector.
		SME government direct loans	The definition of SMEs differs according to sector.
		Non-performing loans, SMEs	The definition of SMEs differs according to sector.
		SME loans requested, authorized and used	The definition of SMEs differs according to sector.
		interest rates, SMEs	The definition of SMEs differs according to sector.
		Collateral, SMEs	The definition of SMEs differs according to sector.

		Loan fees, SMEs	The definition of SMEs differs according to sector.
Colombia	Size of firm: less than 200 employees	Business loans, SMEs	Firm size: enterprises with less than 200 employees
		Non-performing loans, SMEs	Firm size: enterprises with less than 200 employees
		Government guaranteed loans, SMEs	Firm size: enterprises with less than 200 employees
		Interest rate, SMEs	Firm size: enterprises with less than 200 employees
		Collateral, SMEs	Firm size: enterprises with less than 200 employees
Czech Republic	Size of firm: less than 250 employees	Business loans, SMEs	Loan size: amount up to CZK 30 million
		(New business loans, SMEs – flows)	Loan size: amount up to CZK 30 million
		Business loans, SMEs (Outstanding business loans, SMEs – stock)	Firm size: up to 250 employees
		Interest rate, SMEs	Loan size: amount up to CZK 30 million
Denmark	Size of firm: less than 250 employees	Business loans, SMEs	Loan size: amounts up to EUR 1 million
		Short- and long-term loans, SMEs	Loan size: amounts up to EUR 1 million
		Government loan guarantees, SMEs	Firm size: up to 250 employees
		Interest rate, SMEs	Loan size: amounts up to EUR 1 million
Estonia	Size of firm: less than 250 employees	Business loans, SMEs	Loan size: amounts up to EUR 1 million
		Government loan guarantees, SMEs	Loan size: amounts up to EUR 1 million
		Non-performing loans, SMEs	Loan size: amounts up to EUR 1 million
		Interest rate, SMEs	Loan size: amounts up to EUR 1 million
Finland	EU definition (less than 250 employees and annual turnover below EUR 50 million and/ or balance sheet below EUR 43 million)	Business loans, SMEs	Loan size: up to EUR 1 million
		Short- and long-term loans, SMEs	Firm size: less than 250 employees
		Value of government guaranteed loans, SMEs	Firm size: less than 250 employees
		Loans authorised and requested, SMEs	Loan size: up to EUR 1 million
		Interest rate, SMEs	Loan size: up to EUR 1 million
		Collateral, SMEs	Firm size: less than 250 employees
France	EU definition (less than 250 employees and annual turnover below EUR 50 million and/ or balance sheet below EUR 43 million)	Business loans, SMEs	Firm size: number of employees (less than 250), turnover (less than EUR 50 million), total assets of legal units (less than EUR 43 million) and independent; bank must inform the Central Credit Register when it grants a loan of more than EUR 25 000
		Short- medium- and long-term loans	Firm size: number of employees (less than 250), turnover (less than EUR 50 million), total assets of legal units (less than EUR 43 million) and independent; bank must inform the Central Credit Register when it grants a loan of more than EUR 25 000

		Share of the outstanding loans of failing companies, SMEs except micro-enterprises	Firm size: number of employees (less than 250), turnover (less than EUR 50 million), total assets of legal units (less than EUR 43 million) and independent; bank must inform the Central Credit Register when it grants a loan of more than EUR 25 000
		Interest rate, SMEs	Loan size: less than EUR 1 million
		Bankruptcies, SMEs	Firm size: number of employees (less than 250), turnover (less than EUR 50 million), total assets of legal units (less than EUR 43 million) and independent
Georgia	Less than 100 employees and turnover below GEL 1.5 million	Business loans, SMEs	Less than 100 employees and turnover below GEL 1.5 million
		Non-performing loans, SMEs	
		Interest rate, SMEs	
		Collateral SMEs	
Greece	EU definition (less than 250 employees and annual turnover below EUR 50 million and/ or balance sheet below EUR 43 million)	Business loans, SMEs	Firm size: number of employees (less than 250 employees), turnover (less than EUR 50 million) and total assets (less than EUR 10 million)
		Interest rate, SMEs	Loan size: less than EUR 1 million
		Collateral, SMEs	Loan size: less than EUR 1 million
Hungary	EU definition (less than 250 employees and annual turnover below EUR 50 million and/ or balance sheet below EUR 43 million)	Business loans, SMEs	Firm size: number of employees (less than 250 employees), turnover (less than EUR 50 million) and total assets (less than EUR 10 million)
		Overdraft loans, SMEs	Firm size: number of employees (less than 250 employees), turnover (less than EUR 50 million) and total assets (less than EUR 10 million)
		Investment loans, SMEs	Firm size: number of employees (less than 250 employees), turnover (less than EUR 50 million) and total assets (less than EUR 10 million)
		Direct government loans, SMEs	Firm size: number of employees (less than 250 employees), turnover (less than EUR 50 million) and total assets (less than EUR 10 million)
		Government guaranteed loans, SMEs	Firm size: number of employees (less than 250 employees), turnover (less than EUR 50 million) and total assets (less than EUR 10 million)
		Non-performing loans, SMEs	Firm size: number of employees (less than 250 employees), turnover (less than EUR 50 million) and total assets (less than EUR 10 million)
		Average interest rate, SMEs	Loan size: amounts up to EUR 1 million
Ireland	EU definition (less than 250 employees and annual turnover below EUR 50 million and/ or balance sheet below EUR 43 million)	Business loans, SMEs	Firm size
		Short- and long-term loans, SMEs	Loan size: less than EUR 1 million
		Interest rates, SMEs	Loan size: less than EUR 1 million

Israel[i]	Size of firm: less than 100 employees and annual turnover of up to NIS 100 million	Business loans, SMEs	Loan size: amounts of NIS differ depending on the bank
		Interest rate small firms and medium firms	Loan size: amounts of NIS differ depending on the bank
Indonesia	SMEs are defined as enterprises with a maximum turnover maximum of 50 billion rupiah or maximum assets (exclude building land asset) maximum of 10 billion rupiah		
Italy	EU definition (less than 250 employees and annual turnover below EUR 50 million and/ or balance sheet below EUR 43 million)	Business loans, SMEs	Firm size: less than 20 workers
		Short- and long-term loans, SMEs	Firm size: less than 20 workers
		Government guaranteed loans, SMEs	Firm size: less than 250 employees
		Direct government loans, SMEs	Firm size: less than 250 employees
		Loans authorised and used, SMEs	Firm size: less than 20 workers
		Non-performing loans, SMEs	Firm size: less than 20 workers
		Interest rate, average SME rate	Firm size: less than 20 workers
		Collateral, SMEs	Firm size: less than 20 workers
		Venture and expansion capital, SMEs	Firm size: less than 250 employees
		Payment delays, SMEs	Firm size: turnover of up to EUR 50 million and less than 250 employees
Japan	Varies by sector	Business loans, SMEs	The definition of SMEs differs according to sector.
		Bankruptcies, SMEs	The definition of SMEs differs according to sector. Only enterprises with debts of at least JPY10 million are included.
Kazakhstan	Less than 250 employees in addition to an annual income criterium		
Korea	Varies by sector	Business loans, SMEs	The definition of SMEs differs according to sector.
		Short- and long-term loans, SMEs	The definition of SMEs differs according to sector.
		Government loan guarantees, SMEs	The definition of SMEs differs according to sector.
		Direct government loans, SMEs	The definition of SMEs differs according to sector.
		Loans authorised and requested, SMEs	The definition of SMEs differs according to sector.
		Non-performing loans, SMEs	The definition of SMEs differs according to sector.
		Interest rate spread, SME and large firm rates	The definition of SMEs differs according to sector.
		Payment delays, SMEs	The definition of SMEs differs according to sector.
Latvia	EU definition (less than 250 employees and annual turnover below EUR 50 million and/ or balance sheet below EUR 43 million)	Interest rate, SMEs	Loan size: Loans of less than EUR 250000
Lithuania	EU definition (less than 250 employees and annual turnover below EUR 50 million and/ or balance sheet below EUR 43 million)		

Luxembourg	EU definition (less than 250 employees and annual turnover below EUR 50 million and/ or balance sheet below EUR 43 million)	SME loans	Loan size: Loans of less than EUR 1 million
		SME interest rate	Loan size: Loans of less than EUR 1 million
Malaysia	Manufacturing sector: Sales turnover not exceeding RM 50 million or full-time employees not exceeding 200. Services and other sectors: Sales turnover not exceeding RM 20 million or full-time employees not exceeding 75.	SME loans	Firm size: Sales turnover not exceeding RM 50 million or full-time employees not exceeding 200 for firms operating in the manufacturing sector and sales turnover not exceeding RM 20 million or full-time employees not exceeding 75 for firms operating in services and other sectors,
		SME short-term loans	Firm size: Sales turnover not exceeding RM 50 million or full-time employees not exceeding 200 for firms operating in the manufacturing sector and sales turnover not exceeding RM 20 million or full-time employees not exceeding 75 for firms operating in services and other sectors,
		SME long-term loans	Firm size: Sales turnover not exceeding RM 50 million or full-time employees not exceeding 200 for firms operating in the manufacturing sector and sales turnover not exceeding RM 20 million or full-time employees not exceeding 75 for firms operating in services and other sectors,
		SME non-performing loans	Firm size: Sales turnover not exceeding RM 50 million or full-time employees not exceeding 200 for firms operating in the manufacturing sector and sales turnover not exceeding RM 20 million or full-time employees not exceeding 75 for firms operating in services and other sectors,
		SME loans authorised	Firm size: Sales turnover not exceeding RM 50 million or full-time employees not exceeding 200 for firms operating in the manufacturing sector and sales turnover not exceeding RM 20 million or full-time employees not exceeding 75 for firms operating in services and other sectors,
		SME loans requested	Firm size: Sales turnover not exceeding RM 50 million or full-time employees not exceeding 200 for firms operating in the manufacturing sector and sales turnover not exceeding RM 20 million or full-time employees not exceeding 75 for firms operating in services and other sectors,
		SME interest rate	Firm size: Sales turnover not exceeding RM 50 million or full-time employees not exceeding 200 for firms operating in the manufacturing sector and sales turnover not exceeding RM 20 million or full-time employees not exceeding 75 for firms operating in services and other sectors,

Mexico	Firm size: up to 100 or 250 employees, depending on the sector	SME loans	The definition depends on the number of employees and the annual revenues of the borrower
		SME guaranteed loans/direct loans	Firm size: up to 100 or 250 employees, depending on the sector
		SME loans requested and authorized	Firm size: up to 100 or 250 employees, depending on the sector
		SME interest rate	Firm size: up to 100 or 250 employees, depending on the sector
The Netherlands	EU definition (less than 250 employees and annual turnover below EUR 50 million and/ or balance sheet below EUR 43 million)	Business loans, SMEs	Loan size: up to EUR 1 million
		Short- and long-term loans, SMEs	Loan size: up to EUR 1 million
		Government loan guarantees, SMEs	Firm size: up to 250 employees
		Loans authorised and requested, SMEs	Firm size: up to 250 employees
		Collateral, SMEs	Size of firm up to 50 employees
New Zealand	No unique national definition.	Interest rates, SMEs	Loan size: up to NZD 1 million
		Loan authorised, SMEs	Firm size: enterprises with 6-19 employees
		Loan requested, SMEs	Firm size: enterprises with 6-19 employees
Norway	EU definition (less than 250 employees and annual turnover below EUR 50 million and/ or balance sheet below EUR 43 million)	Business loans, SMEs	Firm size: less than 250 employees
Portugal	EU definition (less than 250 employees and annual turnover below EUR 50 million and/ or balance sheet below EUR 43 million)	Business loans, SMEs	Firm size: EU definition (less than 250 employees and annual turnover below EUR 50 million and/ or balance sheet below EUR 43 million, Com Recommendation 2003/361/EC)
		Short- and long-term loans, SMEs	Firm size: EU definition (less than 250 employees and annual turnover below EUR 50 million and/ or balance sheet below EUR 43 million, Com Recommendation 2003/361/EC)
		Government guaranteed loans, SMEs	Firm size: EU definition (less than 250 employees and annual turnover below EUR 50 million and/ or balance sheet below EUR 43 million, Com Recommendation 2003/361/EC)
		Loans authorised and requested, SMEs	Firm size: EU definition (less than 250 employees and annual turnover below EUR 50 million and/ or balance sheet below EUR 43 million, Com Recommendation 2003/361/EC)
		Non-performing loans, SMEs	Firm size: EU definition (less than 250 employees and annual turnover below EUR 50 million and/ or balance sheet below EUR 43 million, Com Recommendation 2003/361/EC)
		Interest rates, SMEs	Loan size: up to EUR 1 million (prior to 2010) and loans up to EUR 0.25 million (in 2010)

		Collateral, SMEs	Firm size: EU definition (less than 250 employees and annual turnover below EUR 50 million and/ or balance sheet below EUR 43 million, Com Recommendation 2003/361/EC)
Russian Federation	Less than 250 employees, not more than RUB 1000 million	Business loans, SMEs	Firm size: Less than 250 employees, not more than RUB 1000 million
		Government loan guarantees, SMEs	Firm size: Less than 250 employees, not more than RUB 1000 million
		Government guaranteed loans, SMEs	Firm size: Less than 250 employees, not more than RUB 1000 million
		Non-performing loans, SMEs	Firm size: Less than 250 employees, not more than RUB 1000 million
Peru	SMEs are defined by annual turnover	Outstanding business loans, SMEs	Defined by annual sales of the borrower
Serbia	Up to 250 employees, turnover up to EUR 10 million, total assets up to EUR 5 million	Business loans, SMEs	Firm size, in accordance with national statistical definition.
		Interest rate, SMEs	Loan size: up to EUR 1 million.
Slovak Republic	EU definition (less than 250 employees and annual turnover below EUR 50 million and/ or balance sheet below EUR 43 million)	Business loans, SMEs	Firm size: less than 250 employees (including natural persons)
		Short- and long-term loans, SMEs	Firm size: less than 250 employees (including natural persons)
		Government loan guarantees, SMEs	Firm size: less than 250 employees (including natural persons)
		Government guaranteed loans, SMEs	Firm size: EU definition (less than 250 employees and annual turnover below EUR 50 million and/ or balance sheet below EUR 43 million, Com Recommendation 2003/361/EC)
		Direct government loans, SMEs	Firm size: less than 250 employees (including natural persons)
		Direct government loans, SMEs	Firm size: less than 250 employees (including natural persons)
		Collateral, SMEs	Firm size: EU definition (less than 250 employees and annual turnover below EUR 50 million and/ or balance sheet below EUR 43 million, Com Recommendation 2003/361/EC)
		Venture capital, SMEs	Firm size: EU definition (less than 250 employees and annual turnover below EUR 50 million and/ or balance sheet below EUR 43 million, Com Recommendation 2003/361/EC)
Slovenia	EU definition (less than 250 employees and annual turnover below EUR 50 million and/ or balance sheet below EUR 43 million)	Short- and long-term loans, SMEs	Firm size: less than or equal to 250 employees and asset value less than or equal to EUR 17.5 million.
		Direct government loans, SMEs	Firm size: less than or equal to 250 employees and asset value less than or equal to EUR 17.5 million.
		Interest rate, SMEs	Firm and loan size: enterprises with less than 250 employees and amounts less than EUR 1 million.

Spain	EU definition (less than 250 employees and annual turnover below EUR 50 million and/ or balance sheet below EUR 43 million)	Business loans, SMEs	Loan size: less than EUR 1 million
		Short- and long-term loans, SMEs	Loan size: less than EUR 1 million
		Government guaranteed loans, SMEs	Firm size: less than 250 employees
		Interest rate, SMEs	Loan size: less than EUR 1 million
		Venture capital, SMEs	Firm size: less than 250 employees
		Payment delays, SMEs	Firm size: EU definition
		Bankruptcies, SMEs	Firm size: EU definition
Sweden	EU definition (less than 250 employees and annual turnover below EUR 50 million and/ or balance sheet below EUR 43 million)	Business loans, SMEs	Firm size: 1-249 employees
		Short- and long-term loans, SMEs	Firm size: 1-249 employees
		Government guaranteed loans, SMEs	Firm size: 0-249 employees
		Government loan guarantees, SMEs	Firm size: 0-249 employees
		Direct government loans, SMEs	Firm size: 0-249 employees
		Loans authorised, SMEs	Firm size: 0-249 employees
		Interest rates, SMEs	Loan size: up to EUR 1 million
Switzerland	Size of firm: less than 250 employees	Business loans, SMEs	Firm size: less than 250 employees
		Government guaranteed loans, SMEs	Firm size: less than 250 employees
		Loans used, SMEs	Firm size: less than 250 employees
		Collateral, SMEs	Firm size: up to 249 employees
		Interest rates, SMEs	Loan size: less than CHF 1 million
Thailand	Number of employees and fixed capital: less than 200 employees and fixed capital less than THB 200 million	Business loans, SMEs	Firm size: sales less than THB 400 million and/or a credit line less than THB 200 million.
		Short- and long-term loans, SMEs	Firm size: sales less than THB 400 million and/or a credit line less than THB 200 million.
		Government guaranteed loans, SMEs	Firm size: sales less than THB 400 million and/or a credit line less than THB 200 million.
		Loans authorised and requested, SMEs	Firm size: sales less than THB 400 million and/or a credit line less than THB 200 million.
		Non-performing loans, SMEs	Firm size: sales less than THB 400 million and/or a credit line less than THB 200 million.
		Interest rate, SME average rate	Firm size: sales less than THB 400 million and/or a credit line less than THB 200 million.
		Payment delays, SMEs	The National definition of SMEs differs according to sector.
		Bankruptcies, SMEs	The National definition of SMEs differs according to sector.
Turkey	Less than 250 employees and TRY 40 million in assets	Business loans, SMEs	Firm size
		SME non-performing loans	Firm size
United Kingdom	Size of firm: less than 250 employees	Business lending, SMEs	Firm size: turnover of up to GBP 25 million
		Interest rates, SMEs	Firm size: turnover up to GBP 25 million
		Collateral, SMEs	Firm size: less than 250 employees, including non-employer enterprises
United States	Size of firm: less than 500 employees	Business loans, SMEs	Loan size: up to USD 1 million.
		Short-term loans, SMEs	Loan size: up to USD 1 million.

		Government guaranteed loans, SMEs	Varies by industry
		Collateral, SMEs	Loan size: up to USD 1 million

Impact of diversity in definitions

The many limitations in data collection above outlined limit the possibility to make cross-country comparisons using the raw data. However, it is possible to observe general trends for the indicators, both within and across countries, using growth rates. When analysing trends, the differences in the exact composition of the indicators are muted by the fact that the changes in the indicators over time are being examined instead of levels. Additionally, if the indicators are analysed as a set, it is possible to form an overview of the country trends in SME financing. It is precisely comparing trends that the Scoreboard sheds light on changing market conditions and policies for financing SMEs and entrepreneurs.

However, again, caution is required in cross-country comparisons, especially as concerns the use of flow variables and stock measures. Flows, which are measured over an accounting period (i.e. one year), capture changes of a given variables and are therefore more volatile than stocks, which measure levels, i.e. the value of an asset at a given point in time, and thus reflect latest flows, as well as values that may have cumulated over time, net of depreciation. The comparison of flows and stock measures can be particularly problematic when growth rates are considered. In fact, a negative growth rate of a flow variable can be compatible with a positive growth rate of the same variable measured in stocks. This would be the case if the stock variables increases over time but the absolute increase by which the stock variables grows becomes smaller. Similarly, a negative growth rate of a loan stock does not necessarily mean a decline in SME lending, but could be attributed to maturing loans exceeding the value of new loans granted. Such difficulties underline the importance of complementing stock data with flows of new loans.

Recommendations for data improvements

Standardised template

To enable more timely collection of data and better cross-country comparison in the future, it is necessary for countries to advance in the harmonisation of data content and in the standardisation of methods of data collection. The adoption of a standardised table for data collection and submission on SME finance has contributed to improve the process of data collection for the Scoreboard, while allowing for some customisation at the country level, and should thus be further pursued, as country coverage increases. The systematic use of the template is furthermore intended to facilitate the timely publication of the data on core indicators on the OECD.Stat website, from which it can then be customised, manipulated and downloaded.

The long-term objectives of timeliness, comparability, transparency and harmonisation of data should continue to be pursued actively by national authorities. To that end, national authorities should work with financial institutions to improve the collection of data on SME and entrepreneurship finance, by:

- Requiring financial institutions to use the national definition for an SME based on firm size.
- Requiring financial institutions to report on a timely basis to their regulatory authorities SME loans, interest rates, collateral requirements, by firm size and broken down into the appropriate size subcategories, as well as those SME loans which have government support.
- Working towards international harmonisation of data on non-performing loans.
- Encouraging international, regional and national authorities as well as business associations to work together to harmonise quantitative demand-side surveys in terms of survey population, questions asked and timeframes; encourage the competent organisations to undertake yearly surveys.
- Promoting the harmonisation of the definition of venture capital in terms of stages of development.

Core indicators

Since the Scoreboard pilot exercise was launched in 2009-10, with the participation of 11 countries, important progress has been made in terms of standardisation and comparability of information. As country coverage increases, it is important that good practices in data collection and reporting be shared among countries, but also that further advancement be made in the harmonisation of core indicators. A number of areas can be identified to improve the monitoring over time of trends at the country level and across countries.

First, it is of paramount importance to improve reporting of SME loan variables. Key areas for refinement include:

- Separate reporting of financial information for non-employer and employer-firms, so as to harmonise the financial data with the SME definition employed in national statistics. The separation would also allow for a more in-depth evaluation of financing trends at the country level, distinguishing between funding that is directed to businesses that generate employment from that directed to self-employers, which may however represent an important share of the country's business activity.
- Collection of stock and flow data for SME loans. These two indicators are complementary and should be jointly analysed in order to draw a comprehensive picture of the evolution of the SME lending portfolio.
- Information on the composition of lending portfolios, broken down by different products (overdrafts/ lines of credit/ leases/ business mortgages or credit cards/ securitised loans). Greater granularity in the reporting of business loans would allow for the identification of the underlying elements of the SME business loan portfolio. This represents a necessary first step towards pursuing greater harmonisation in the definition of SME loans across countries, or, at least identifying a common "base composition" for more meaningful cross-country comparisons.

Second, it is also necessary to fill the gaps in available data and work towards more comprehensive information for other core indicators in the Scoreboard:

- Government guarantees: Provide consolidated figures, which take into account the entire range of public guarantee programmes, while excluding double counting related, for instance, to the counter-guarantee of the same lending portfolio. Include additional information on the scope and coverage of public guarantee schemes, in particular information on the volume of outstanding guarantees, the public contribution to the fund's capitalisation, and the value of the loans supported by public guarantees. The Scoreboard data should be complemented, in the policy section of country profiles, by the monitoring of the take-ups and phasing out of these guarantee schemes.
- Government guaranteed loans: Provide the corresponding loans backed by the reported government guarantees so as to allow for the calculation of a leverage ratio. Optimally, the guaranteed portions of these loans should be also reported.
- Non-performing loans (NPLs): Provide the NPL ratio for SME loans, together with the overall NPL ratio of the business loan portfolio or the NPL ratio for large firms. The latter would be used as a benchmark against which the performance and quality of the SME loan portfolio is measured.
- Asset-based finance: Obtain data broken down by firm size or a functioning proxy of firm size. Currently, business associations usually do not make the distinction according to the use of these instruments by firm size, which limits the understanding of the importance of these non-bank financial instruments for SMEs.
- SME loan fees: Provide information on the standard practice of the commercial banking sector with respect to loan fees charged to SME loans in addition to the interest rate, at a national level. If possible, use demand-side surveys to collect information on this indirect cost on SME lending.
- Collateral: Improve the description of what constitutes collateral and use demand-side survey information to compensate for lack of supply-side data on collateral.

Medium and long-term objectives

In the medium to long term, it is necessary for countries to continue to make progress in the harmonisation of definitions and to improve transparency and accounting practices by financial institutions. In this regard, the following steps should be considered by governments to improve the collection of data on SME and entrepreneurship finance:

- Require financial institutions to use the national definition for an SME based on firm size.
- Require financial institutions to report on a timely basis to their regulatory authorities SME loans, interest rates, collateral requirements, by firm size and broken down into the appropriate size subcategories, as well as those SME loans which have government support.
- Work towards international harmonisation of data on non-performing loans.
- Encourage international, regional and national authorities, as well as business associations to work together to harmonise quantitative demand-side surveys in terms of survey population, questions asked and timeframes; encourage the competent organisations to undertake yearly surveys.
- Promote the harmonisation of the definition of venture capital in terms of stages of development

www.ingramcontent.com/pod-product-compliance
Lightning Source LLC
Chambersburg PA
CBHW061209240926
51846CB00006B/1161